IMAGES of America

Cherry Run Valley

Plumer, Pithole, and Oil City

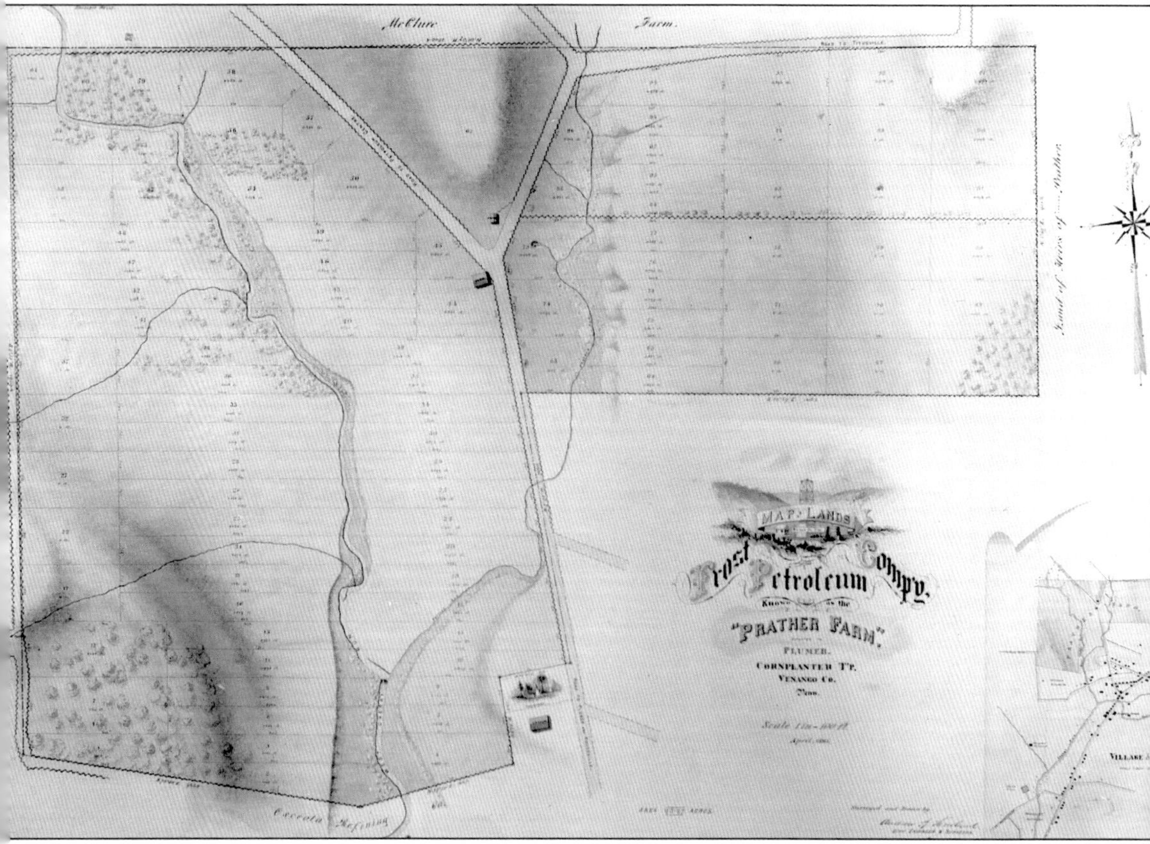

Andrew B. Houland was commissioned by the Frost Petroleum Company in 1865 to survey and draw this map of the Prather farm in Plumer. The farm was divided into subplots that were purchased or leased to oil speculators, who often times would sublease these plots into shares as small as a 1/64 interest in a real oil well. The inserted overleaf of the village of Plumer was later updated and reprinted by *The Beers Atlas of the Oil Region*. The Beers map of Plumer appears on page 42.

IMAGES
of America

CHERRY RUN VALLEY

PLUMER, PITHOLE, AND OIL CITY

Steve Karns

ARCADIA
PUBLISHING

ISBN 978-0-7385-0494-0

Published by Arcadia Publishing
Charleston, South Carolina

Printed in the United States of America

Library of Congress Catalog Card Number: 00106708

For all general information contact Arcadia Publishing at:
Telephone 843-853-2070
Fax 843-853-0044
E-mail sales@arcadiapublishing.com
For customer service and orders:
Toll-Free 1-888-313-2665

Visit us on the Internet at www.arcadiapublishing.com

I dedicate this book to Dick Turk, a fine man with a kind soul.
Thanks to Dick and to my daughter, Sara Karns.

CONTENTS

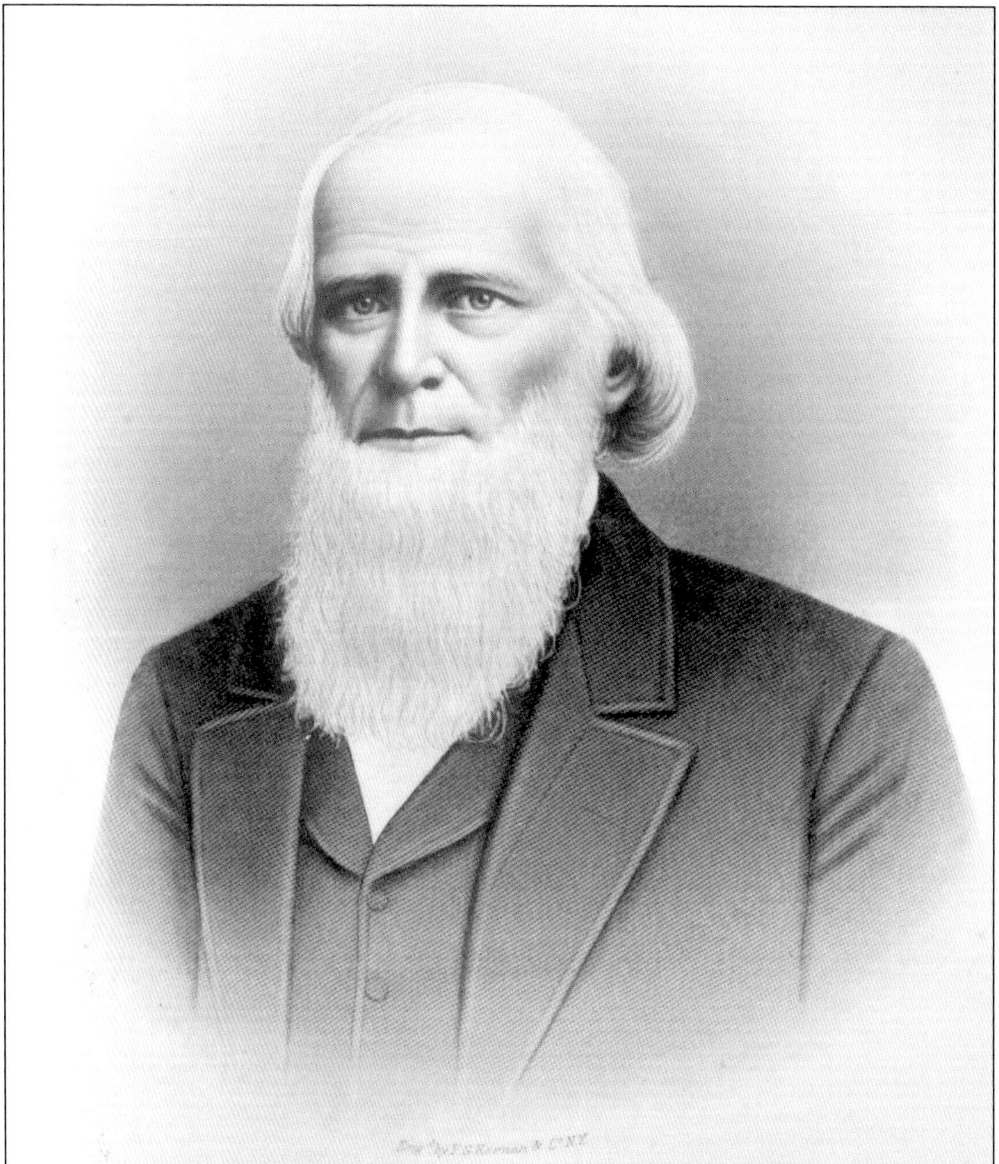

Henry McCalmont, one of the earliest settlers in the Cherry Run Valley, named the village of Plumer in honor of Arnold Plumer, pictured above, an ardent Democrat who served as a U.S. representative from 1837 to 1839 and again from 1841 to 1843. Originally from Franklin (the county seat of Venango County), Plumer was a very influential national figure and held appointed offices under both President Van Buren and President Buchanan. When Plumer died in 1869, he left the largest estate "ever accumulated by any one man in Venango County."

INTRODUCTION

Cherry Run Valley is located in the heart of Venango County, Pennsylvania, which is situated in the northwestern portion of the state. Cherry Run is one of the major tributaries that feeds Oil Creek, which flows into the Allegheny River at the site of what is now Oil City. Pithole Creek, another tributary to the Allegheny River, runs parallel to Cherry Run, lying just 2 miles east of it. The French who first explored the region found a valley covered in primeval forests of oak, maple, and hemlock, and claimed that "there was no more beautiful scenery to be found in the world." Native Americans graced the valley thousand of years ago, using the river and its tributaries as water highways. An abundant wealth of wildlife roamed the forests and filled the streams. Today, deer and bear are back in increasing numbers; the trout streams are world renowned.

This pastoral setting was interrupted in 1859, when word spread throughout the world that oil was being pumped from the earth. Col. Edwin L. Drake and his driller, Uncle Billy Smith, had found success at Watson Flats on Oil Creek near Titusville. Oil would bring $20 a barrel to those who made the effort to drill for it. Cherry Run Valley boasted a population of less than 300 in 1850 and, by 1860, it swelled to over 2,000. Although there are no census records, it is thought the population peaked in 1865 at 10,000 to 20,000 as thousands of hardened veterans from the Civil War came to the valley seeking adventure and fortune. The valley was clear-cut, as every piece of timber was needed to fuel the boilers and build the framed buildings that appeared overnight. The forests were depleted so quickly that lumber had to be imported from distant towns and villages. The wildlife that had been so abundant before was harvested to near extinction throughout the oil region. Laborers were recruited from places like New York and Boston to build the railroads and work in the factories. Factories that instantly went up to support the oil industry's need for pipe and steam engines and barrels by the hundreds of thousands. The oak barrels used to store whiskey were depleted in just a few weeks, and out of necessity, a new industry was born. The going rate for laborers was $3 per day, but they were hard to keep. When they saw the oil gushing from the well heads and watched the money flow like water, they would head off to make their own fortunes.

Towns rose from buckwheat fields, and cities grew from small crossroad villages. Speculators and reporters from distant cities would pay $100 a night to sleep two to a bed in ramshackle hotels with extravagant names like the Metropolitan, the Imperial Hotel, the Astor House, and the New Yorker. Deals worth millions were sealed with a handshake and contracts were written without regard to their authenticity. New markets were created to ship the now overabundant oil as well. A vast market for petroleum was found in Europe, as oil soon became one of our country's leading exports. It was a commodity, a new form of currency. Every significant leader in the American petroleum industry of the 19th century was heavily involved in the oil regions of Venango County, including John Rockefeller, John Archibold, Samuel Dodd, Joseph Seep, and Daniel O'Day. Quaker State and Pennzoil are two of the many hundreds of oil companies that were founded here. The National Transit Company, headquartered in Oil City, was a major branch of the Standard Oil Company. From its offices, the flow of oil was controlled and regulated as it moved through thousands of miles of pipeline across the country. The dominance of the oil region would reach a zenith in the 1920s and would revive itself as it supported the war effort in the 1940s. Most of the oil industry has moved on; in fact, Pennzoil sold its last refinery in the region in June 2000.

Cherry Run Valley: Plumer, Pithole, and Oil City looks at the history of the heart of the oil region of Venango County through the images of its people. The influence of its location and the vision of its people affected the direction of the oil industry. From 1864 to 1865, Cherry Run Valley was the capital of the oil industry in the world. It boasted four large refineries, the world's first successful pipeline, and the world's first and most famous oil boom town, Pithole. In 1864, incredible minds gathered in Plumer and made decisions that captured the country's imagination. The phenomenon of Pithole far exceeded anything these gentlemen could have planned or projected. Pithole was the benchmark that would judge the mettle of oil pioneers for years.

Plumer on Cherry Run was the largest town in Cornplanter Township and, by 1845, already had a gristmill, a hotel, and several stores. It seemed destined to become a major town with a balance of industry, business, and agriculture, but oil changed that destiny. While Plumer had an incredible boom with oil, that surge faded, and Plumer never gained the prominence it once held. Plumer influenced the rise of Oil City, which went on to become the hub of all oildom. Oil City became the industrial center of the oil region and, as it was well situated on the Allegheny River, it was the logical place to receive and ship goods. The railroad companies built major yards there, and the hills surrounding the city were best suited as residential neighborhoods. It has survived several major floods and fires and a turbulent economy that still defines the make-up of the city.

Cherry Run Valley is quiet now—the run flows with trout, and deer are plentiful in the forests that cover the hillsides. Old central power plants and abandoned pumping jacks stand as a tribute to her past. Oil is still pumped from solitary wells daily, but in ever diminishing numbers. Pithole is the site of a state museum, and the village of Plumer, with its beautiful churches and old residences, stands at the entrance to Oil Creek State Park. Oil City is cradled in the Allegheny Valley with houses sweeping up the hillsides. The valley is now a popular place for visitors who enjoy its natural beauty and rich history.

I wish to thank everyone who contributed to the making of this book: Jim Stoudt, who took all the current pictures that appear in the book; Lee Prindle, who did the copy stand and darkroom work; Gina Wig; Lois Horner; Jack Horner; June Pearson; John and Margie Hummel; the Russells; Don Saltzman; Bill Grove; Edith Leach Gesin; Roxanne Hitchcock; Carolee Michener; Kay Ensle; Pat Warner; Joe and Jerri Saunders; the Venango Historical Museum; the Oil City Genealogical Society; the Drake Well Museum; Sue Beates; Mabel Huber; Bill Huber; Jeff and Denise Huber; Judy Etzel; Carol and Kenny Cubbon; John Cubbon; and Dick Turk and his family.

One

PLUMMERVILLE

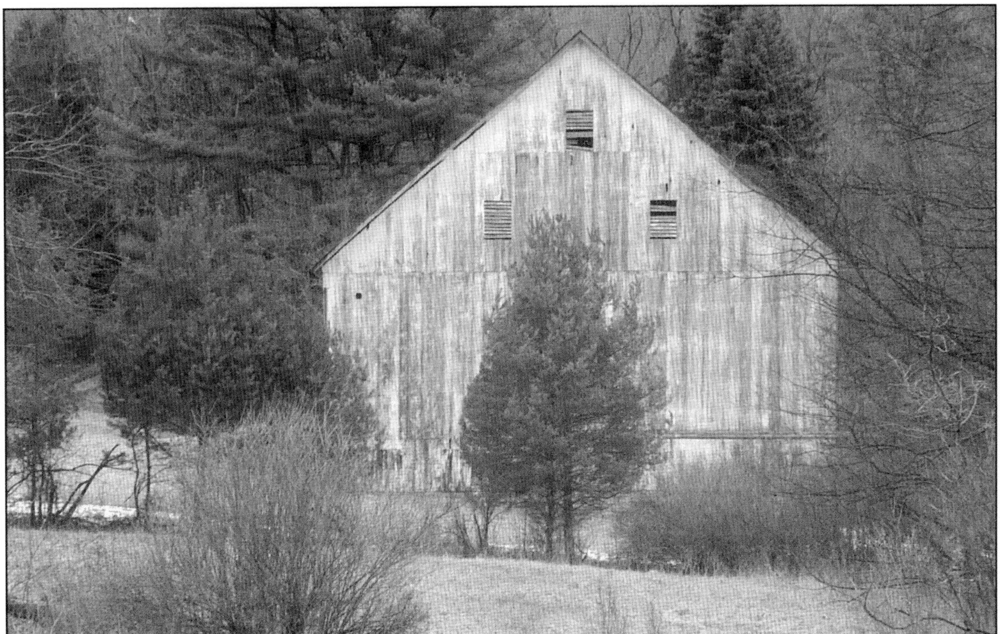

In the first half of the 19th century, Plumer, then known as Plummerville, was the largest settlement in Cornplanter Township. The village spread over the gentle hills that lined both banks of Cherry Run Creek, situated nearly 3.5 miles from the creek's mouth. The village's location on the hillsides spared it from the ravages of devastating floods that had plagued Venango County's other major towns. Plummerville was ideally located on the Franklin Warren Pike and served as the major overnight stop between those two cities for more than a century. Pictured is the barn of Peter Berry, much as it looked when Berry raised it over 120 years ago. It is now used by the state forestry department in its management of state game lands. This site was designated as the one-millionth acre of land procured by the commonwealth and set aside as state game lands. (Photographed by Jim Stoudt.)

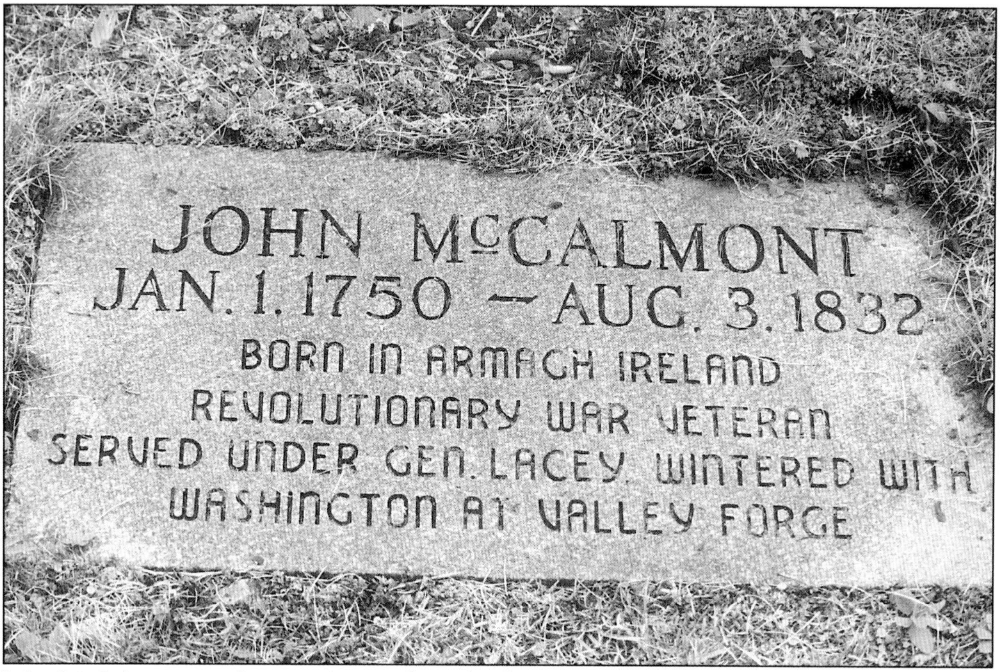

John McCalmont was born in Armanch, Ireland, in 1750, and spent the majority of his life in Venango County. He served in the Continental Army and wintered with General Washington at Valley Forge. McCalmont died in 1832 and is buried in the Plumer cemetery near his son, Henry McCalmont, who founded the village of Plumer in 1821. (Photographed by Jim Stoudt.)

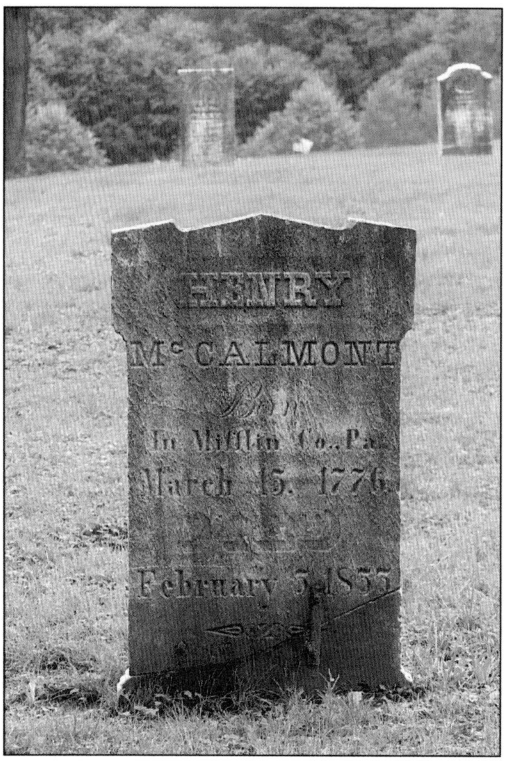

In 1821, when Henry McCalmont settled along Cherry Run, John Ricketts had already built a primitive sawmill farther up the run on 300 acres of land he had purchased from the Holland Land Company in 1810. McCalmont built the Plumer Hotel (House) as an inn and a house of entertainment in 1843, and served as a justice of the peace until his death. McCalmont donated the land for the Plumer Cemetery after a nameless traveler died at his inn. Henry had him buried on the hillside overlooking the village, on land that adjoined the Seceder Church. This church became the United Presbyterian Church of Plumer. (Photographed by Jim Stoudt.)

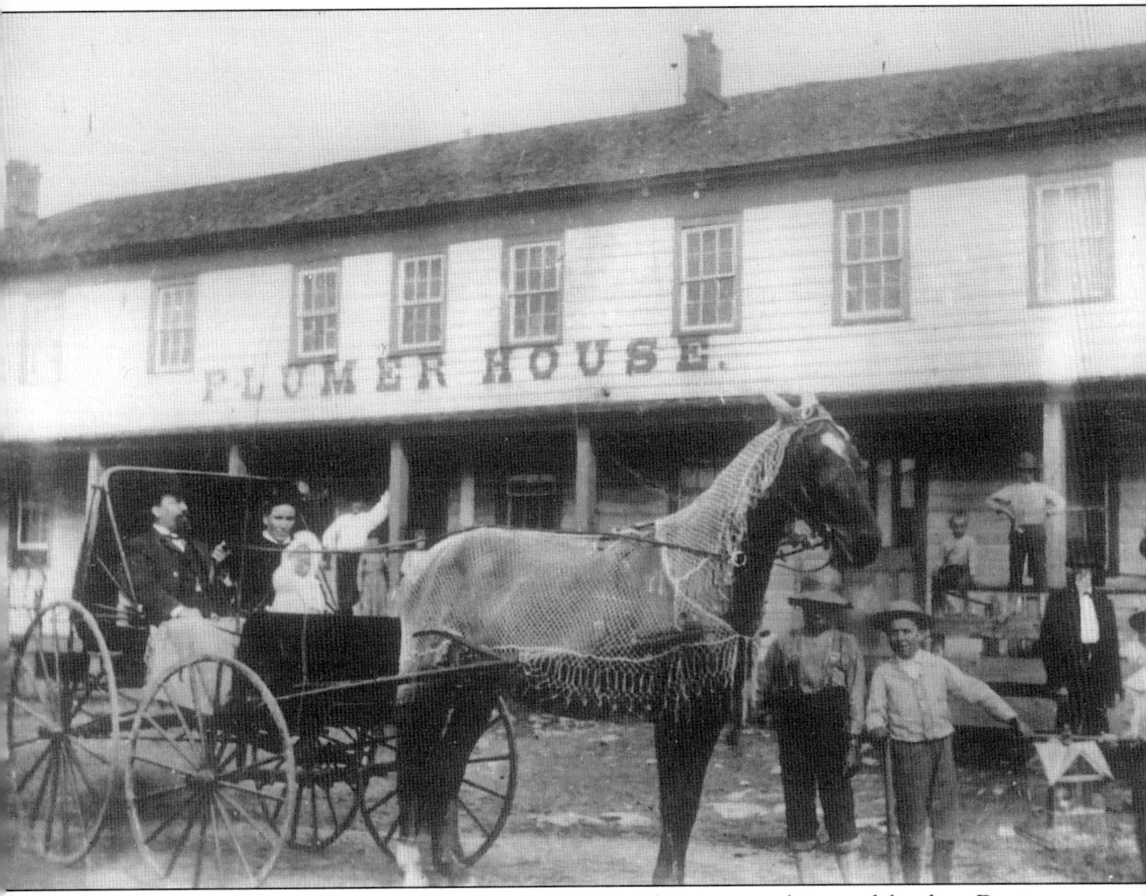

The Plumer House flourished as an inn until 1889, when it was destroyed by fire. During its 46 years, it had a succession of innkeepers, and many a weary traveler graced its doors. Dr. E.P. Crooks, the innkeeper from 1877 to 1888, is shown with his wife, Margaret Alexander, and their children. In addition to his medical career, Dr. Crooks had great success as an oil producer in and around Petroleum Centre. (Photograph courtesy the Venango Historical Society.)

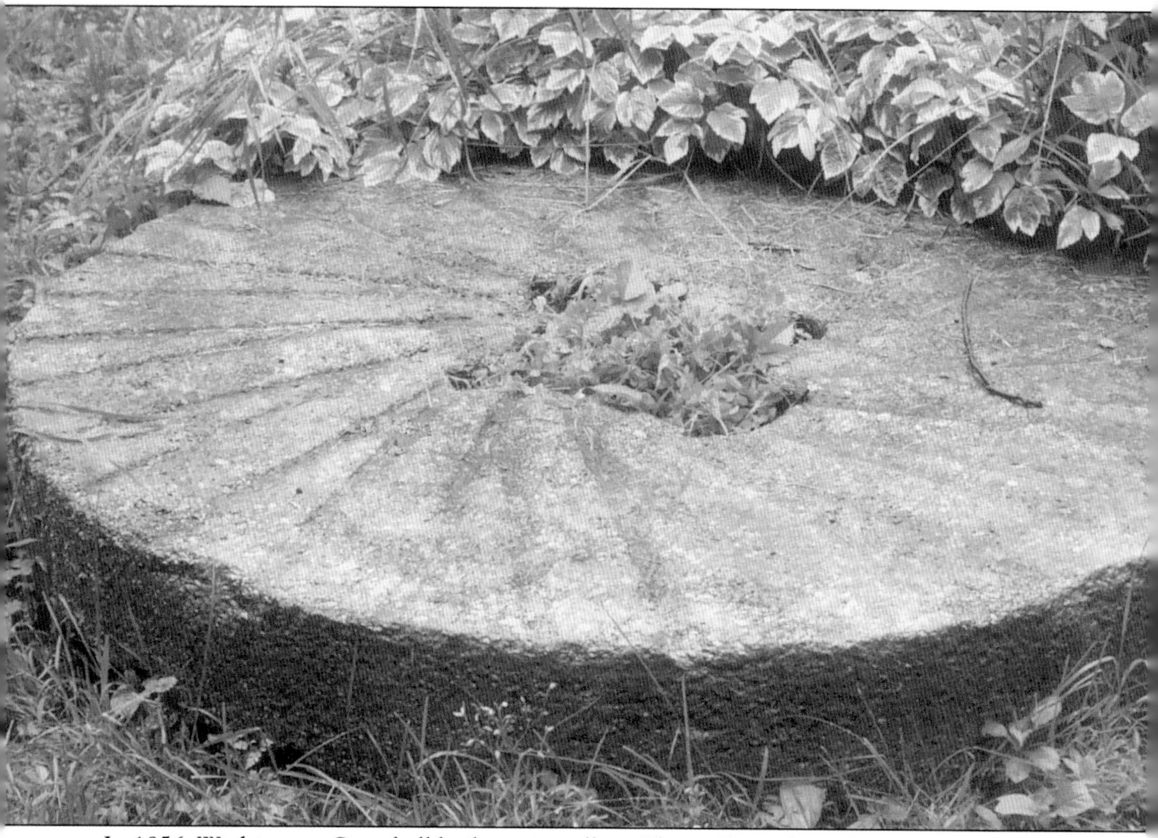

In 1856, Washington Campbell built a gristmill on Cherry Run where the run crossed the road to Eagle Rock. This millstone is one of two that can still be seen behind the Nelson house in Plumer. Campbell's son, George Campbell, became a blacksmith and an oil rig builder in Plumer. James Sutton built the first store in Plummerville in 1851, opposite the Plumer Hotel. The Prather brothers—George, Abram, and John—ran the third store that had been erected by Henry McCalmont in the early 1850s. Their father, Abram C. Prather, had established a tannery in 1815, which was then known as the best equipped in the county. It flourished into the 1830s, when the elder Prather retired. Many of the families living in and around the Cherry Run Valley today can still trace their roots to the early settlers of the Cherry Run Valley. (Photographed by Jim Stoudt.)

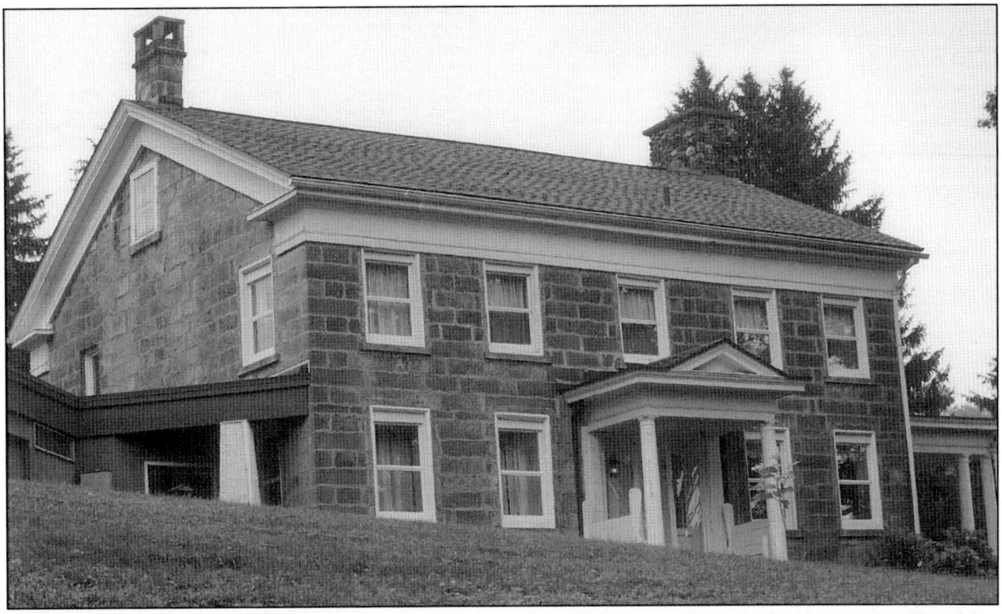

The oldest dwelling still standing in Plumer is the Old Stone House, built on the Franklin Warren Pike, in 1841, by Thomas Turner, who originated from New York State and settled in Plummerville before 1840. The area on the eastern side of the Franklin Warren Pike became known as Turner Hill. The Reverend John R. Slentz and his wife, Margaret, purchased the property on January 30, 1861. Reverend Slentz had settled in Plumer in 1852, to minister to the Presbyterian congregation there. It is believed that the Slentzes used the Old Stone House as a ladies' seminary. The house was used as a hostelry until 1890, by which time it had fallen into disrepair. In 1948, Dr. Earl Magee purchased the house and, while modernizing the home in 1967, he chanced upon a hidden basement that supported the legend that the house had served as a stop on the Underground Railroad. (Photographed by Jim Stoudt.)

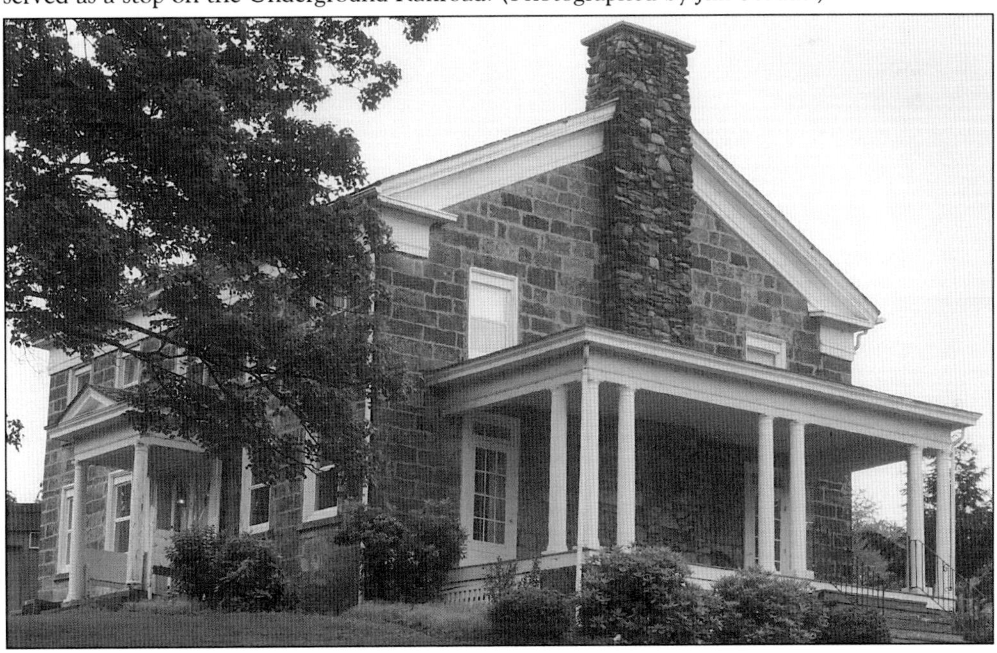

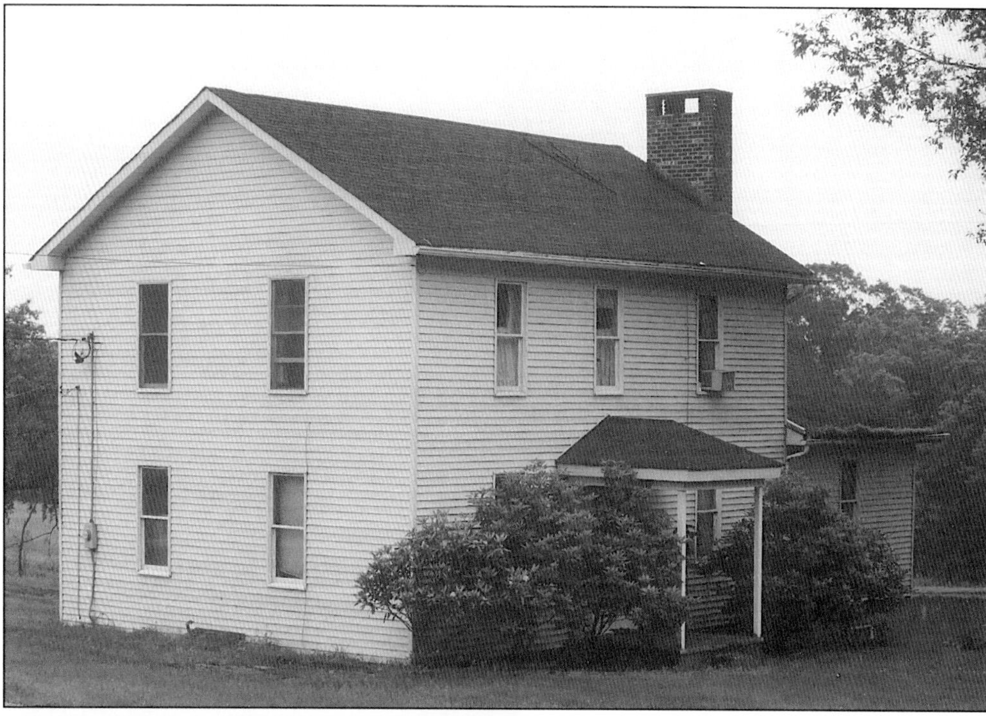

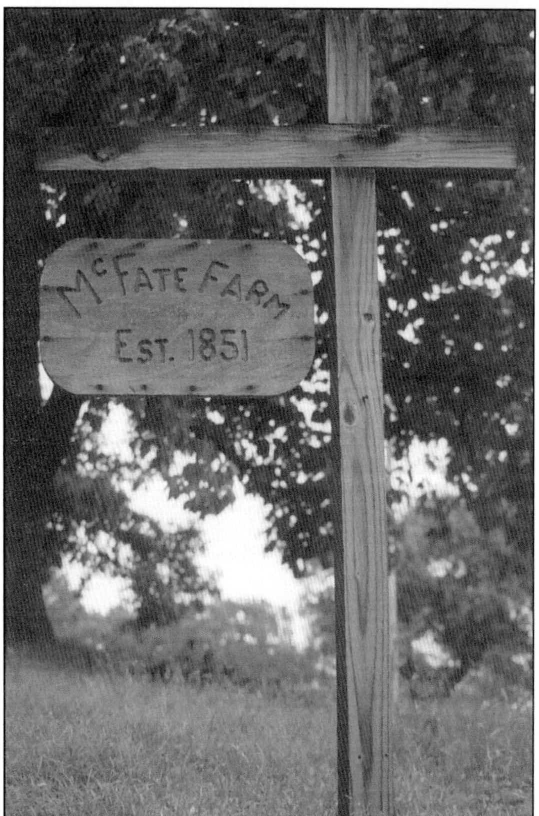

This homestead was built by the McFate family in 1851. The McFates settled on the eastern side of Cherry Run. Their homestead extended all the way to the Allegheny River at Walnut Bend. On December 20, 1864, John McFate was found murdered on the road on his way home from Oil City. It has been long thought that McFate was too boastful about his oil fortunes. The mistake cost him his life. (Photographed by Jim Stoudt.)

Two

The Cherry Run Valley Flows with Oil

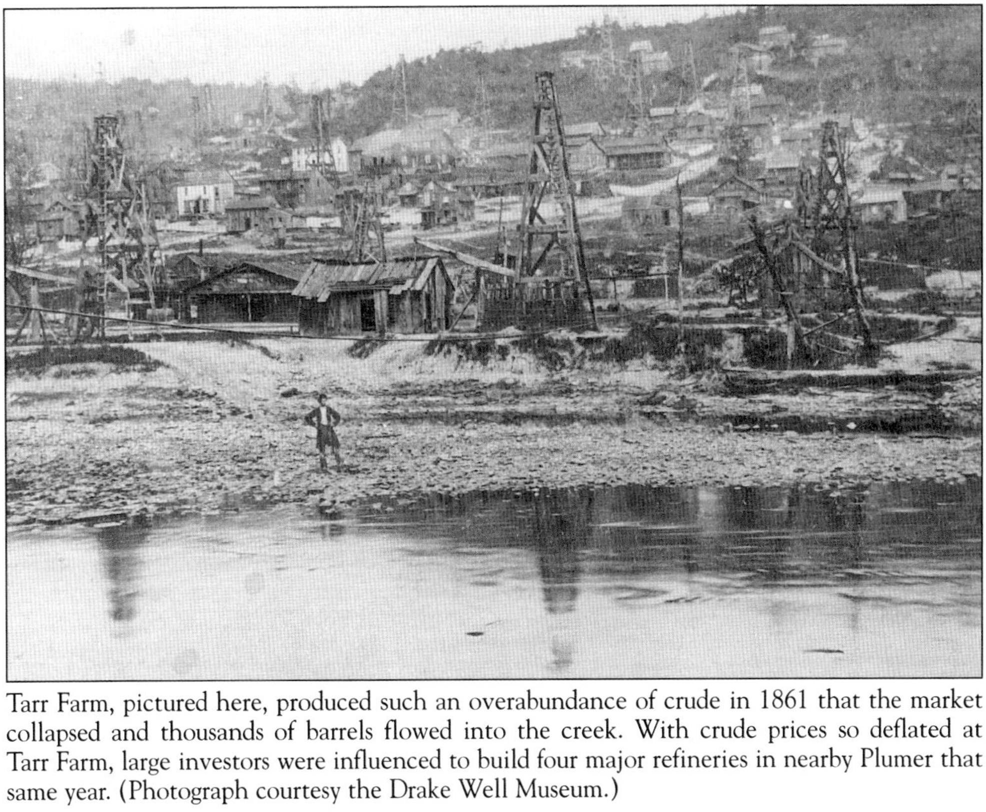

Tarr Farm, pictured here, produced such an overabundance of crude in 1861 that the market collapsed and thousands of barrels flowed into the creek. With crude prices so deflated at Tarr Farm, large investors were influenced to build four major refineries in nearby Plumer that same year. (Photograph courtesy the Drake Well Museum.)

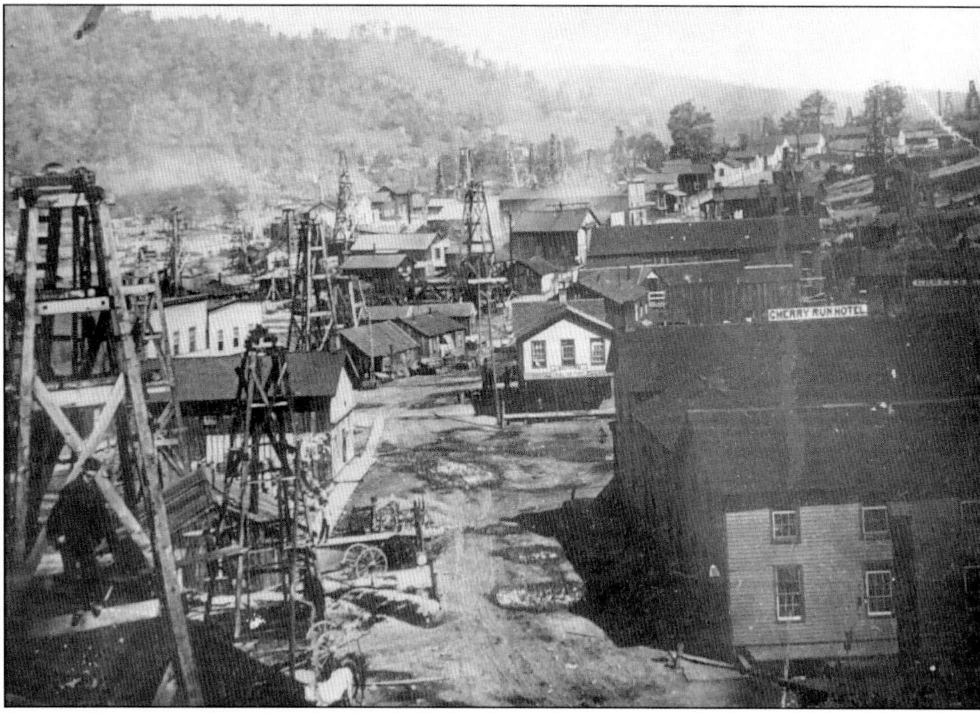

Rouseville, situated on the mouth of Cherry Run, was growing almost as quickly as Plumer. Derricks lined both sides of the run as far as Plumer, 3.5 miles away. In 1865, a correspondent from New York exclaimed, "The derricks along Cherry Run stood as close as masts on the East River." (Photograph courtesy the Oil City Genealogical Society.)

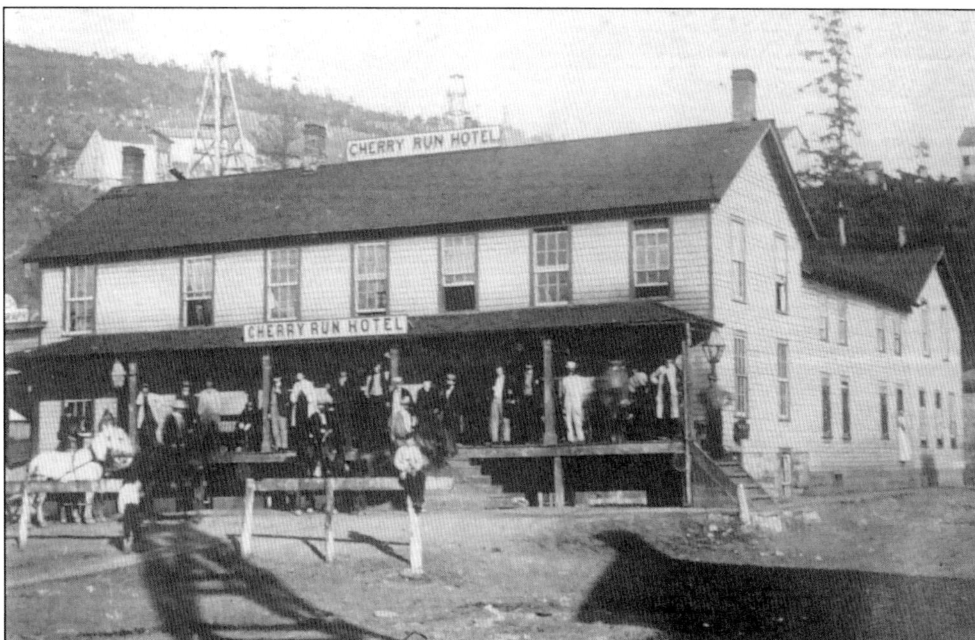

The Cherry Run Hotel in Rouseville was built by Francis Kane, a longtime innkeeper in Plumer. (Photograph courtesy the Venango Historical Society.)

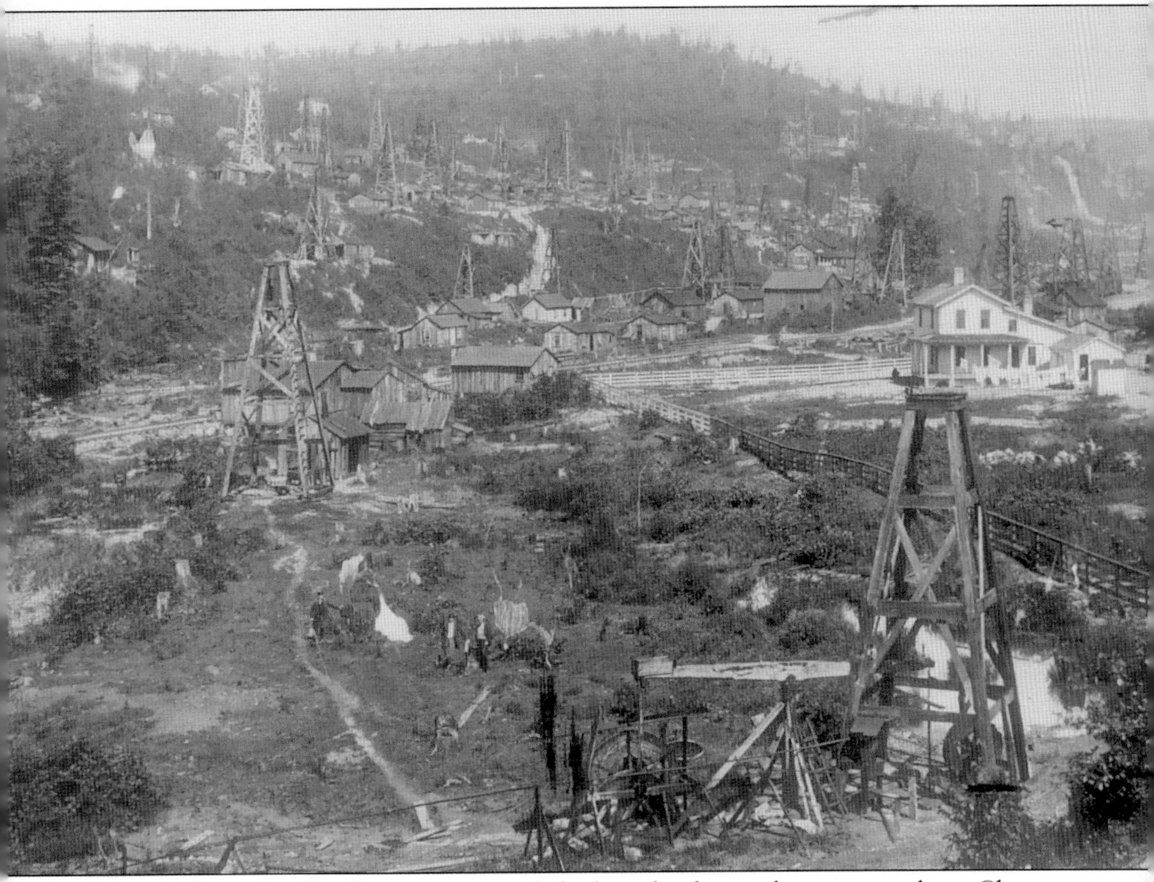

In 1864, William Reed's efforts were rewarded when the first gusher was struck on Cherry Run, 1.5 miles south of Plumer. The Reed and Criswell well on Cherry Run was producing 300 barrels of oil per day, and by November 1864 the well was sold for $650.000. Just a year previously, the well and two adjacent acres of land could not be sold for $1,500. The Smith farm just north of the Reed Well was owned by Beers and Cornen, who refused an offer of $4 million for their rights to the farm in the summer of 1865. Cherry Run had become the favorite place for oil seekers. The farmhouse above is engulfed in a sea of derricks. (Photograph courtesy the Venango Historical Society.)

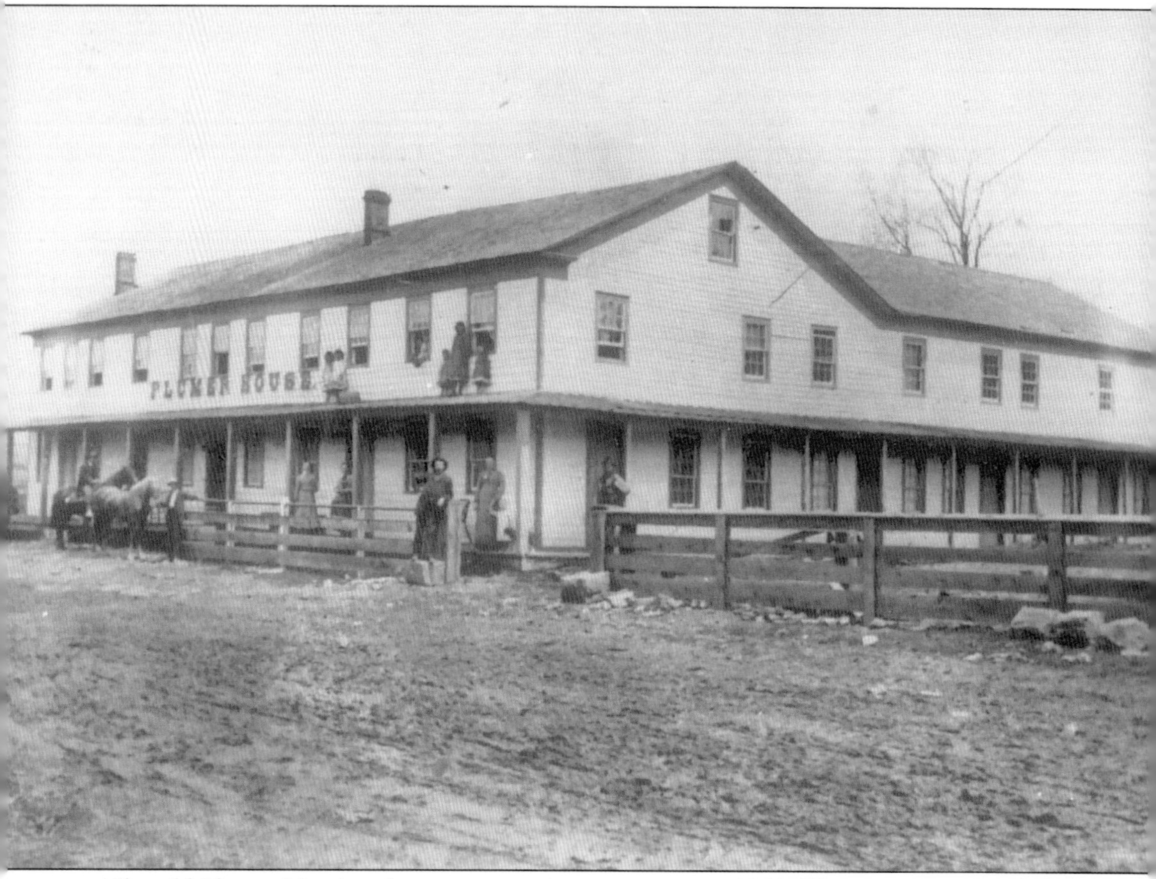

The old Plumer Hotel underwent extensive expansion in 1864. The renovation tripled the number of beds, doubled the dining room, and boasted of a pocket billiard parlor room. For all the hard work done, the nearby Pavilion House, owned by Robinson and Masseth, was still found to be "second to none for neatness, comfort, and copious ventilation. It is in fact a pavilion of stout tent cloth with a board floor." Plumer now boasted of eight hotels, two telegraph offices, a newsstand, four refineries, and several general stores. The population was in excess of 5,000 people, and with transients and laborers counted, it was counted at 8,000. Circuses and carnivals would often set up in the field adjacent to the Plumer Hotel. (Photograph courtesy the Venango Historical Society.)

Adam Weber from Kirchberg, Germany, came to Plumer as the Civil War concluded. After his service in the Union Army, his search for a new start found him employed at the Humboldt refinery in Plumer. He remained with the refinery until its close in the late 1860s. Over the next few years, he manufactured cigars, a business that evolved into a career in merchandising. He would go on to be a successful oil producer.

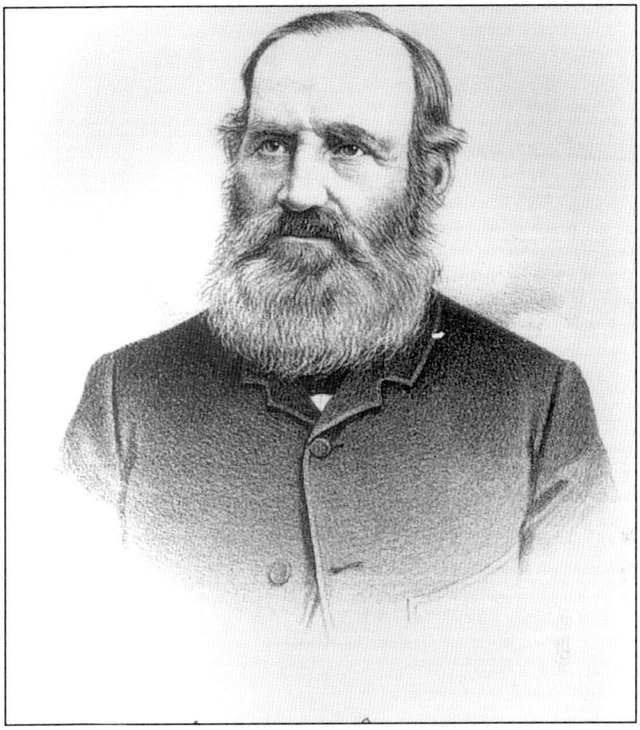

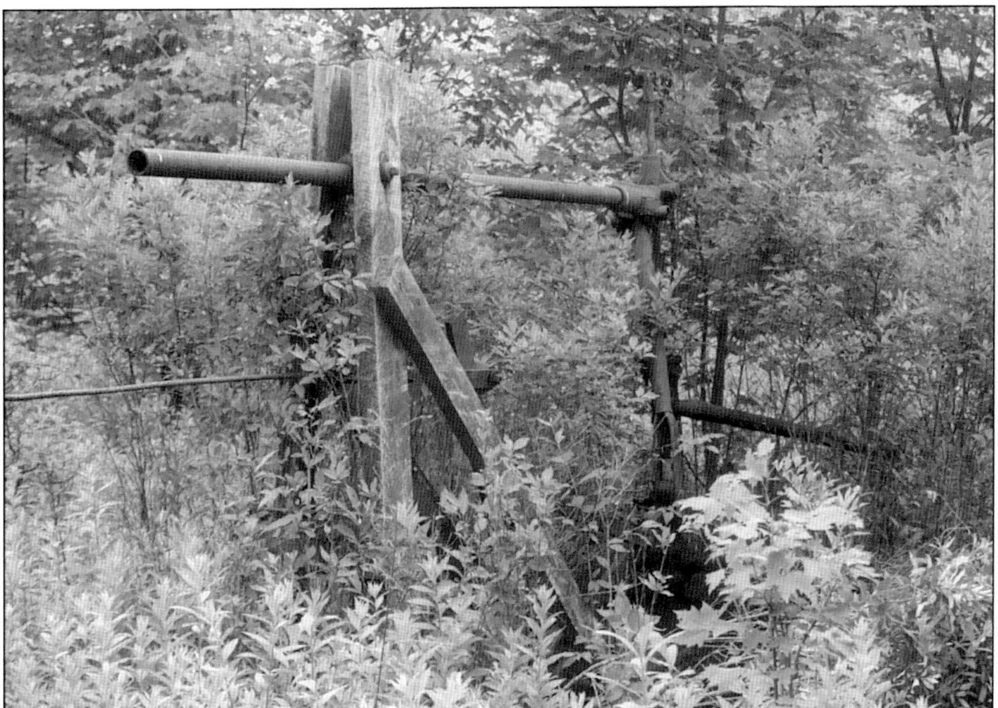

The pumping jack of the Weber well is shown in this contemporary photograph. The well was first bored via horsepower in 1865. The well, still producing, is the second oldest active well in the world. It is located on the Boyle farm, one-half mile east of Plumer. (Photographed by Jim Stoudt.)

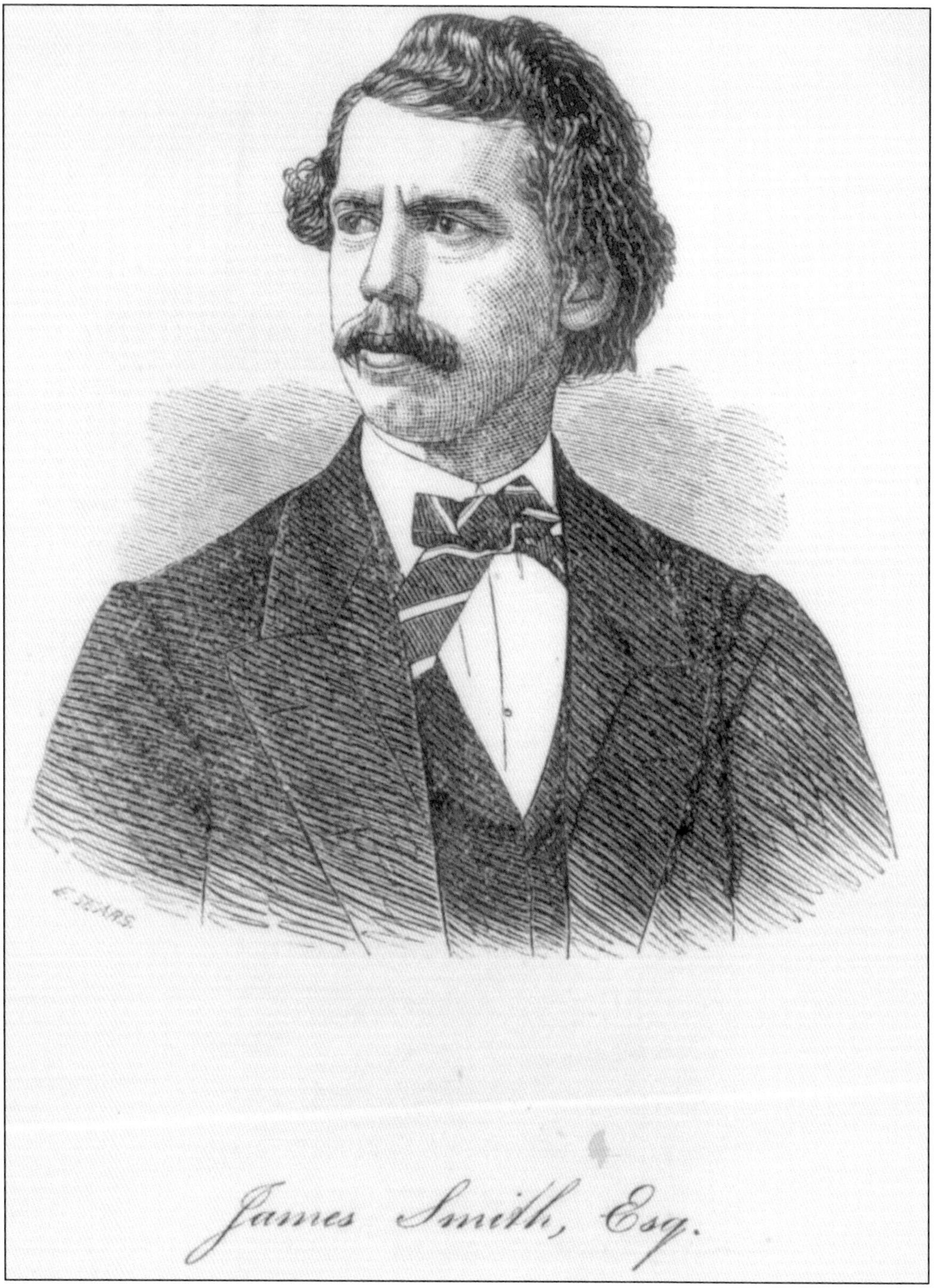

James Smith, from Brantford, Canada, came to the oil region in February 1865 and located in Plumer. He was employed by the firm of Hamlin, Moore, and Company as a machinist. In 1867, with C.C. Barker, he gained patent rights to both the Morahan and the Roberts sand pumps. By 1868, he bought out the firm and controlled the sand pump market for the next ten years. Eventually, the company merged with the Boston Iron Works in Franklin, Pennsylvania, where he relocated his work in the 1870s.

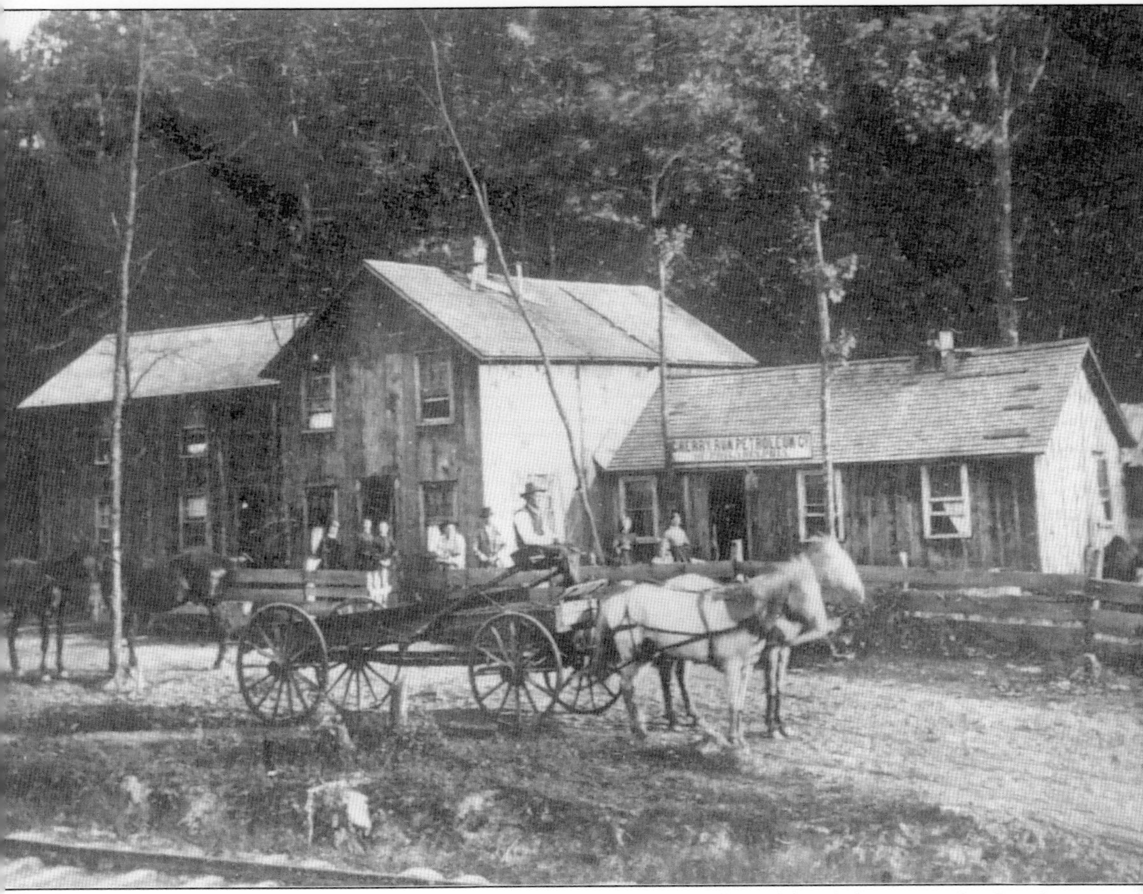

The Cherry Run Petroleum Company owned the majority of the oil lands between the Reed Well and the Humboldt Works. In November 1864, after word of a successful strike, the stock of the Cherry Run Petroleum Company rose from $7 to $32 per share. This was astounding news to those who only a short time previously had thought the investors "only fit for a lunatic asylum." In the lower left corner are the railroad tracks that were soon completed through to Plumer by C.V. Culver. (Photograph courtesy the Venango Historical Society.)

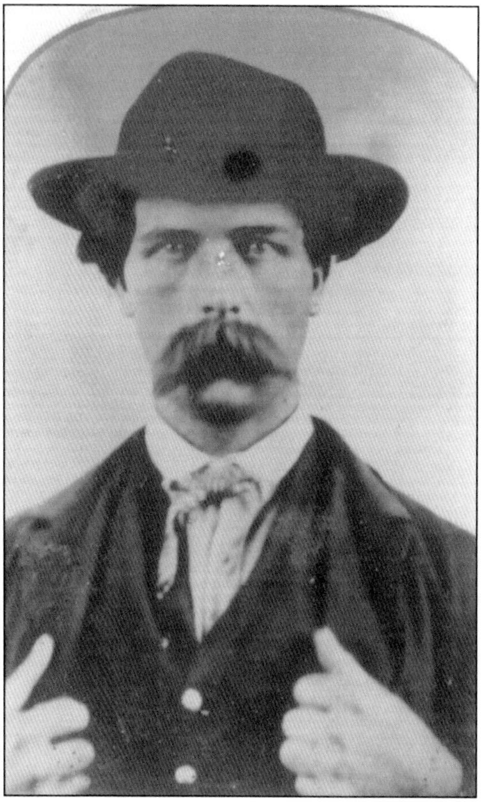

Patterson Sankey, at left, and James Walter, below, were drillers and roustabouts who drifted through Plumer in 1865. Little is known of their lives or their final whereabouts. They were both emblematic of the many Civil War veterans who came to the oil regions seeking their fortunes. (Photographs courtesy Roxanne Hitchcock.)

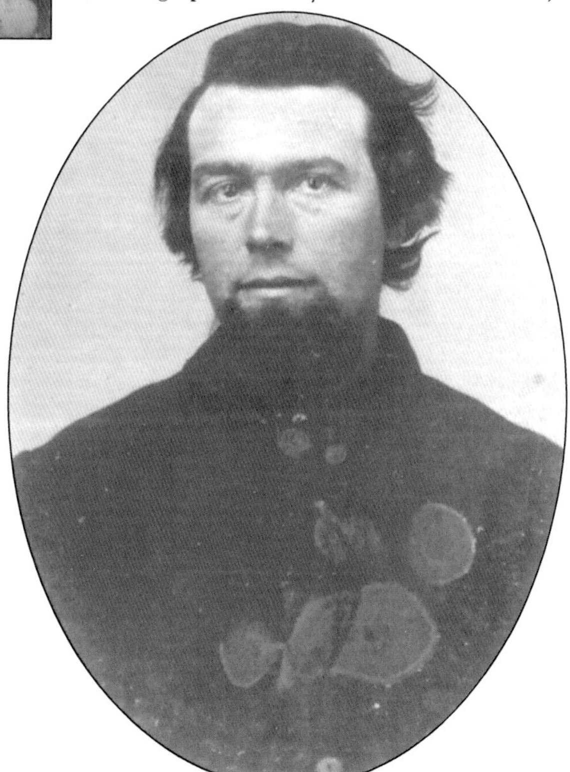

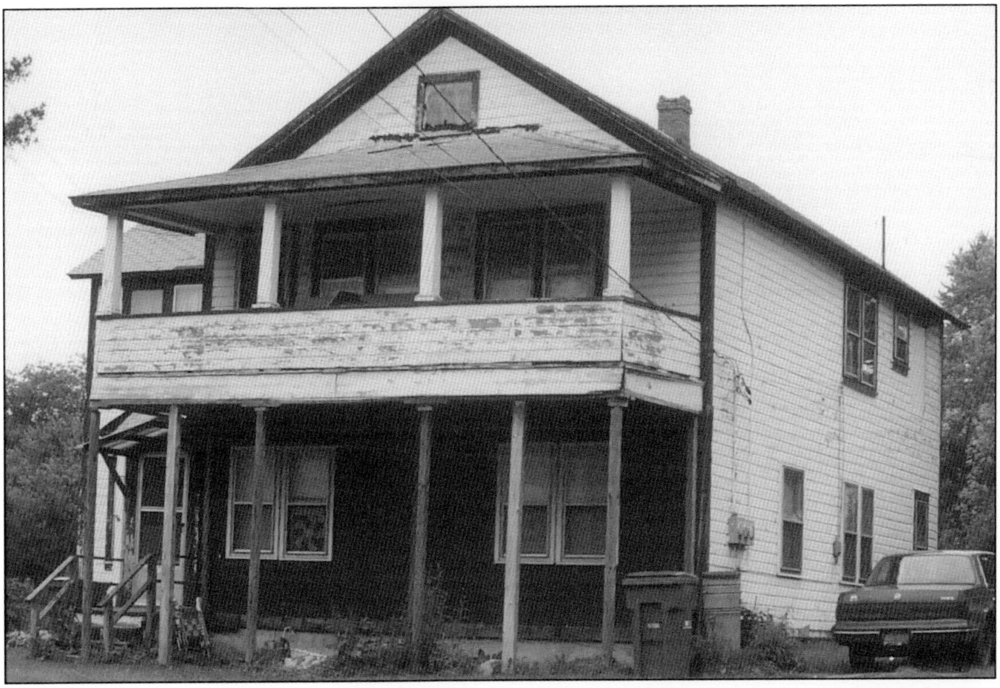

This residence, located just south of the Eagle Rock Road in Plumer, is most commonly known as the Forbes store. It was built in 1925 on the old foundation of a store originally built by James McCray in the 1860s. (Photographed by Jim Stoudt.)

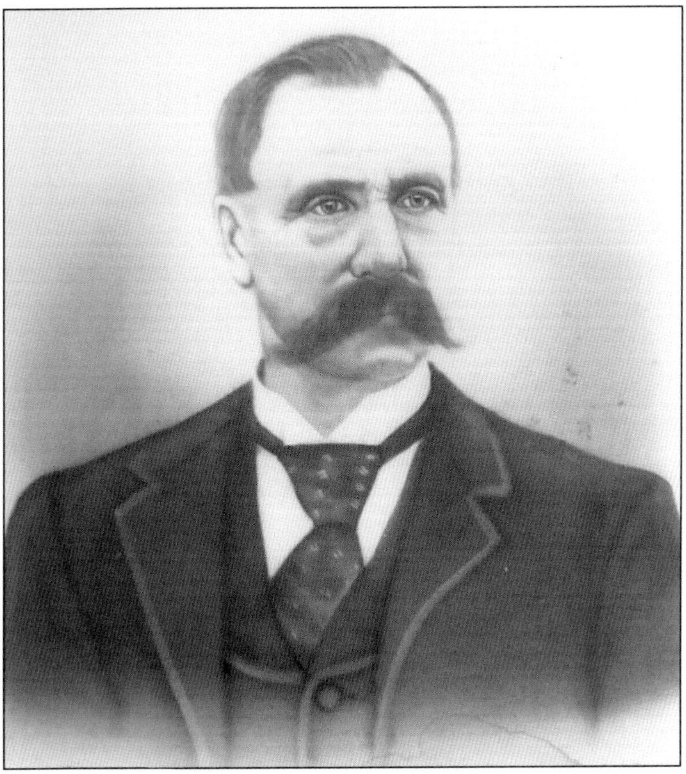

James McCray, the son of William McCray, spent the early part of his life on the family farm between Petroleum Center and Plumer. He went on to become successful as an oil producer. His sons and grandsons settled in Plumer and later joined the ministry.

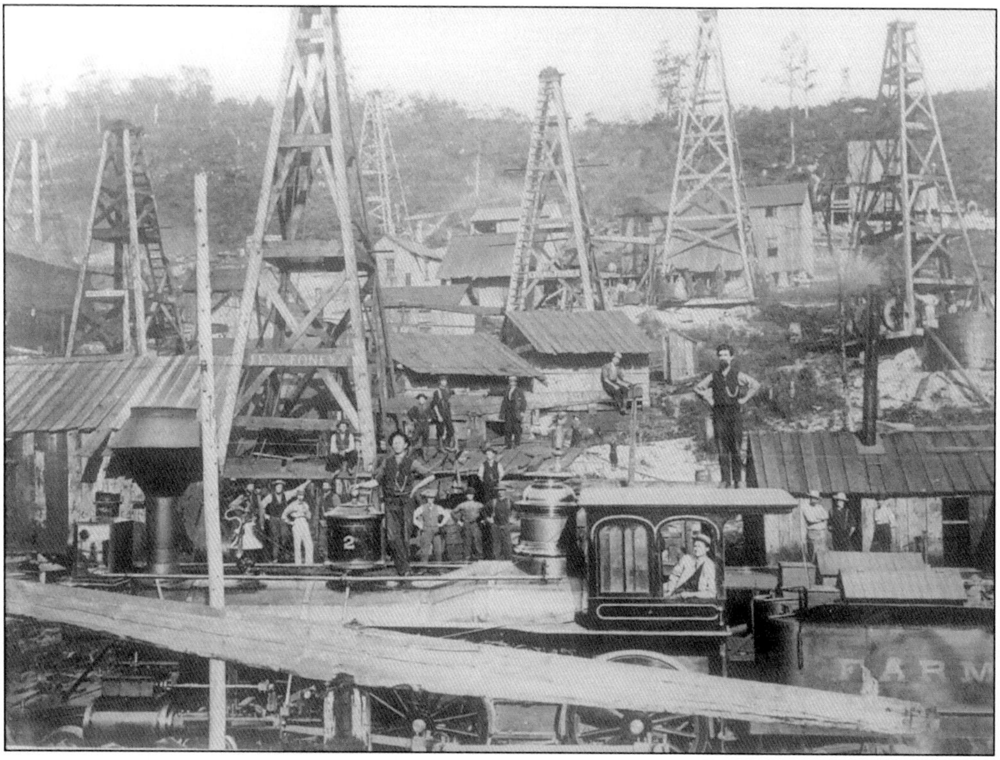

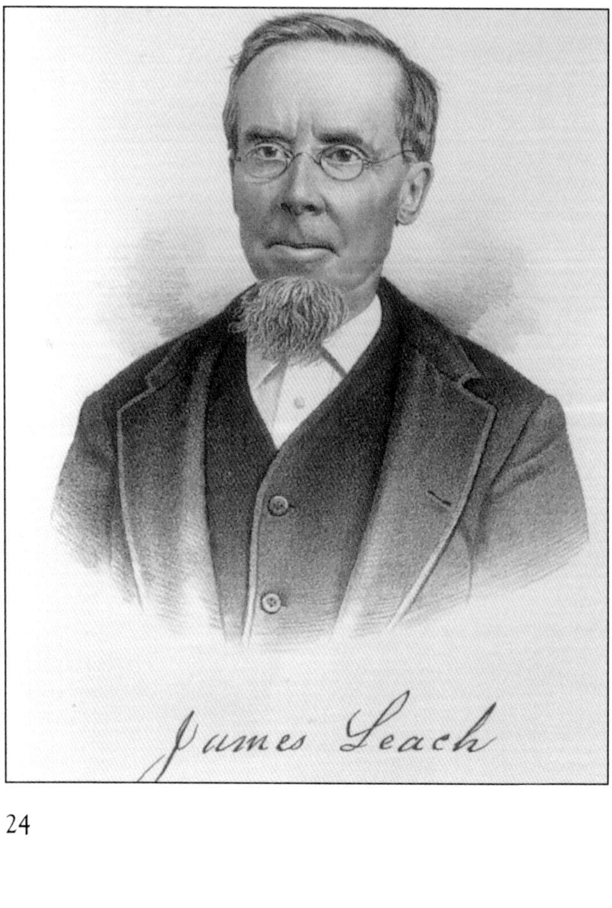

James Leach was born in Lancastershire, England, in 1825. He first came to Plumer in January 1865 with his family. His father, Rev. Daniel Leach, was the Methodist pastor in Plumer. Above, James is shown standing under the derrick and wearing a white shirt and hat. The well was located south of Plumer on Cherry Run. James was elected the justice of the peace of Plumer in 1877 and served until his death in 1898. His wife, Mary Ewing, owned and operated the old Prather store on Eagle Rock Road until her death in 1920. (Top image courtesy the Venango Historical Society.)

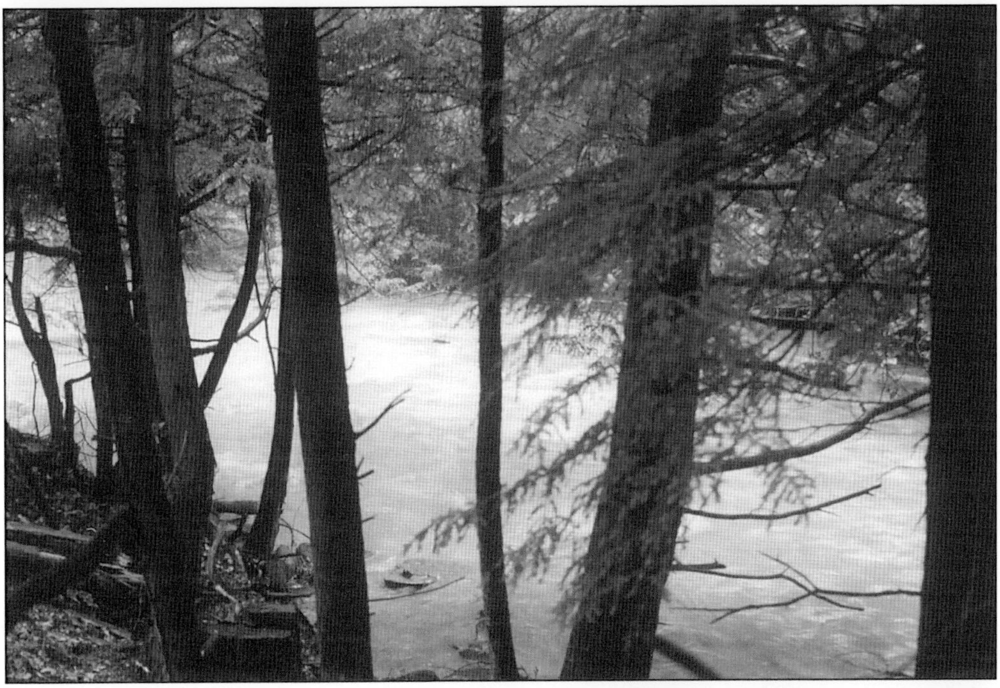

Phillip Hatch was raised on his father's farm on Allender Run, located near Pithole Creek. He married Mary Prather of Plumer and joined with the Prather brothers in building a refinery in Oleopolis. In the 1870s, he purchased the Prather farm in Plumer and served as postmaster from 1878 to 1885. He was a longtime trustee of the Methodist Church in Plumer. (Top image photographed by Jim Stoudt.)

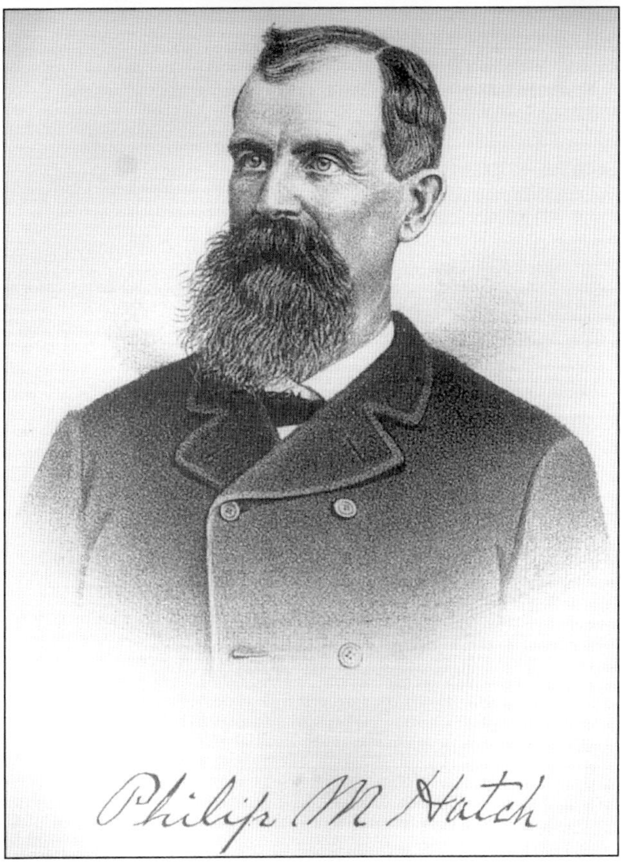

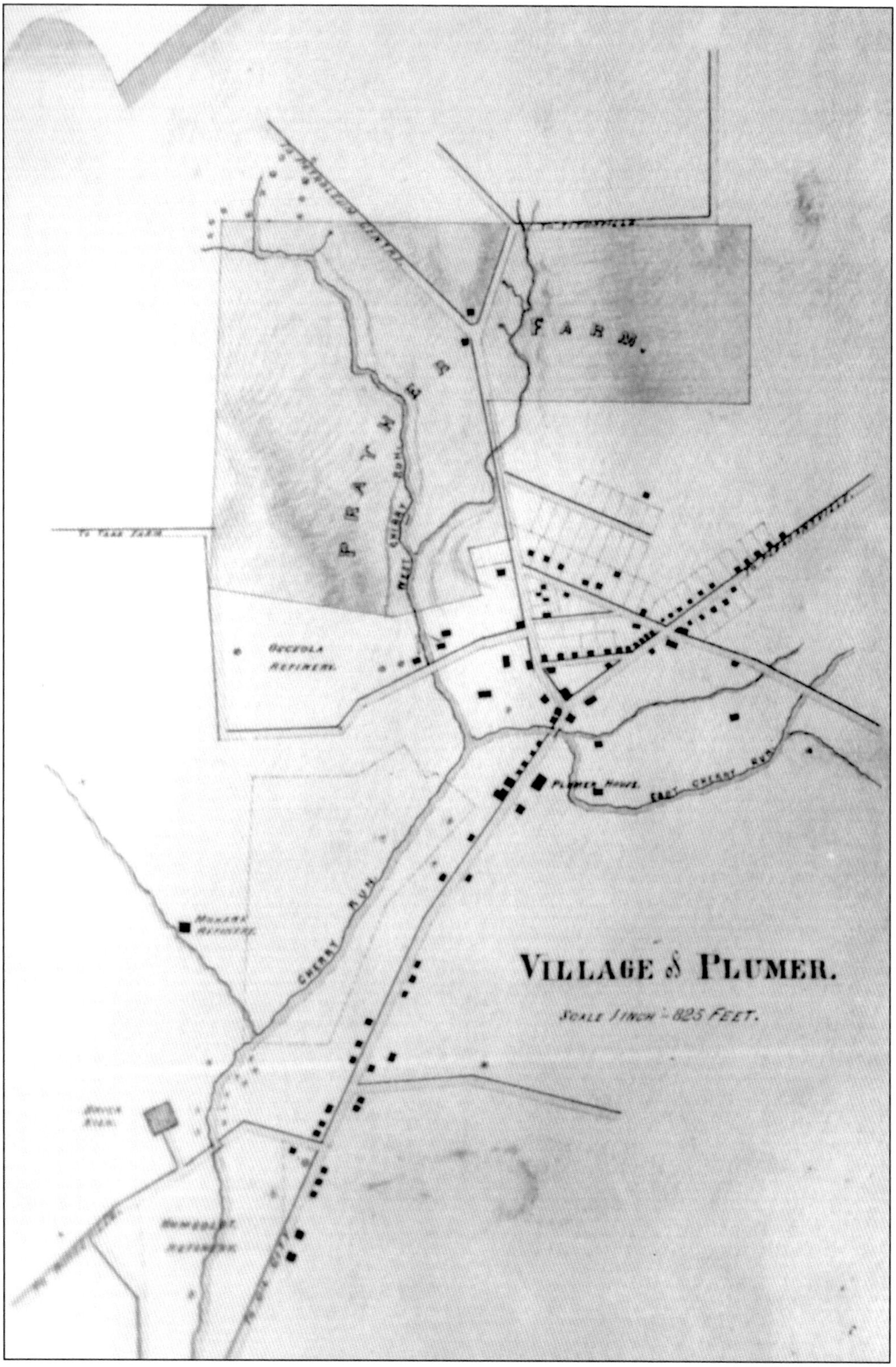

This map of the village of Plumer was published *c.* 1865. (Courtesy the Drake Well Museum.)

Three

PITHOLE'S RISE

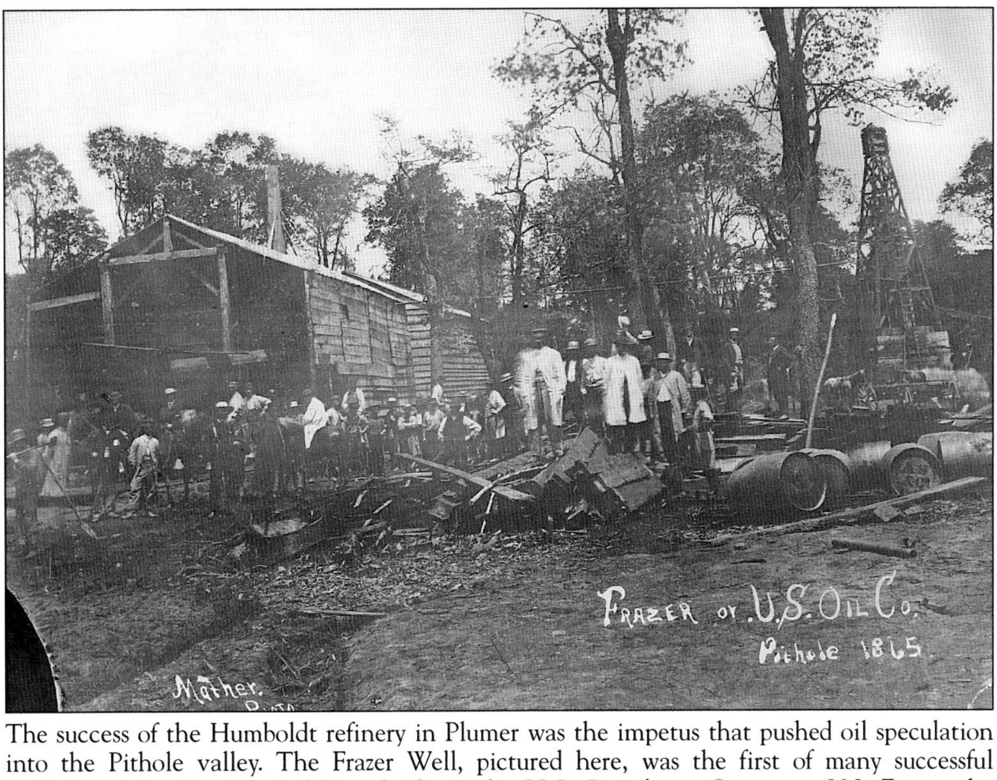

The success of the Humboldt refinery in Plumer was the impetus that pushed oil speculation into the Pithole valley. The Frazer Well, pictured here, was the first of many successful wells bored by the Humboldt's subsidiary, the U.S. Petroleum Company. I.N. Frazer, the superintendent of the newly formed U.S. Petroleum Company, stands beside the tree on the right of the photograph. (Photograph courtesy the Drake Well Museum.)

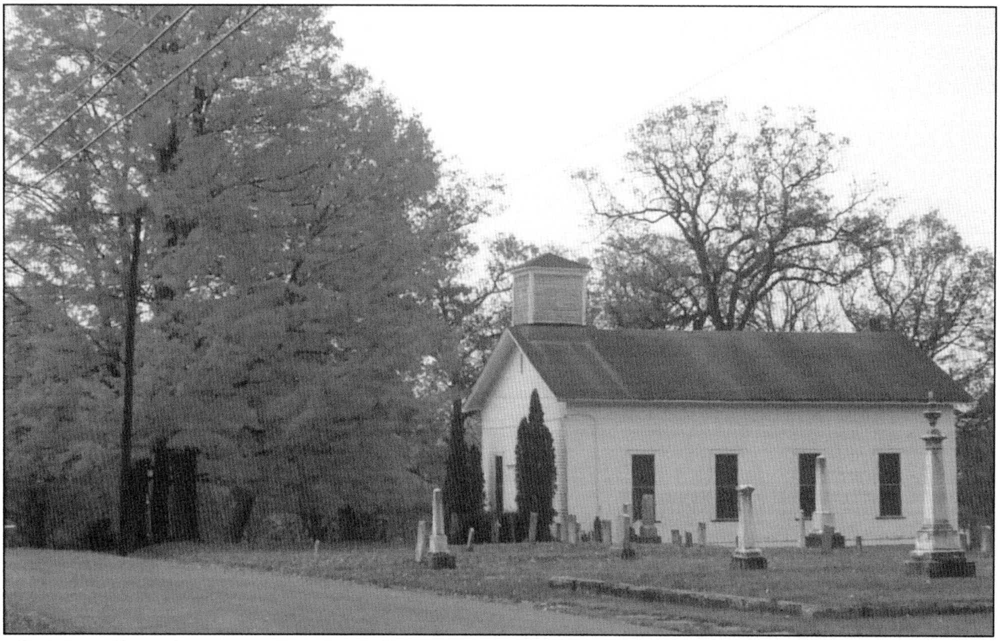

The United Presbyterian Church of Plumer was built in 1862. It replaced the old Seceder Church, which was established in 1823. The present sanctuary was endowed by George C. Prather, who additionally funded the Presbyterian church, built in Pithole in 1865. Reverend Slentz was the pastor for both congregations. (Photographed by Jim Stoudt.)

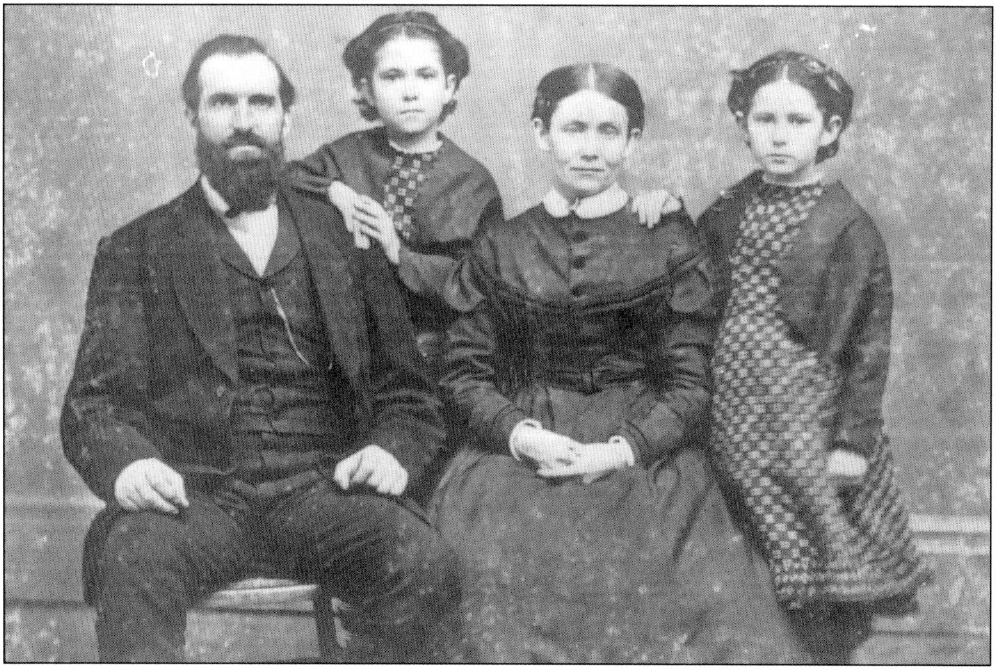

Reverend Steadman was the first Methodist minister in Pithole, coming to the area in 1865. Thomas Duncan donated the property for both the Methodist church and the one in Pithole. Reverend Steadman was well known as the pastor who delivered the eulogy for Pres. Abraham Lincoln's funeral in Springfield, Illinois. (Photograph courtesy the Drake Well Museum.)

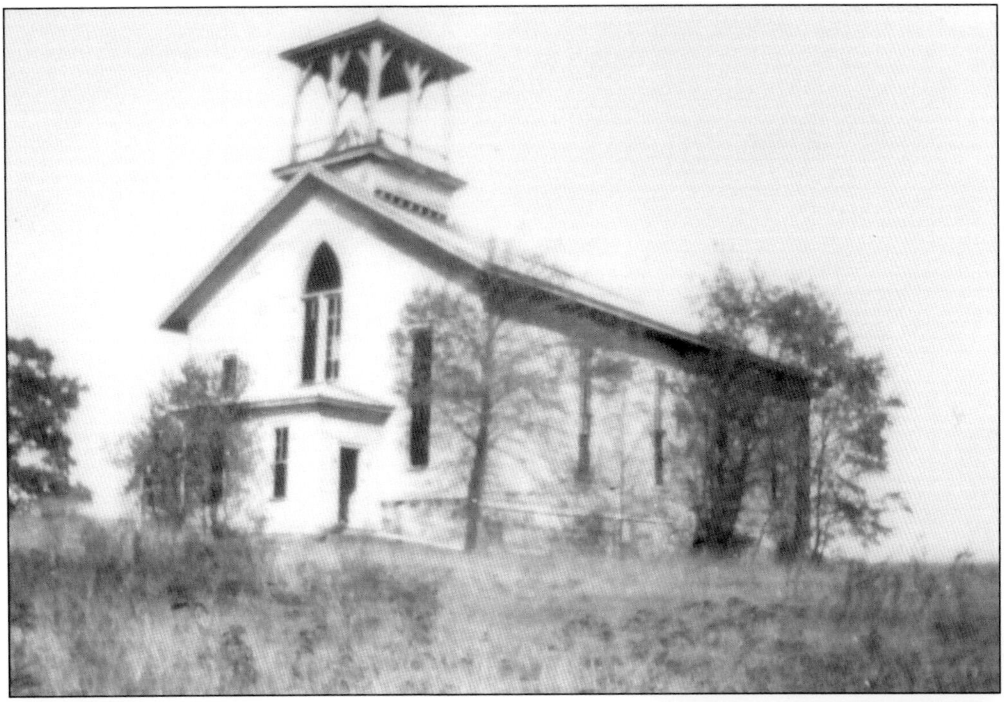

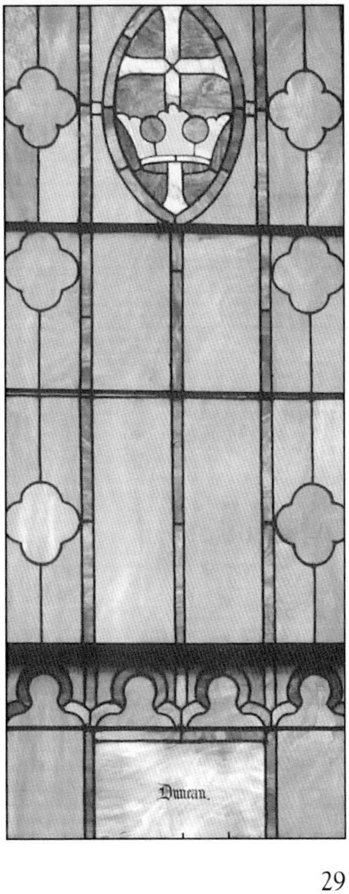

Shortly before it was demolished in the 1930s, the Methodist church of Pithole appeared as it did above. The stained-glass window shown at the right was originally installed in the Plumer Methodist church in 1865. Thomas Duncan, the church's benefactor, left an endowment of several thousand dollars to maintain both sanctuaries. (Image at right photographed by Jim Stoudt.)

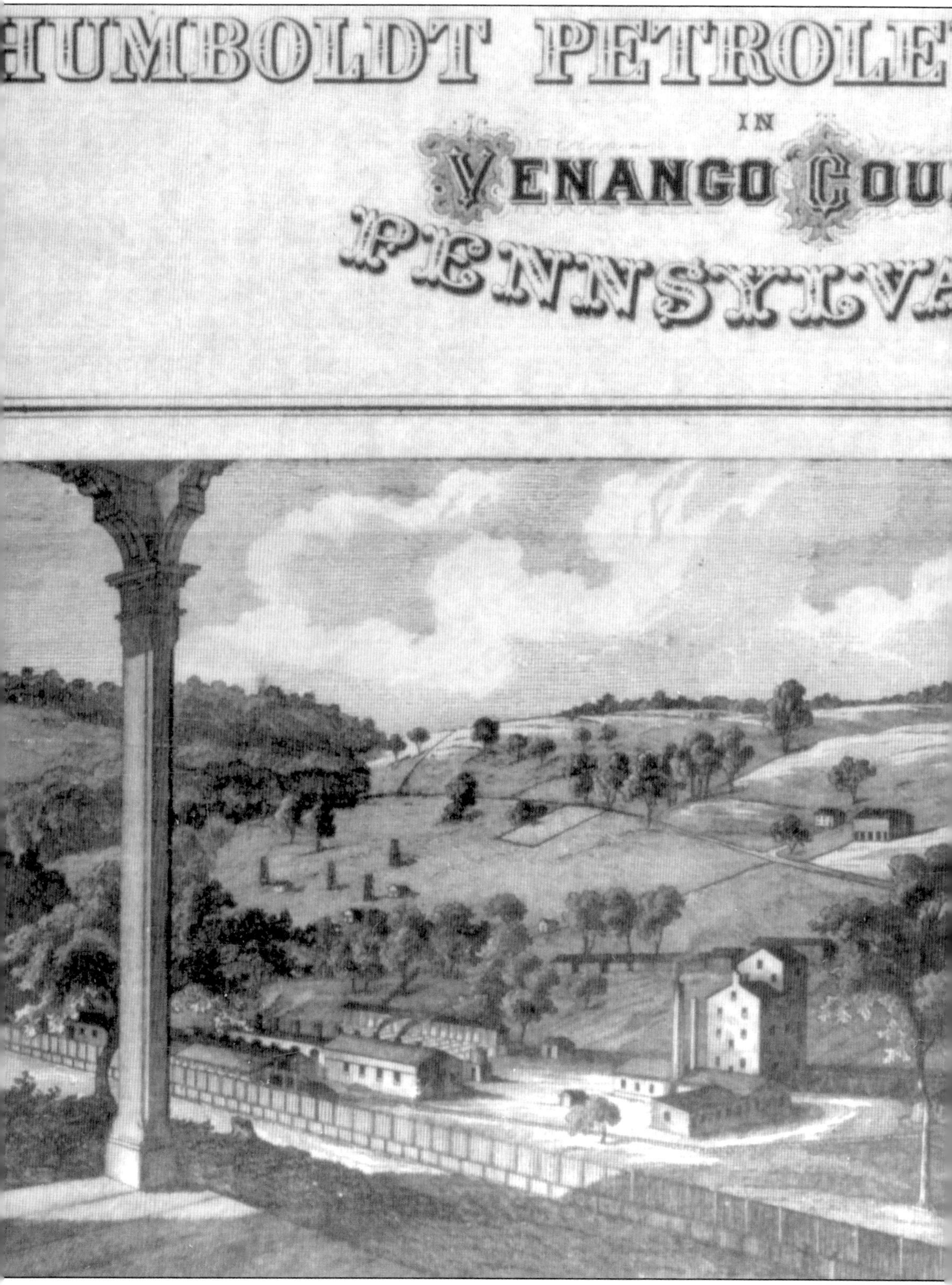
HUMBOLDT PETROLE
IN
VENANGO COU
PENNSYLVA

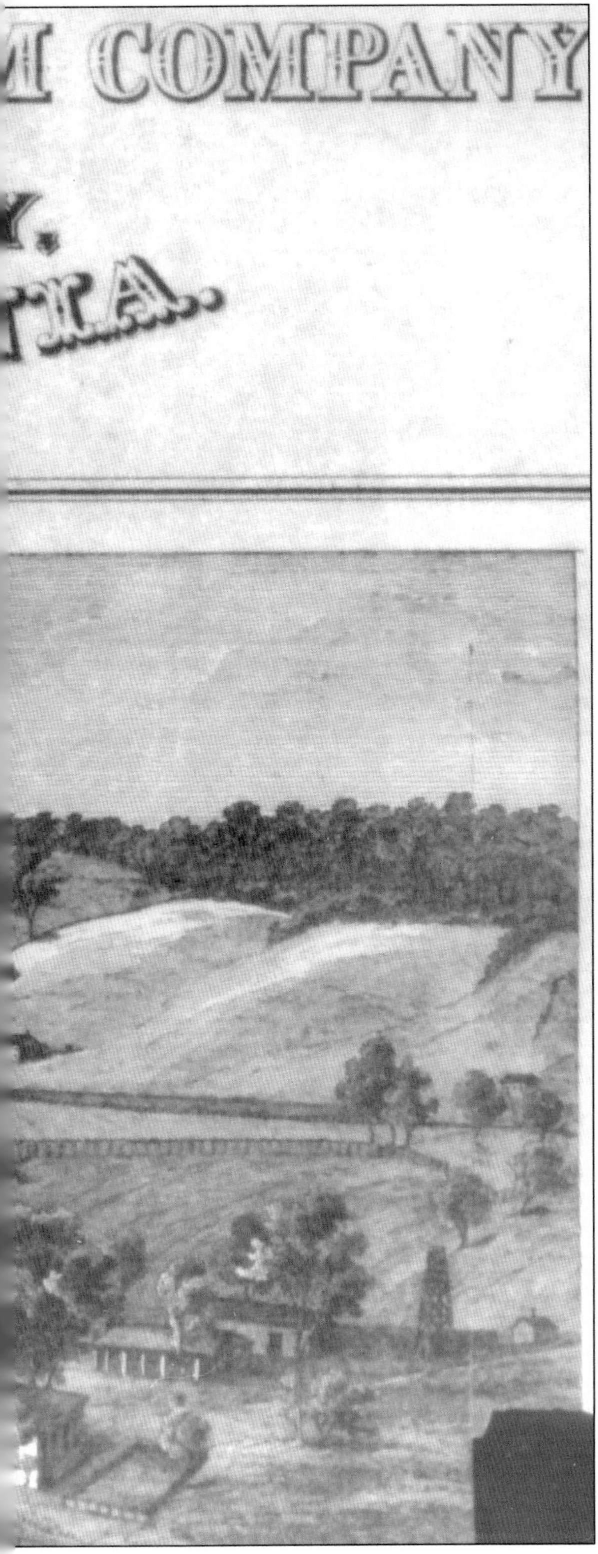

In the fall of 1861, Jon Bruns of Bremen, Germany, came to Plumer to purchase property on which to build the largest and most modern refinery in the world. With the financial backing of Rudolph, Otto, Louis, and Thomas Ludovici (brothers and Wall street bankers), Bruns was able to construct a refinery that produced more refined oil in 1862 than all the refineries in Cleveland combined. So complete were the works that the grounds contained two complete cooper works, dormitories for employees, a brick works producing 10,000 bricks per day, an aniline dye works, and storage capacity for 30,000 barrels of crude oil. The main works occupied an area of about 19.5 acres and was entirely surrounded by a close-boarded wood fence, 8 feet high. The works was made entirely of quarried cut stone; the stills were designed to prevent destruction by fire. Bruns named the works after Alexander von Humboldt, the most celebrated German naturalist and explorer of the 17th and 18th centuries. In 1799, Humboldt spent the next five years of his life exploring the Americas, where he catalogued thousands of unknown species of animals, plants, and minerals. After Humboldt met with Thomas Jefferson, Jefferson was heard to say that Alexander von Humboldt was the greatest man he had ever seen. Given the success of the Humboldt works, three other refineries were soon constructed in Plumer. From 1861 through 1866, Plumer was the oil refining capital of the world. In May 1864, Bruns dissolved his partnership with the Ludovici brothers and returned to New York. The Ludovicis merged the works with outside investors from New York and continued as general managers. Without Bruns, however, the works was unable to keep pace with newer refineries and eventually ceased operation in 1868. Nothing is known of Bruns's life after that, but his refinery would serve as the model for John Rockefeller and his Standard Oil empire.

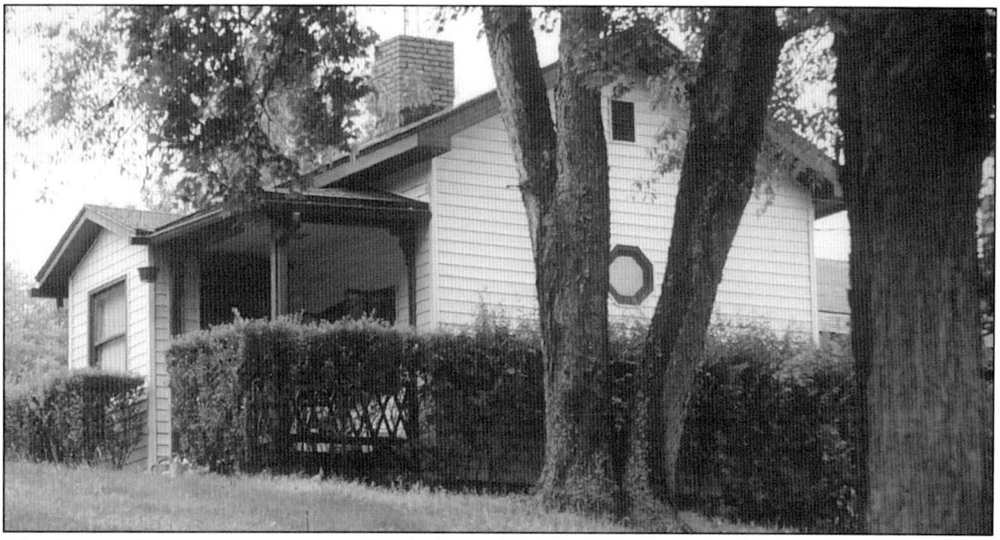

This home, shown as it appears today, belonged the superintendent of the Humboldt refinery, Allen Norton Leet. Leet brought great ingenuity to the Humboldt. He designed the works to incorporate the natural flow of the hillside to move crude oil, refined oil, and naphtha from tanks to still and then into barrels and bottles without the need for pumps. When coal and wood was too expensive to use as fuel for the stills, he created an injection system that fired the boilers using gasoline refined from crude—gasoline that would have been burned off as a waste by-product. The efficiency of the refining process became the envy of many modern-day refineries. With the capacity of the refining increasing every day, the need for crude pushed the Humboldt refinery to search the Pithole valley for additional reserves of the precious commodity. (Photographed by Jim Stoudt.)

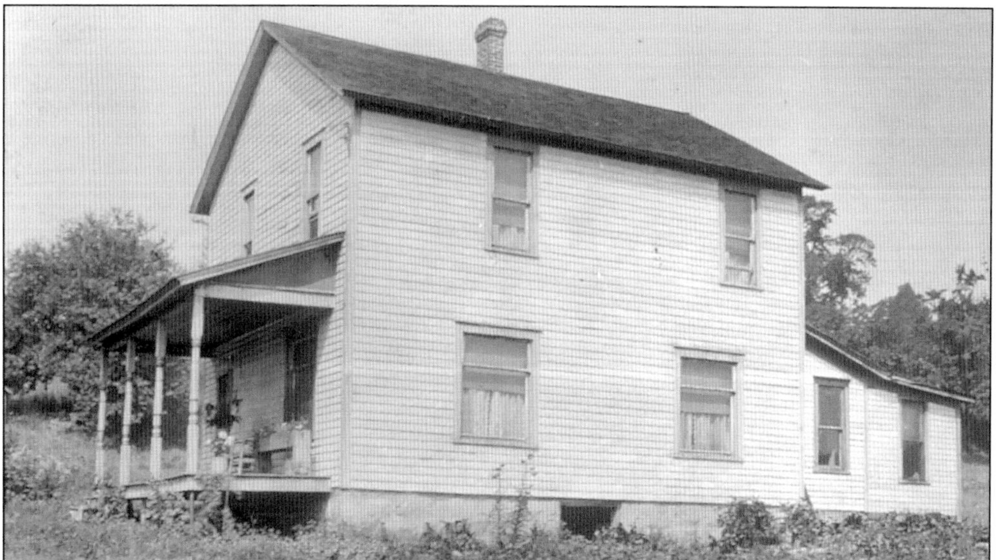

Frederick Ensle, a master cooper from Germany, was brought to Plumer in 1862 to build and operate the cooper shops at the works. He built his home, pictured here, on land just adjacent to the Humboldt property. Frederick's sons stayed in Plumer and, with William Huber, became successful oil producers and operators. (Photograph courtesy Bill Huber.)

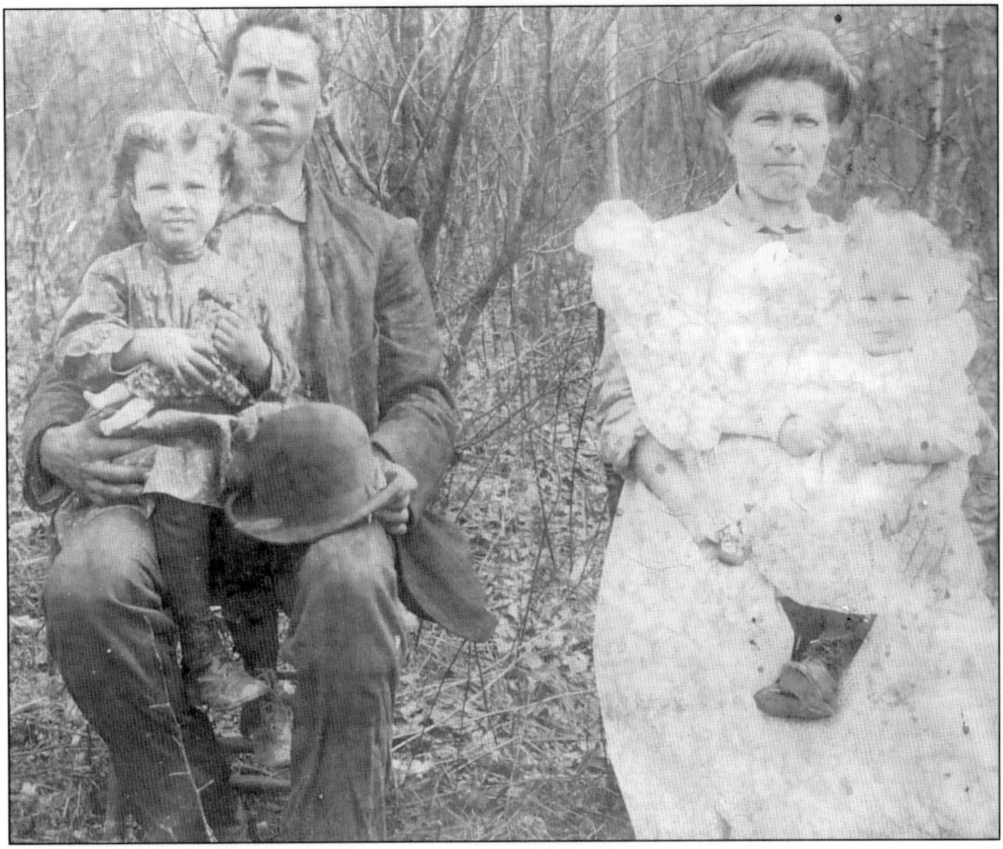

William Haupt, his wife, and their daughters, Etta and Louise, came to Plumer in 1862. William was a stone mason from Germany and was in charge of cutting and laying the massive cut stone used in building the Humboldt refinery. He later designed and built the two stone arch bridges that cross Pithole Creek and continue to support daily automotive traffic today. (Photograph courtesy Bill Grove.)

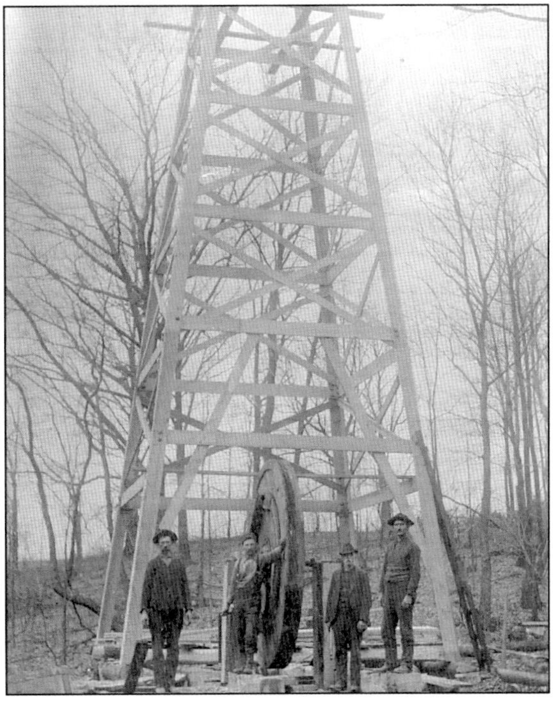

Frederick Ensle's sons and William Huber build a standard rig on the old Ensle homestead, *c.* 1905. (Photograph courtesy Bill Huber.)

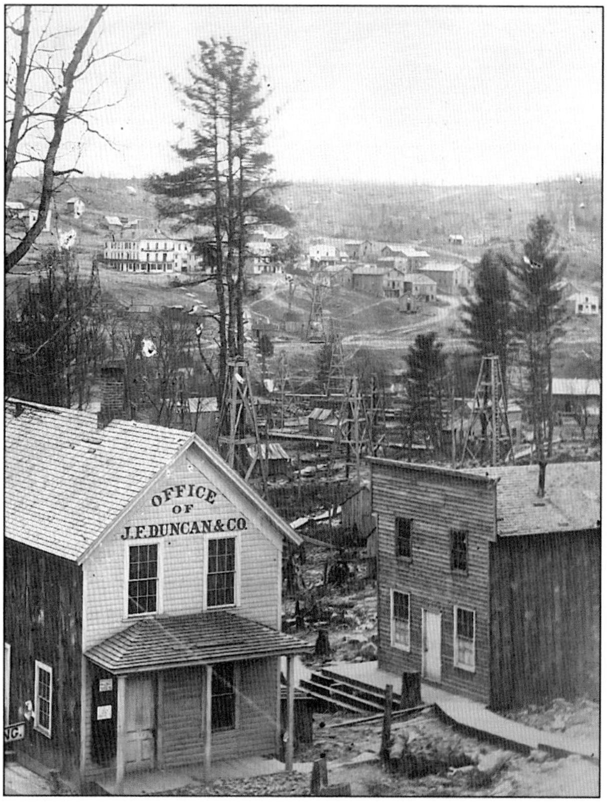

This view of Pithole, taken in the spring of 1866, looks across the flats to Prather City on the far hillside. To the right of Duncan's office is the newly built jail. In the distance, the short-lived Bonta House can be seen. The Bonta House was soon sold for the salvage rights, as it was to be demolished. (Photograph courtesy the Drake Well Museum.)

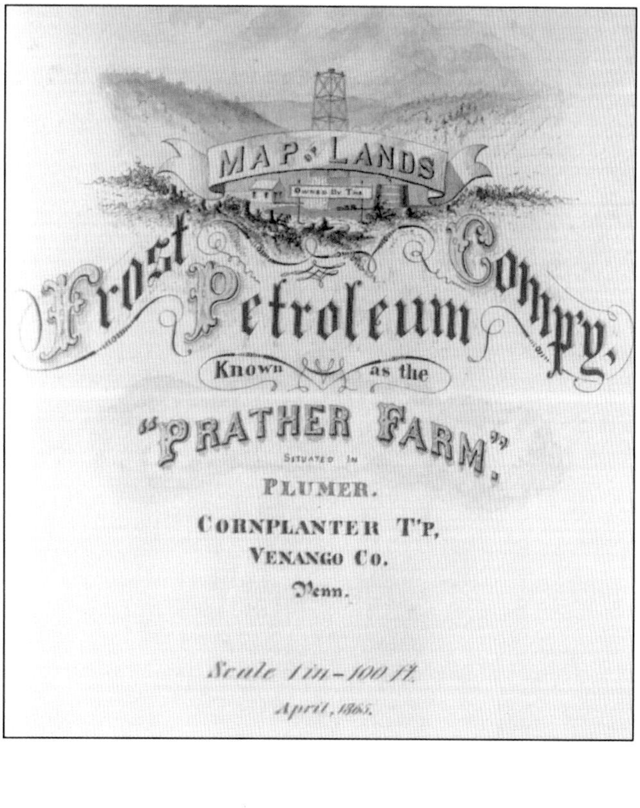

This masthead appeared on the map of the Prather farm in 1865. George Prather and Thomas Duncan had profited greatly from land speculation in and around Plumer from 1865 to 1866. Town lots in Plumer sold for more than $150 per foot and were hard to obtain at that price. Tracts of land adjacent to the Humboldt works had been sold for more than $12,500 per acre without any successful oil developments having been made. With this capital, they purchased the farm of Thomas Holmden of Pithole for $100,000 and sold the property a year later for about $2 million.

In 1862, Mr. Hutchins arrived from New York with a new rotary pump he had designed. Along with Mr. Fostor, he contracted to build a 2-inch wrought-iron pipeline from Tarr Farm to the Humboldt refinery in Plumer. Using three of his rotary pumps, he successfully pumped the crude more than 2 miles in distance and up an elevation of more than 400 feet. This was the first oil pipeline to ever use pumps to transport crude oil. The Warren brothers, who had built a large refinery in Plumer near the Humboldt works, built the second pipeline to transport refined oil in 1863. The 2-inch pipeline was totally gravity fed and carried the refined oil more than 3 miles from Plumer to the Allegheny River. (Map courtesy the Drake Well Museum.)

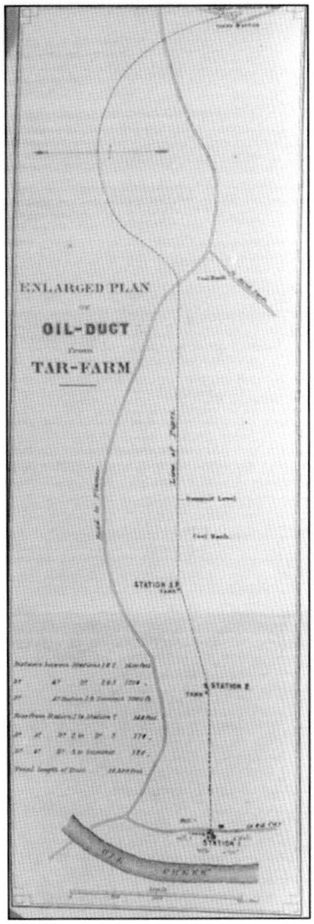

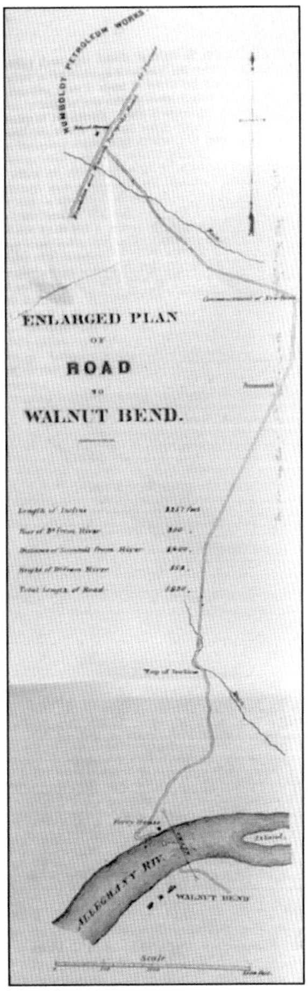

Jon Bruns facilitated the movement of refined oil by building a private road to Walnut Bend on the Allegheny River. Steamboats would load the refined oil, naphtha, and aniline dye directly on board and ship it to Pittsburgh some 90 miles away. The majority of the products refined at the Humboldt works were shipped to Bremen, Germany. Bruns, in spite of initially high construction costs, still realized a profit of $50,000 in the Humboldt refinery's first year of operation. (Map courtesy the Drake Well Museum.)

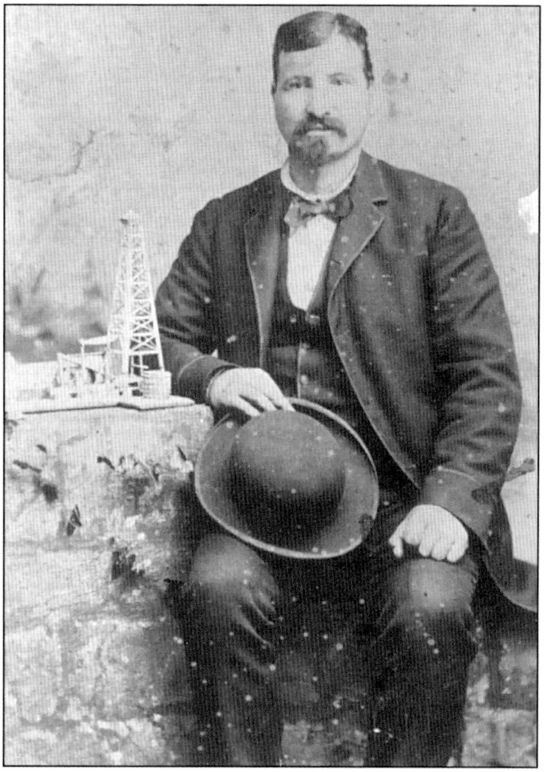

Josiah Winger, pictured here in 1883, first began drilling wells at Walnut Bend in 1861. His third well was drilled by horsepower with "a fine cream colored horse brought up from Pittsburgh via steam boat." Years later, Winger would delight in telling how he "had to toss stones at the flanks of the old nag to keep him moving." Winger was an active driller until his death in 1917, earning him the title of the world's oldest driller. He is pictured with one of the four models of rigs he presented to Edwin Bell, the founder of the first Drake Memorial Museum in 1913. (Photograph courtesy the Drake Well Museum.)

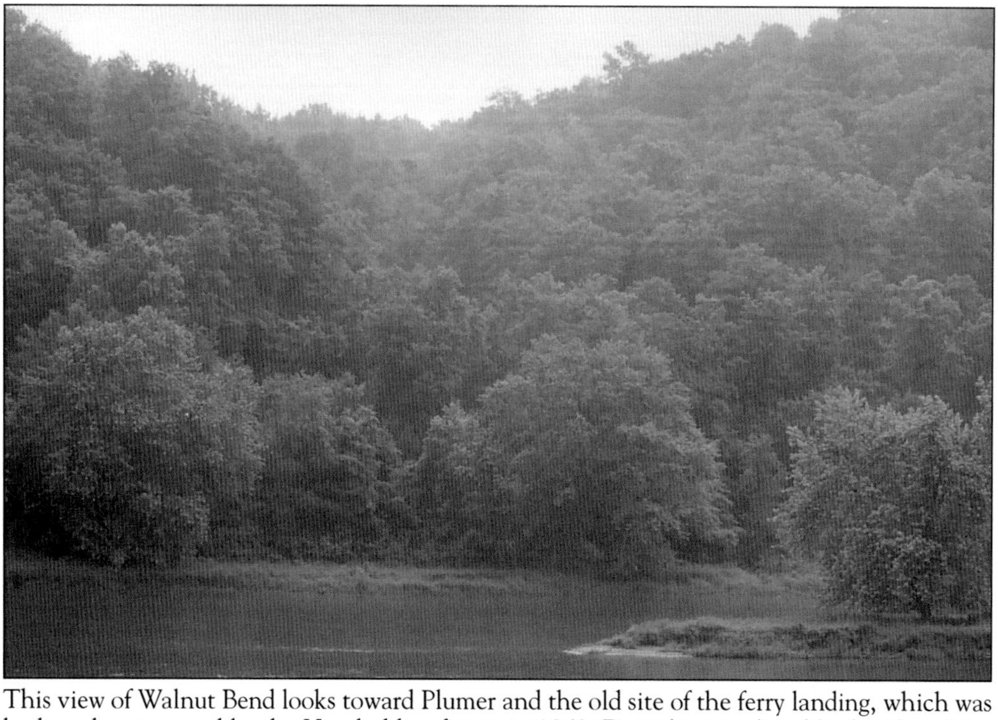

This view of Walnut Bend looks toward Plumer and the old site of the ferry landing, which was built and maintained by the Humboldt refinery in 1862. Derricks once lined both sides of the Allegheny River and even up the steep hillsides. (Photographed by Jim Stoudt.)

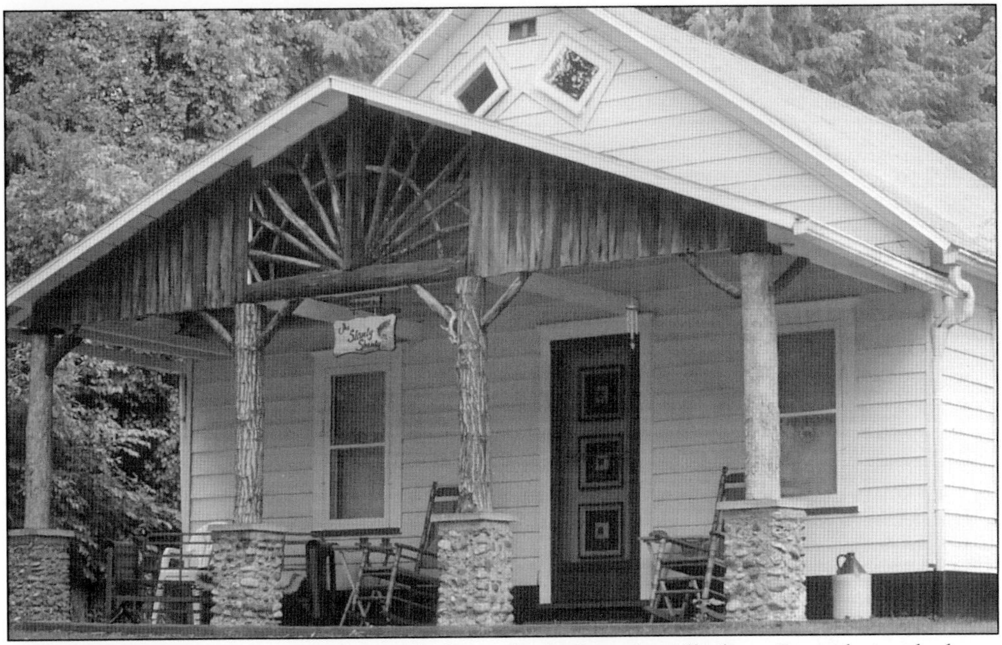

This Arts and Crafts–style cabin is typical of many built along the Allegheny River during the latter half of the 1800s and the early 1900s. The cabin at Walnut Bend was built over the foundation of one of the Humboldt houses, originally built in 1863. (Photographed by Jim Stoudt.)

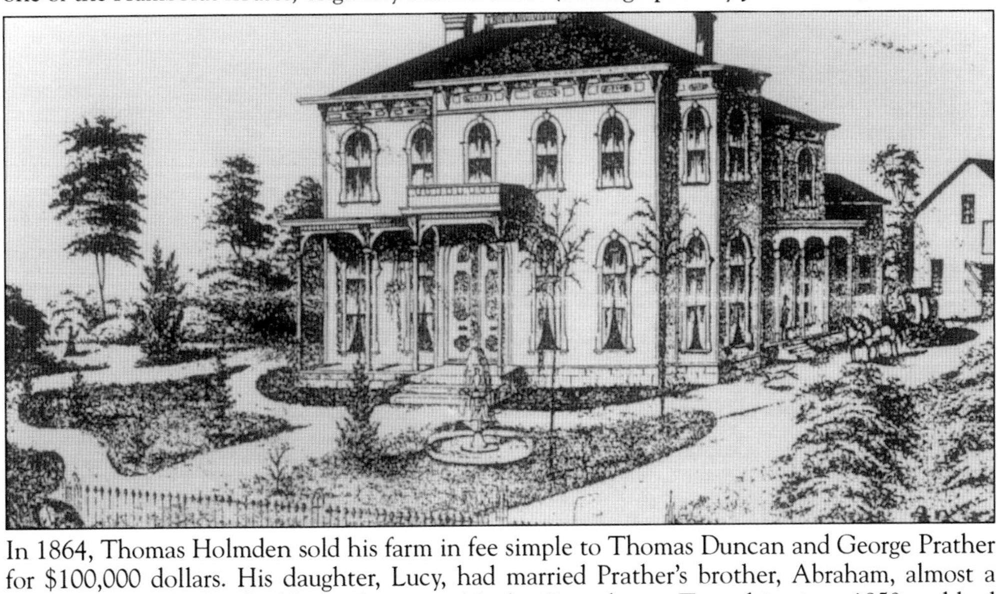

In 1864, Thomas Holmden sold his farm in fee simple to Thomas Duncan and George Prather for $100,000 dollars. His daughter, Lucy, had married Prather's brother, Abraham, almost a year earlier. Holmden had been the constable for Cornplanter Township since 1859 and had served as the county commissioner since 1863. He was a well-known and respected figure in Venango County and had followed the oil industry for more than three years. When he was approached by representatives of the Humboldt refinery to begin exploration on his farm along Pithole Creek, he was eager to lease the mineral rights for a one-quarter interest. He moved to Cleveland and built this fine residence in the late 1860s, near the property of Thomas Duncan and George Prather. Holmden remained an active political figure in Cleveland until his death. (Photograph courtesy Richard Hammil.)

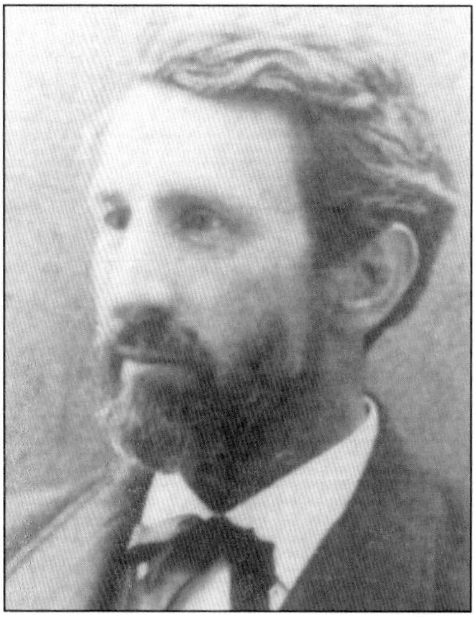

Charles Vernon Culver came to the oil region from Ohio in 1862. In the next two years, he had successfully resurrected the Bank in Meadville and founded nearly a dozen more banks in the oil region and a major banking institution in New York City. He purchased the land for the First National Bank of Plumer in 1864 and sat on the board of a dozen other banks. He was such a popular and charismatic figure that, in the fall of 1865, at the age of 35, he was elected to Congress. Culver pleaded to be removed from the ballot and was quoted as saying, "I'd rather pay $50,000 than accept the nomination." Despite this claim, he was elected in 1865.

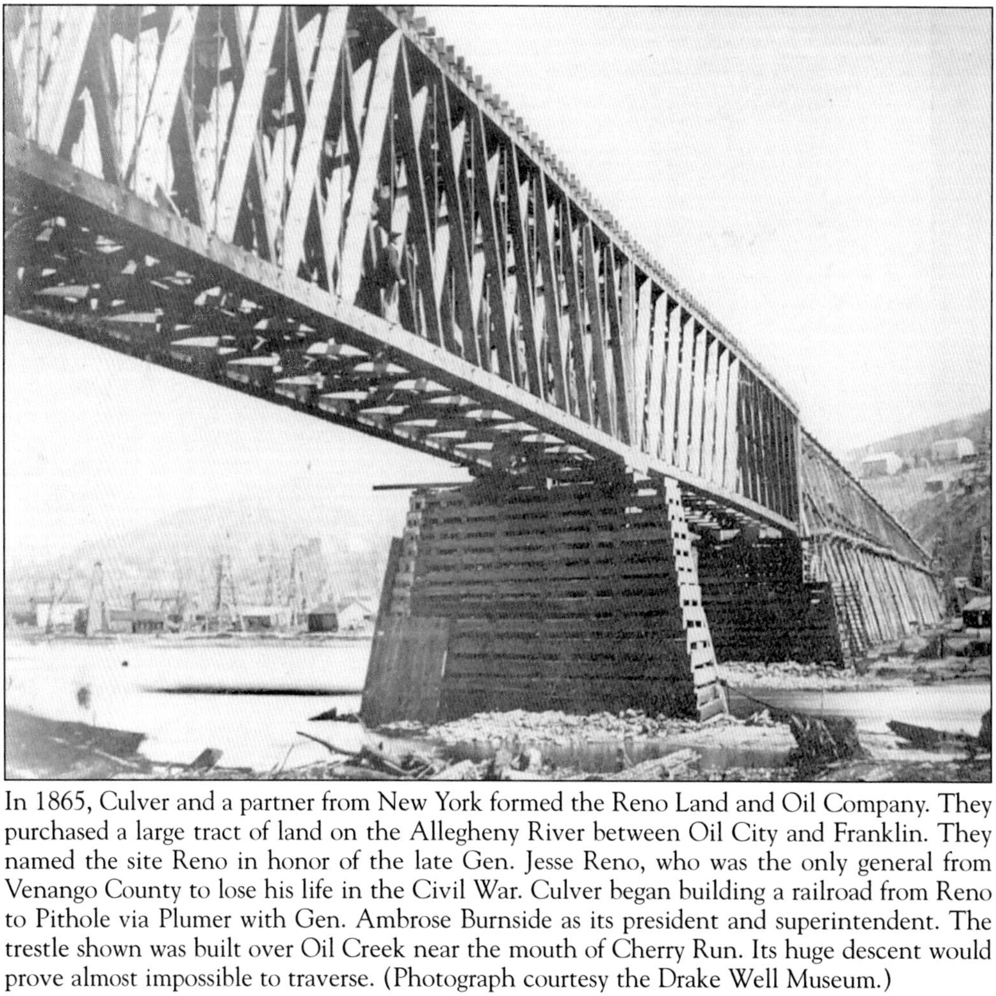

In 1865, Culver and a partner from New York formed the Reno Land and Oil Company. They purchased a large tract of land on the Allegheny River between Oil City and Franklin. They named the site Reno in honor of the late Gen. Jesse Reno, who was the only general from Venango County to lose his life in the Civil War. Culver began building a railroad from Reno to Pithole via Plumer with Gen. Ambrose Burnside as its president and superintendent. The trestle shown was built over Oil Creek near the mouth of Cherry Run. Its huge descent would prove almost impossible to traverse. (Photograph courtesy the Drake Well Museum.)

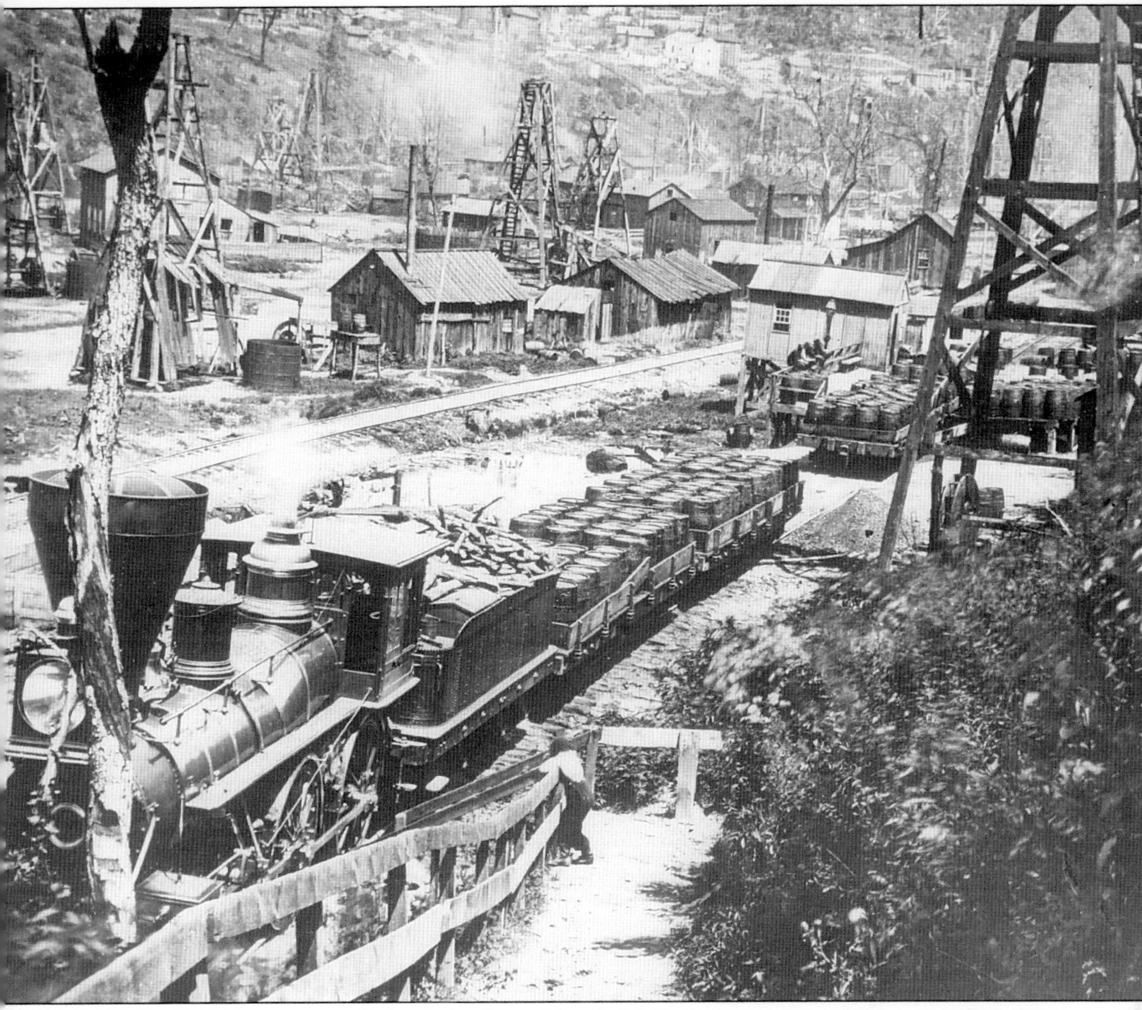

After an unfortunate run on Culver's banks in March 1866, Culver was unable to complete the railroad to Pithole. The railroad that ran to Plumer went on to operate for only a few years. In June 1866, the deputy sheriff of Cornplanter Township went to Plumer and seized one of the Culver locomotives due to non-payment. When word reached Culver in Reno, Culver took several armed employees with him and met the sheriff in Rouseville, where he had moved the seized locomotive. After a two-day, armed standoff, Culver and his men backed down and returned to Reno. After a lengthy legal battle, Culver was imprisoned with his wife by his side in jail. Congress never found any evidence to censure Culver and he was soon exonerated. Culver remained in Franklin as an oil operator, but never again realized the success he once had. (Photograph courtesy the Venango Historical Society.)

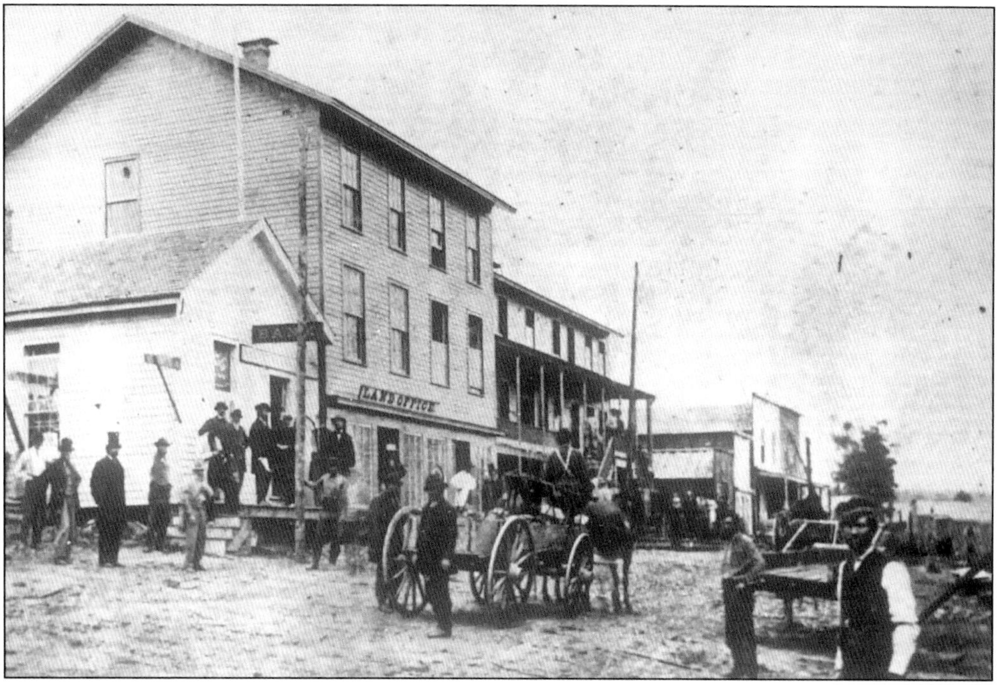

Culver's First National Bank of Plumer was made up of a very strong group of Plumer businessmen and refiners. With George Prather as the president, it weathered the collapse of Culver's other banking institutions. In the summer of 1865, Prather and J.J. Wadsworth, the head cashier at the Plumer Bank, formed the Prather and Wadsworth Bank of Pithole, shown above. The First National Bank of Plumer provided the majority of the financial underwriting that capitalized the rapid growth of Pithole. In June 1865, Pithole grew from a few wells along the creek to a town of more than 900 buildings and more than 10,000 inhabitants. (Photograph courtesy the Drake Well Museum.)

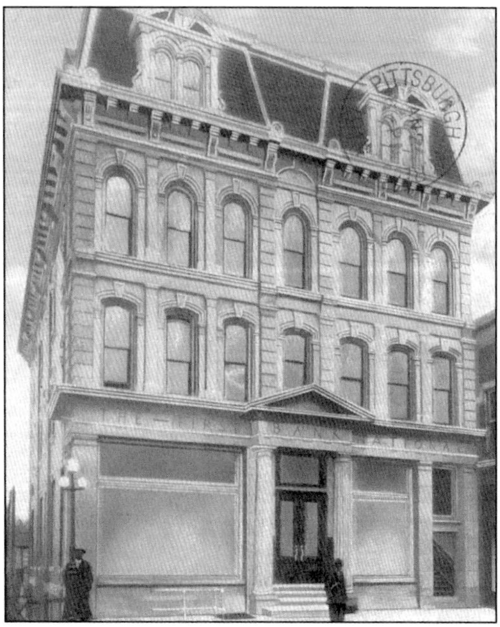

In just two years, Pithole—which once boasted over 50 hotels, 3 theaters (the Murphy Theatre was adorned with Tiffany chandeliers and scenery from New York), and countless taverns—was a near ghost town, with fewer than 200 inhabitants. Fires wiped out large sections of town and destroyed countless wells on the creek. Speculators were following the migration to new towns like Shamburg and Grease City, where it was easier to do business and have a good time. George Prather sold his interest in the Pithole Bank in 1866, closed his bank in Plumer in 1868, and built this beautiful building in Sharon, Pennsylvania, to house his bank. (Photograph courtesy John and Margie Hummel.)

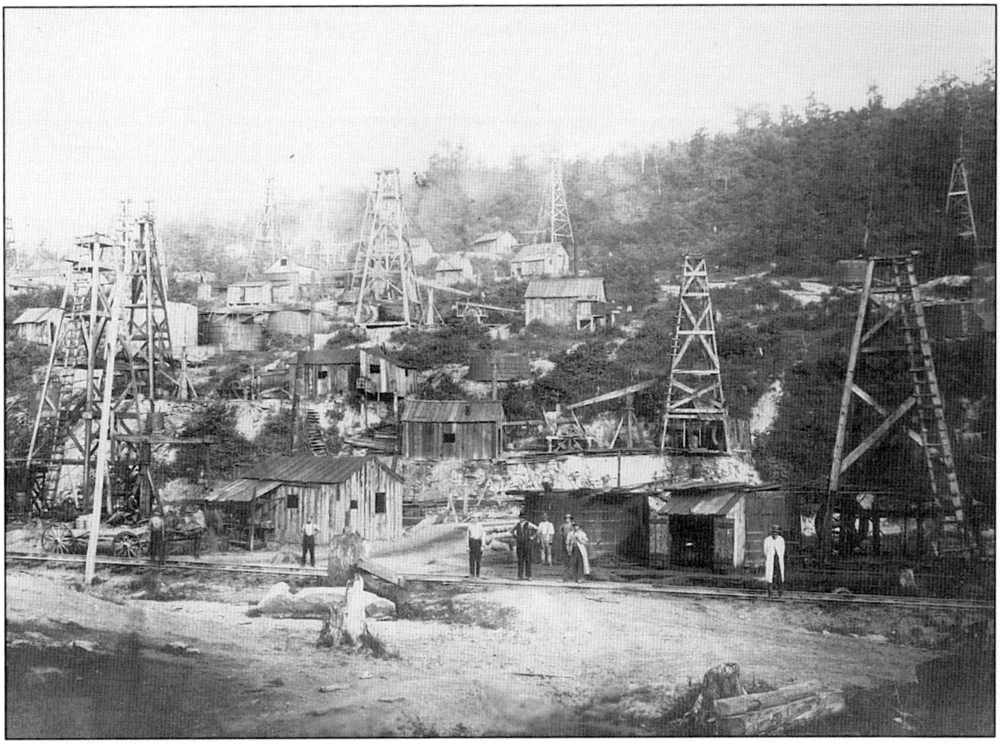

Tarr Farm was immune to most of the rapid decline and continued as a major producing field for a number of years. (Photograph courtesy the Venango Historical Society.)

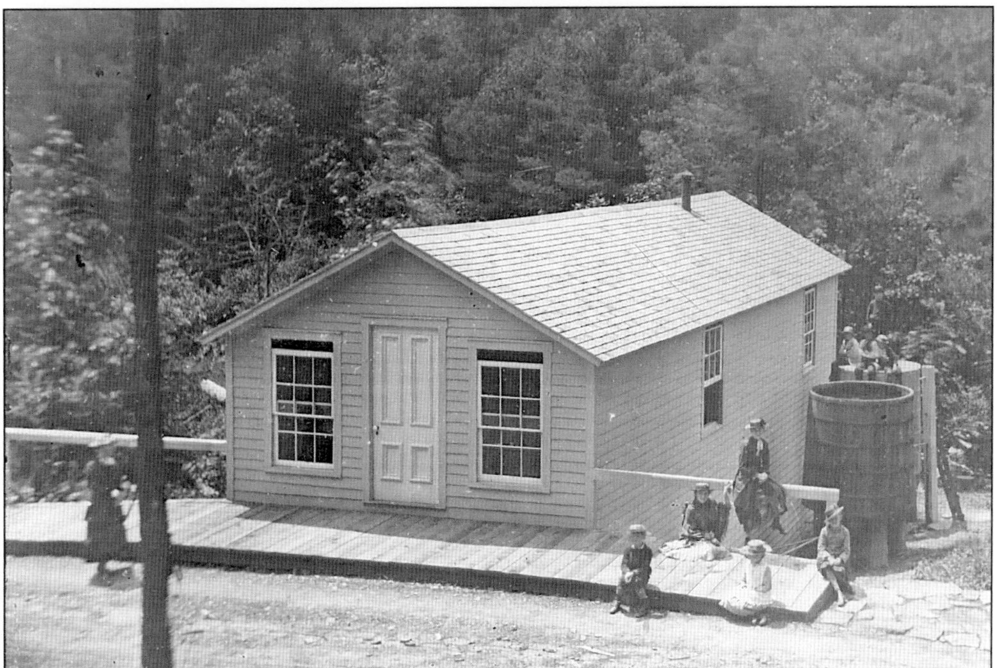

This pastoral setting at Tarr Farm almost belies the fact that this building was a tavern. (Photograph courtesy the Drake Well Museum.)

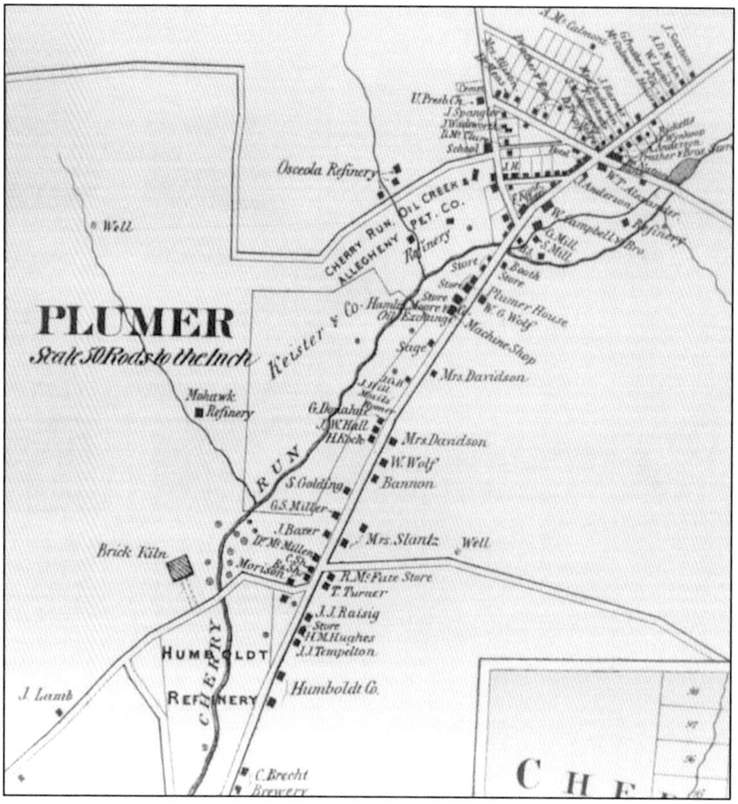

The Beers Atlas of the Oil Region, published in 1865, shows Plumer when it was the hub of all oildom. Plumer spawned Pithole, and unlike countless other boom towns—including Pithole, Redhot, Cashup, and Prather—Plumer never vanished. It continues to be a beautiful village along the banks of Cherry Run.

PLUMER

BUSINESS DIRECTORY.

ABBOTT & ARNITT........Dealers in Groceries and Feed.
ADAMS, J...................Blacksmith.
ALEXANDER & GALEY...Dealers in Groceries and Provisions.
BARKER, C. C..............Agent Cherry Run, Oil Creek and Allegheny Petroleum Co.
BARNES, JAMES A.........Wagon Maker.
BOOTH, P. J................Dealer in General Merchandise.
BROWN, THOMAS H.......Supt. Reliance Petroleum Co.
BURDICK, S. M............Proprietor of Burdick House.
DRAKE, A...................Dealer in Dry Goods.
DUNCAN, THOS. G........Merchant, Oil Dealer, &c.
HAMLIN & MOORE........Manufacturers of Drilling and Mining Tools.
HILL, JOHN.................Blacksmith.
HUGHES, H. M.............Dealer in Groceries and Feed.
KANE, FRANCIS...........Cherry Run Hotel.
KOCH & BRO., J. A........Carpenters and Joiners.
MASON, L. D. V.............Supt. United States Petroleum Co.
McFATE, R. W.............Dealer in General Merchandise.
MILLER, G. S...............Proprietor Saloon.
MILLER, H. C...............Miller's Saloon.
MILLS & SWAN.............Land Agents, Plumer.
MINOR & DURSTON.......Land Agents, Plumer.
MOORE, M. M...............Resident.
PRATHER & BROS.........Merchants, Oil Dealers, &c.
RAISIG, J. J.................Pastor Lutheran Church.
RICKETTS, JOHN...........Oil Dealer and Producer.
RUSLING, G. M.............Civil Engineer and Surveyor.
SAGE, J.......................Resident.
TEMPLETON, J. J..........Carpenter and Joiner.
WILSON W. N...............Harness Maker.
WOLF, W. G.................Proprietor of Plumer House.
WYNKOOP, J. F............Oil Dealer.

PLAN OF LANDS
on
CHERRY RUN.

30 Rods   Scale 30 Rods to the Inch.

Entered according to Act of Congress, in the year 1865 in the Clerks Off…

Four

Cherry Run Valley through the End of the 19th Century

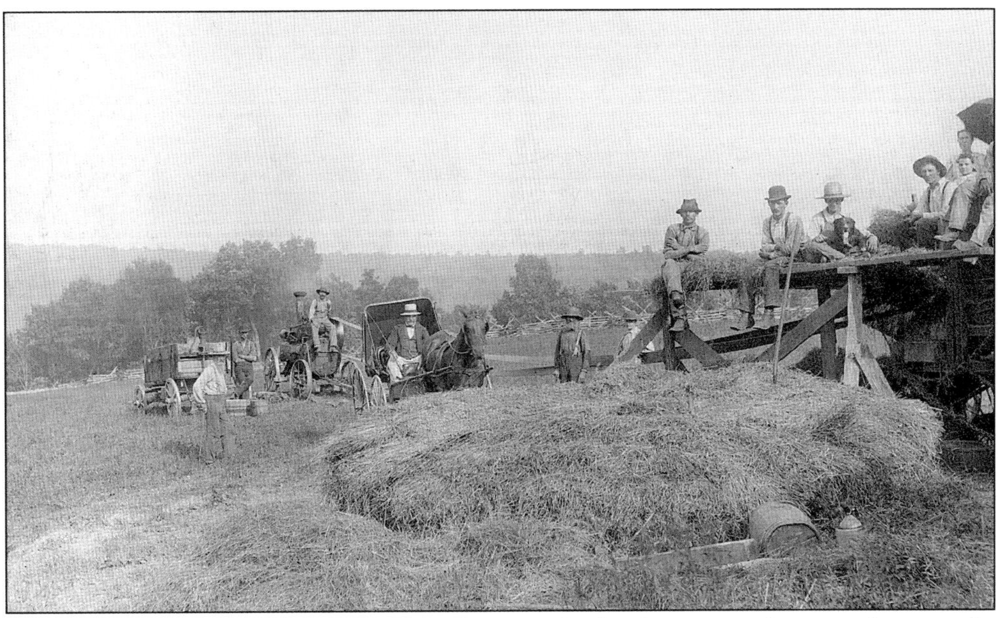

Peter Berry's farm is shown *c.* 1880. Note the steam boiler that was used to provide power for the harvesting machinery. Although most of the trees were clear-cut and crude oil had polluted most of the creeks and streams, the land was still fertile. By the 1880s, the streams were running pure and full of native trout. Many families that had come to the valley seeking instant fortune in the oil fields stayed to till the land and raise children. (Photograph courtesy Dick Turk.)

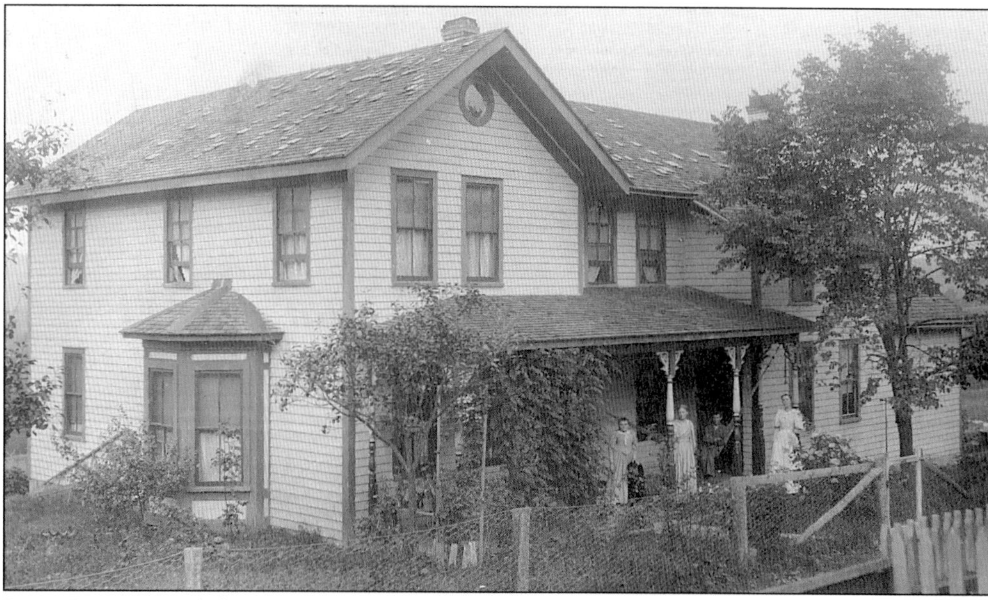

Peter Berry moved from Erie County, New York, in 1868, and became a tool dresser near Tidioute. After much effort, he gained success with the Grandin brothers in Forest County. In 1882, they struck a well producing 1,000 barrels of oil a day. In 1884, Berry was elected to the state legislature by the widest margin in Forest County. He built this homestead near Plumer in 1889. (Photograph courtesy Dick Turk.)

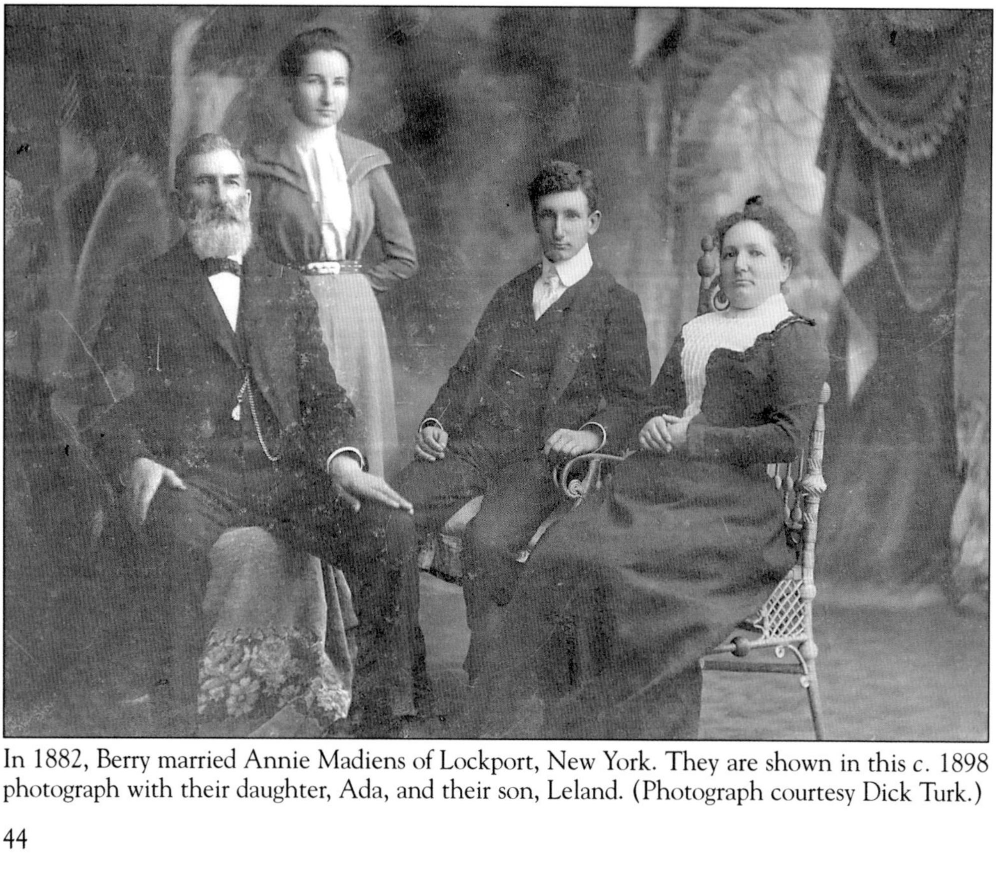

In 1882, Berry married Annie Madiens of Lockport, New York. They are shown in this *c.* 1898 photograph with their daughter, Ada, and their son, Leland. (Photograph courtesy Dick Turk.)

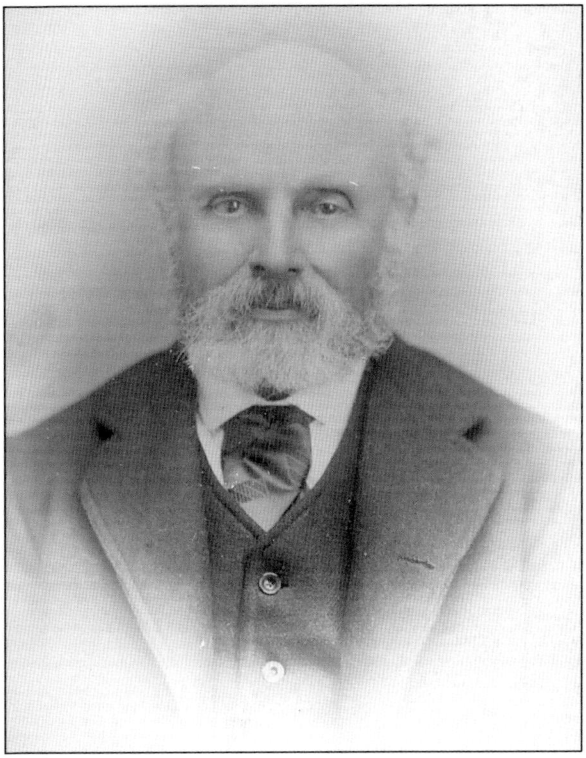

Karl Brecht, pictured at right, was from Wurtemberg, Germany. A brewer by trade, he moved to Plumer in 1861, where he purchased a farm and built a brewery. The brewery was adjacent to the Humboldt works on the Franklin Warren Pike. His eldest son, Christian, ran the brewery in Plumer until 1879, when he moved to Rocky Grove to continue operations there. Karl Brecht lived in Plumer the rest of his life. Below is the Brecht homestead, which was torn down in the 1960s. (Photographs courtesy Don Saltzman.)

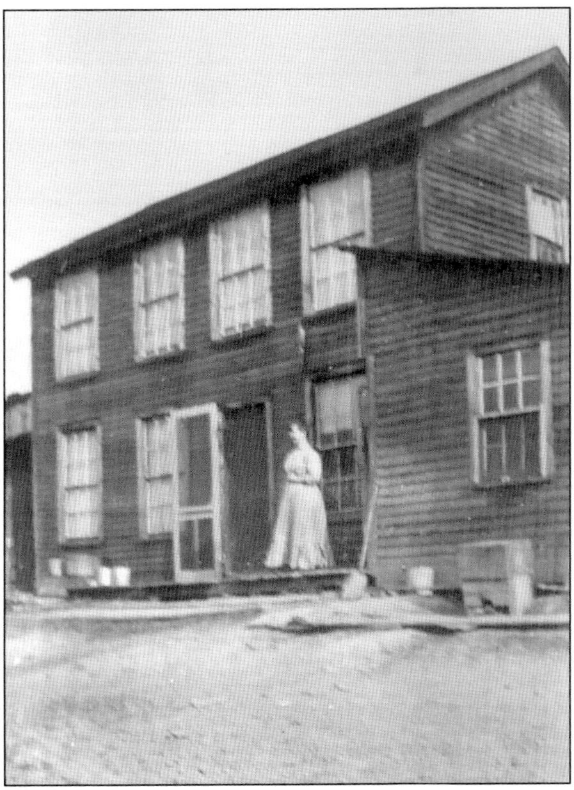

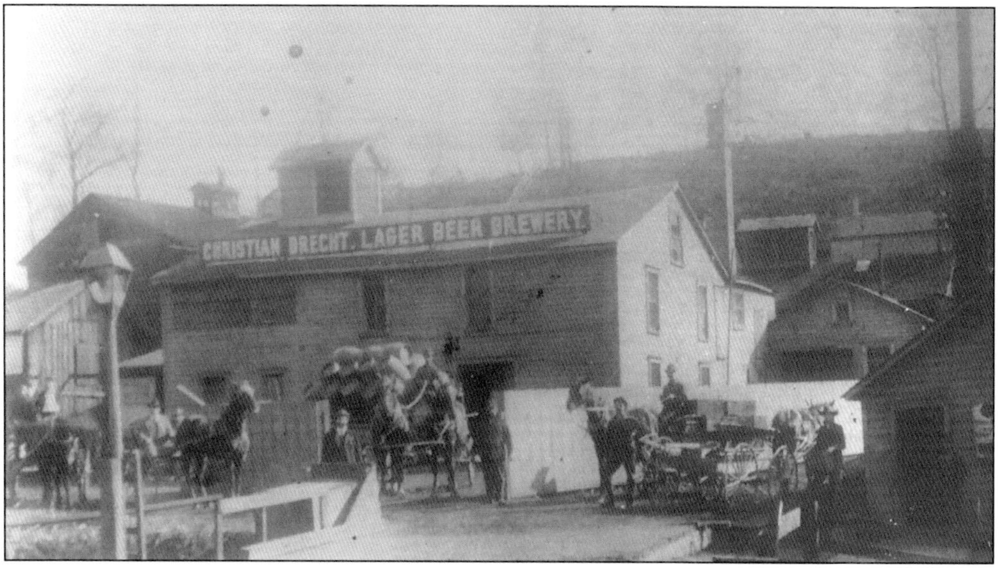

Christian Brecht opened this brewery after he moved to Rocky Grove from Plumer. (Photograph courtesy the Venango Historical Society.)

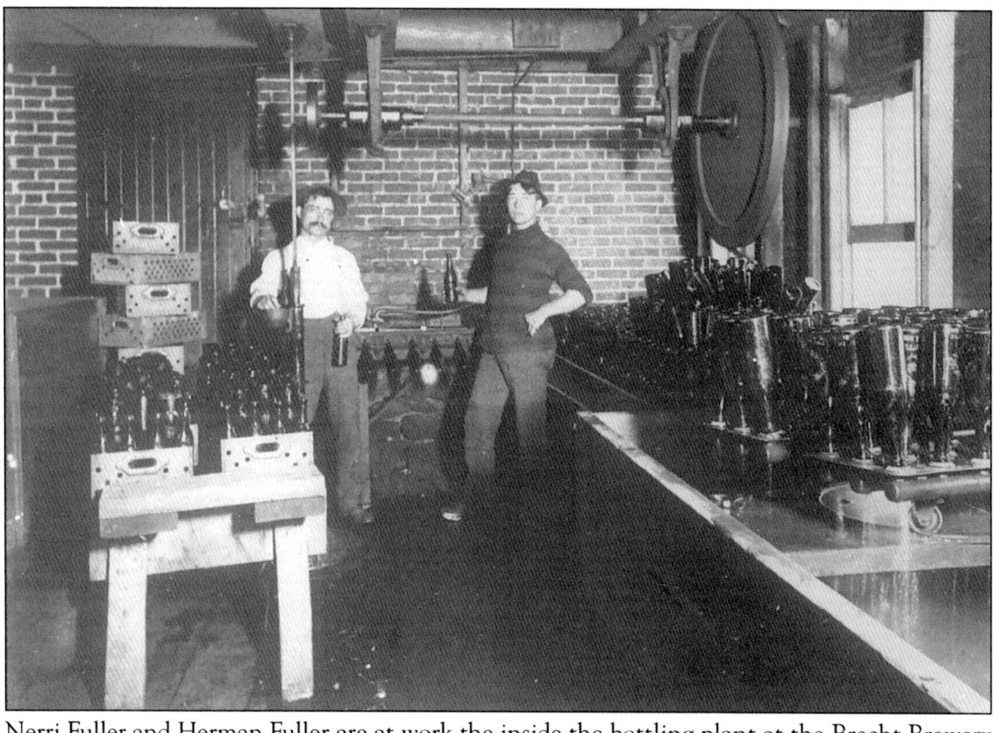

Nerri Fuller and Herman Fuller are at work the inside the bottling plant at the Brecht Brewery in Rocky Grove. (Photograph courtesy the Venango Historical Society.)

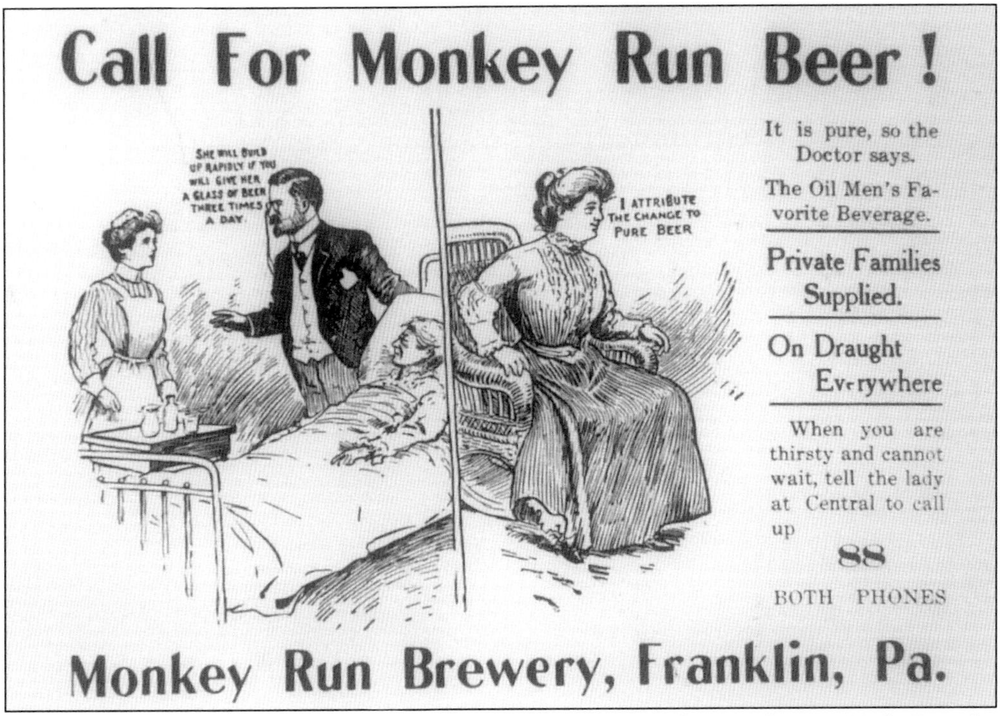

Monkey Run Beer was a competitor of the Cabinet Pilsner and Muencheneur Hofn Brau for which Christian Brecht was famous. Brecht's advertisements read, "The best I ever drank!"

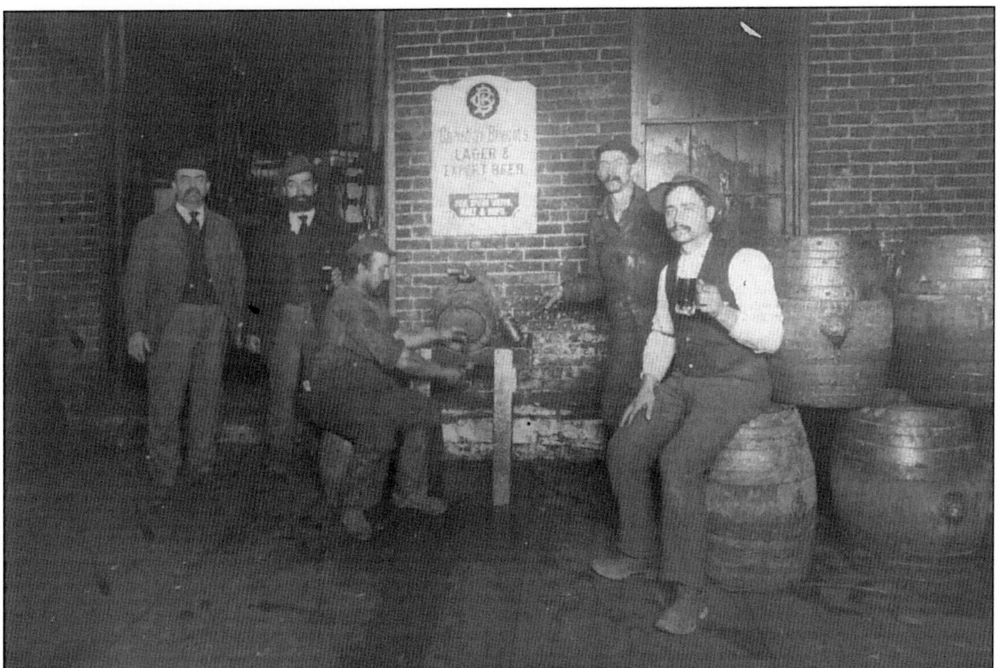

The Brecht employees sample the latest lager Christian brewed. Identified by the Venango Historical Society are, from left to right, Christian Brecht, Mr. Gerhardt, unidentified, George Ressler, and Neri Fuller. (Photograph courtesy the Venango County Historical Society.)

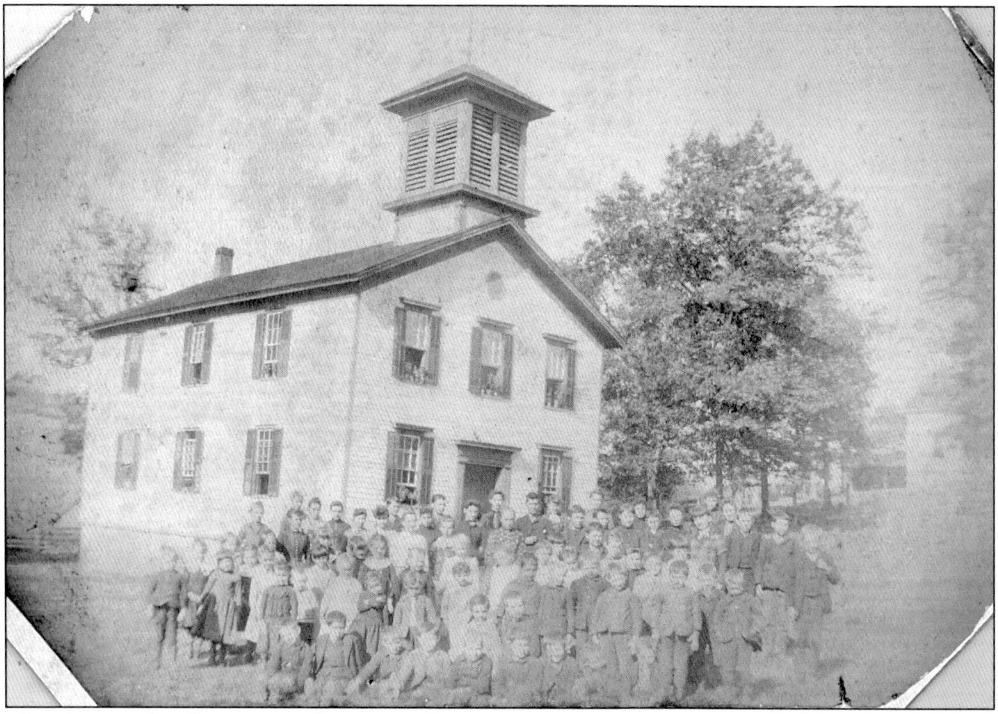

The Plumer schoolhouse, seen here c. 1870s, was built in 1871. (Photograph courtesy Dick Turk.)

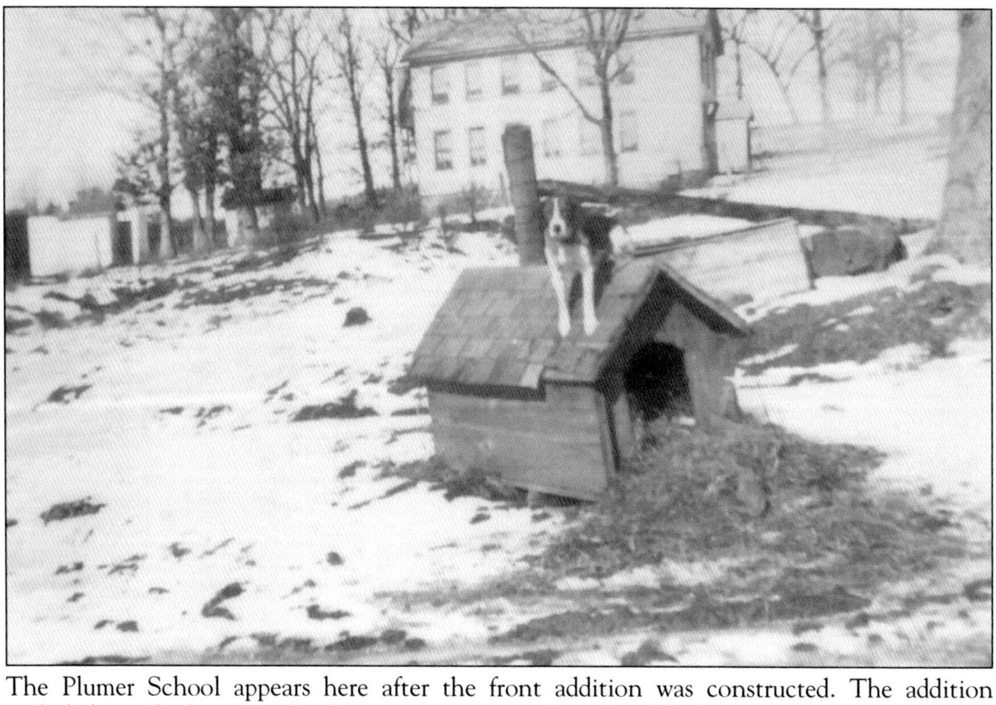

The Plumer School appears here after the front addition was constructed. The addition included two bathrooms, the first running water the school had ever known. (Photograph courtesy John Russell.)

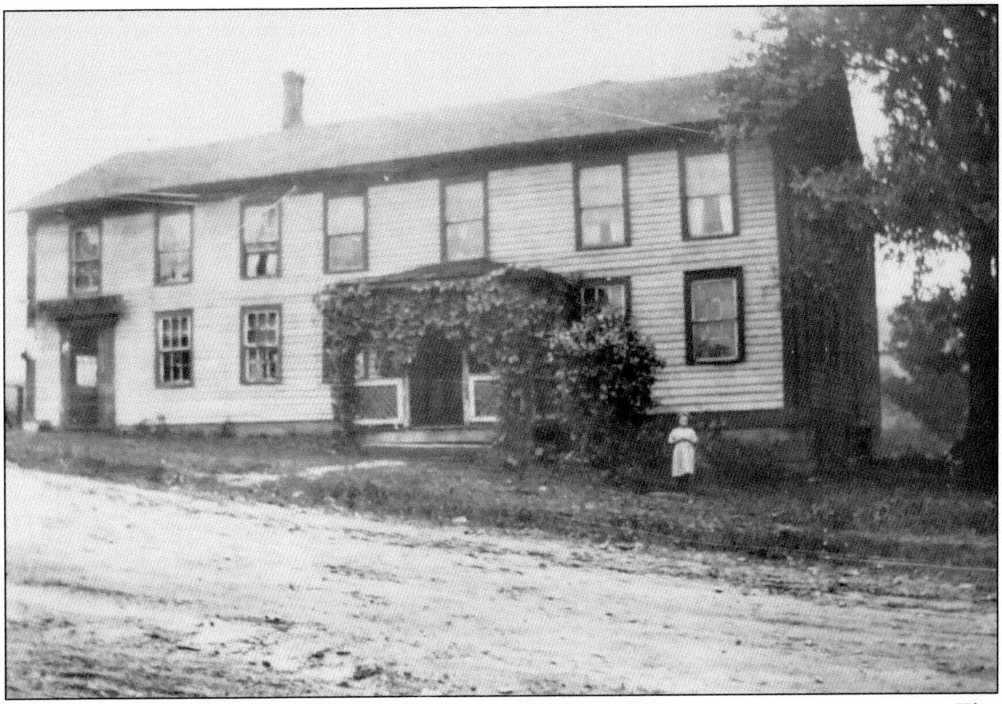

The former Prather house was located on Eagle Rock Road in Plumer, shown here *c*. 1900. The little girl on the porch is Edith Leach Gesin's older sister. The store was owned and operated by James Leach, Edith's grandfather. (Photograph courtesy the Oil City Genealogy Society.)

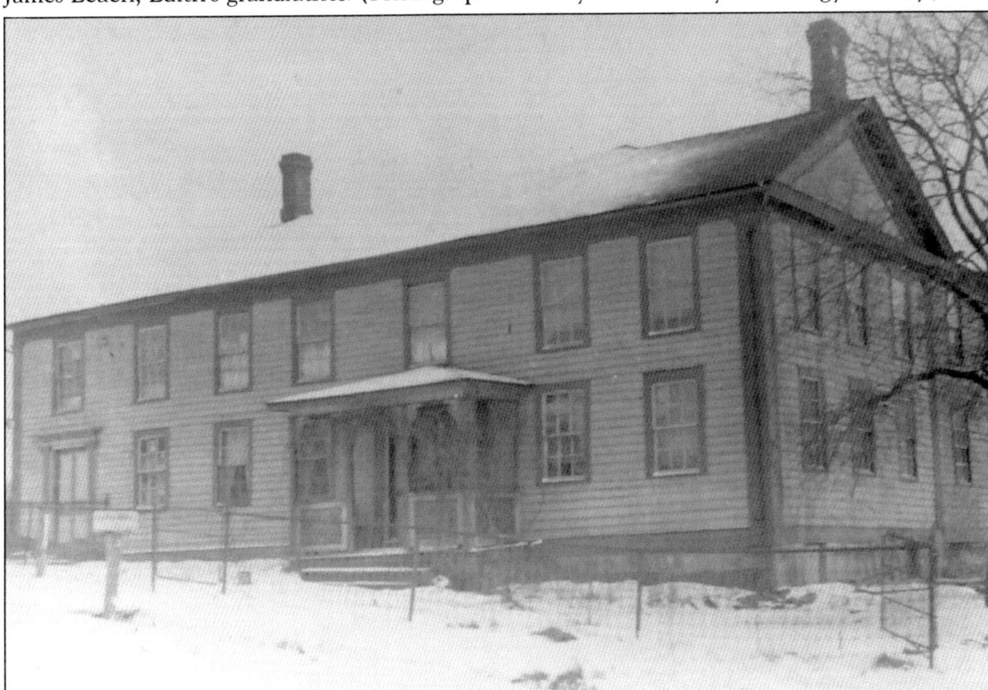

In 1900, the Leach store added another wing to the rear of the store that housed a billiard parlor. (Photograph courtesy the Venango Historical Society.)

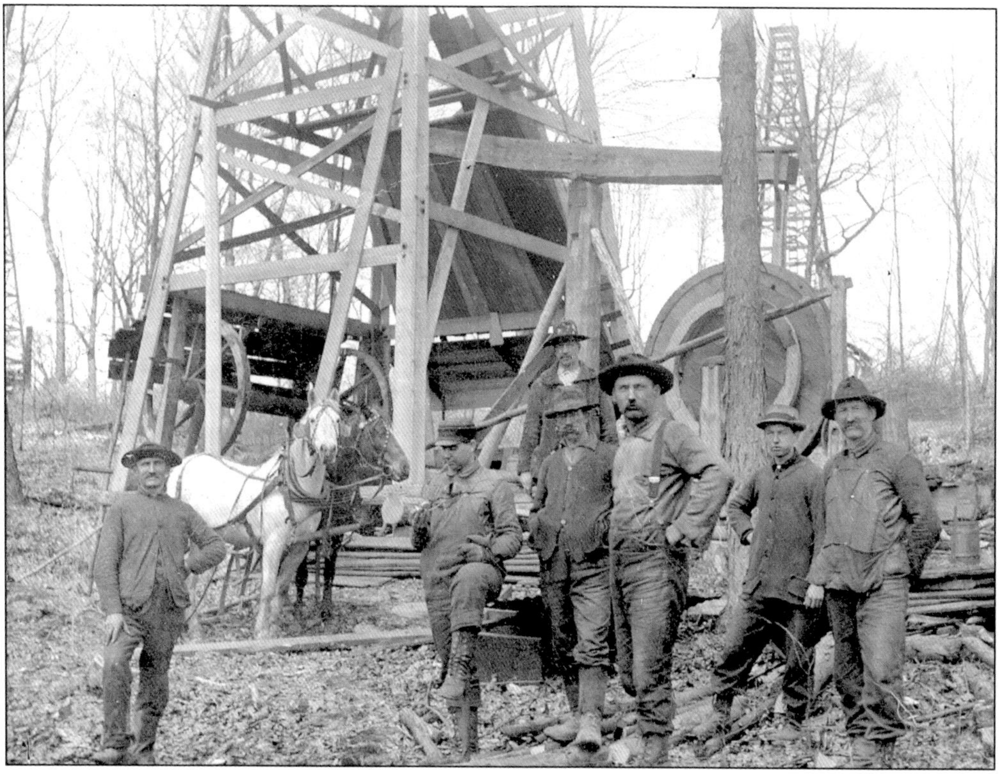

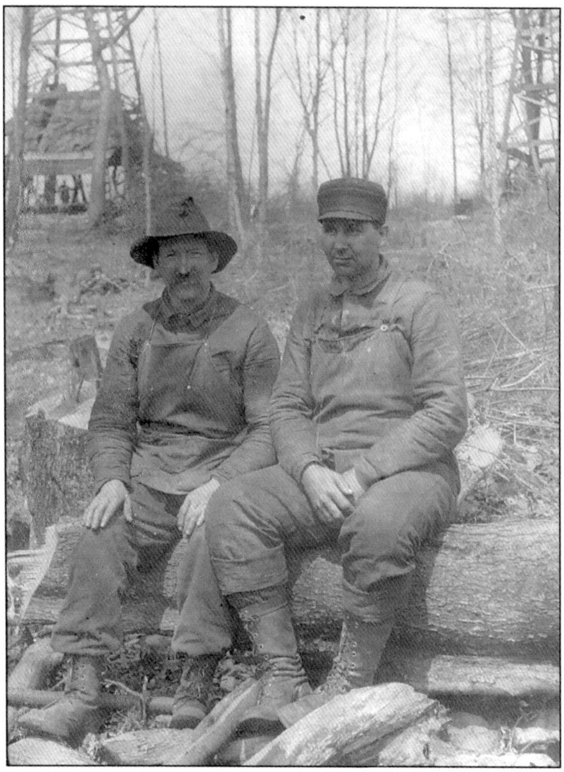

Three standard rigs were photographed on the Ensle lease, *c.* 1905. John Christie is just left of center, checking his watch. William Huber is to the extreme right. The other men are the Ensle brothers, and the crew's horses are Blanche and Alice. (Photograph courtesy Bill Huber.)

William Huber and John Christie take a short break, *c.* 1905. (Photograph courtesy Bill Huber.)

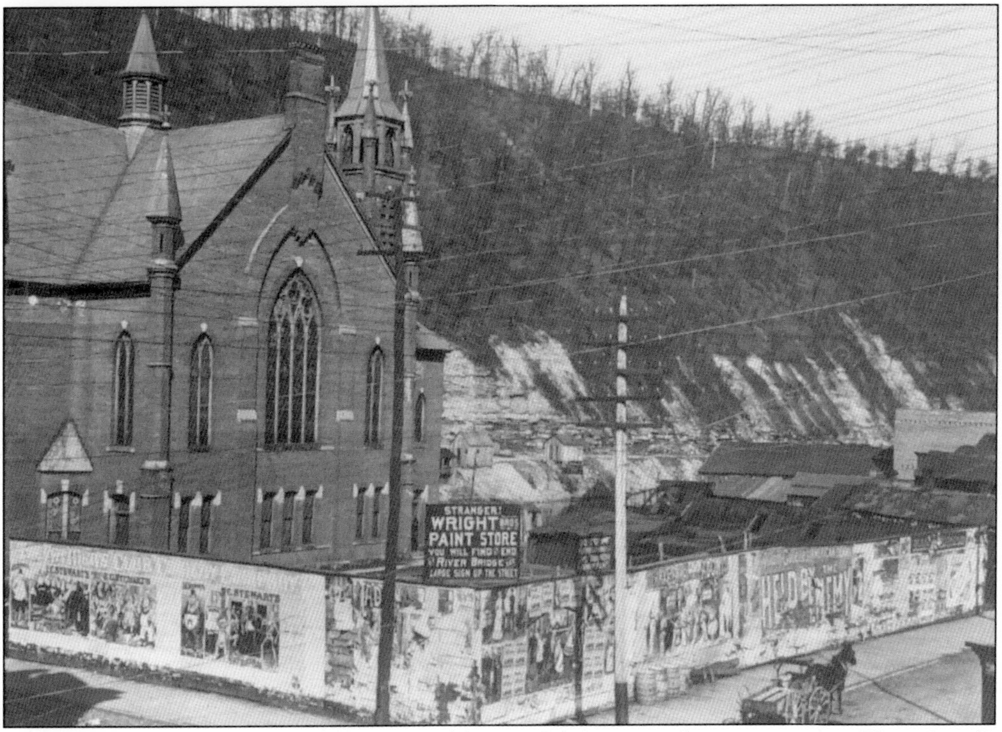

In this 1889 view, the National Transit Building at Oil City is under construction. The sidewalk barricades have already become covered in advertising posters.

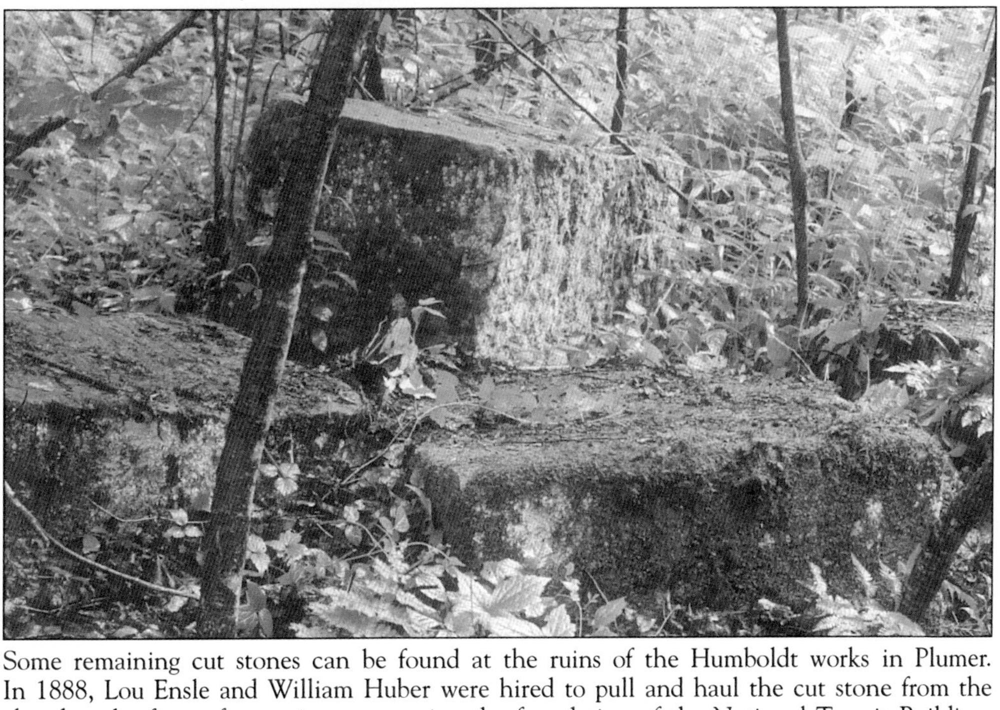

Some remaining cut stones can be found at the ruins of the Humboldt works in Plumer. In 1888, Lou Ensle and William Huber were hired to pull and haul the cut stone from the abandoned refinery for use in constructing the foundation of the National Transit Building. (Photographed by Jim Stoudt.)

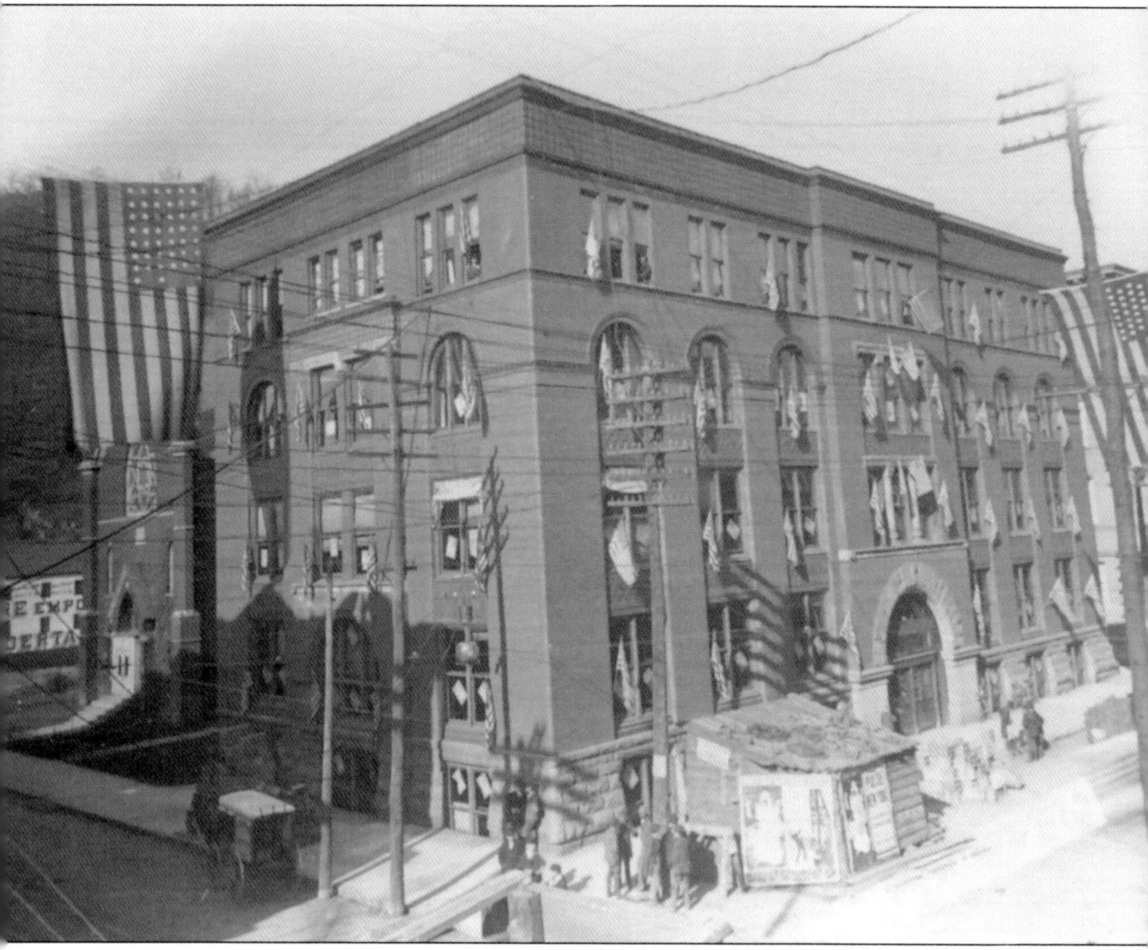

The National Transit Building nears completion, *c.* 1890. The National Transit Company was one of the largest subsidiaries of the Standard Oil Company. The entire transfer and flow of oil through the pipelines across America was controlled here at the National Transit Building. (Photograph courtesy the Oil City Genealogical Society.)

Five

Plumer Views

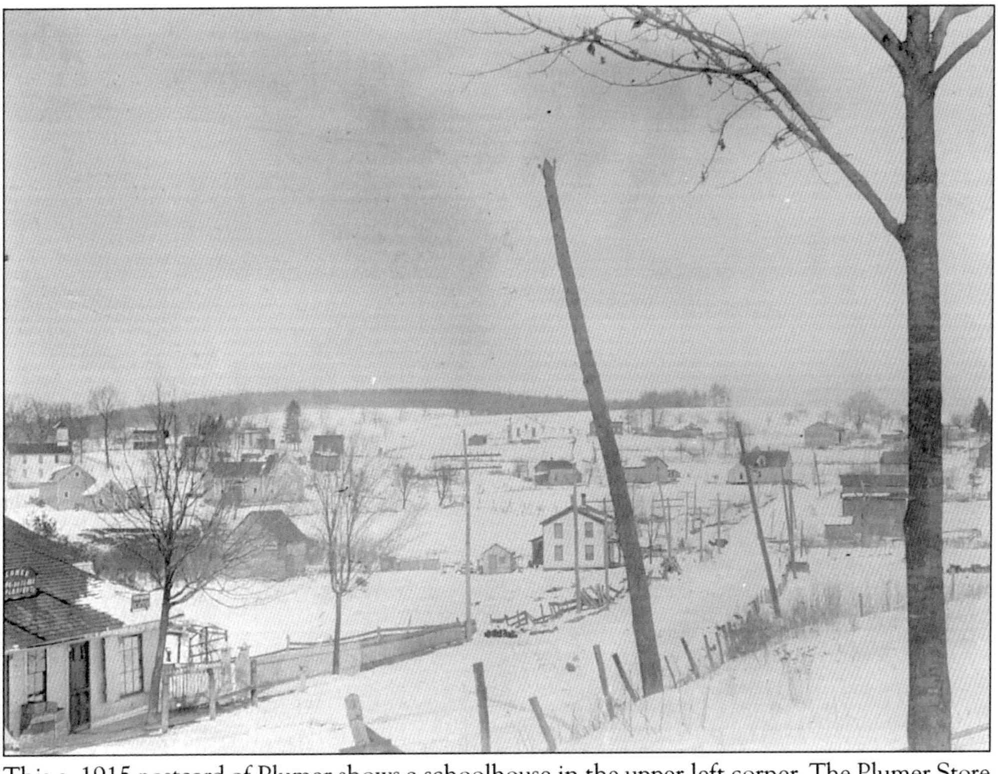

This *c.* 1915 postcard of Plumer shows a schoolhouse in the upper left corner. The Plumer Store is to the lower left corner. The Methodist church is to the upper right center. The hillside was still showing the effects of clear-cutting in the 1860s. (Photograph courtesy Bill Huber.)

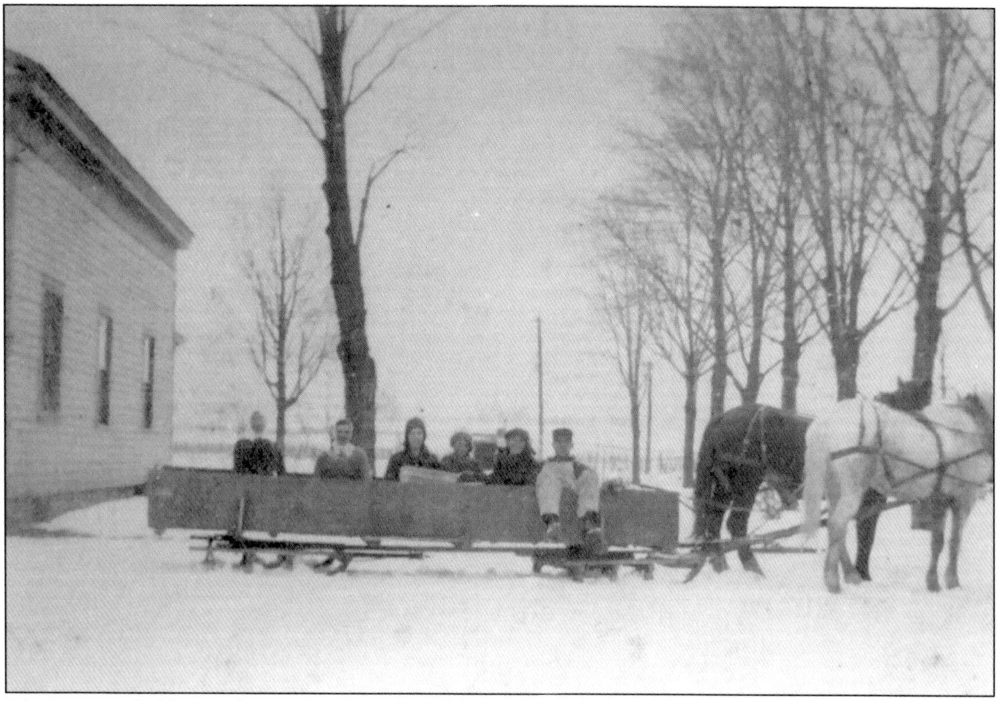

The Haupt children take a ride in a horse-drawn sled in the side yard of the Plumer Presbyterian church, *c.* 1920. (Photograph courtesy Bill Grove.)

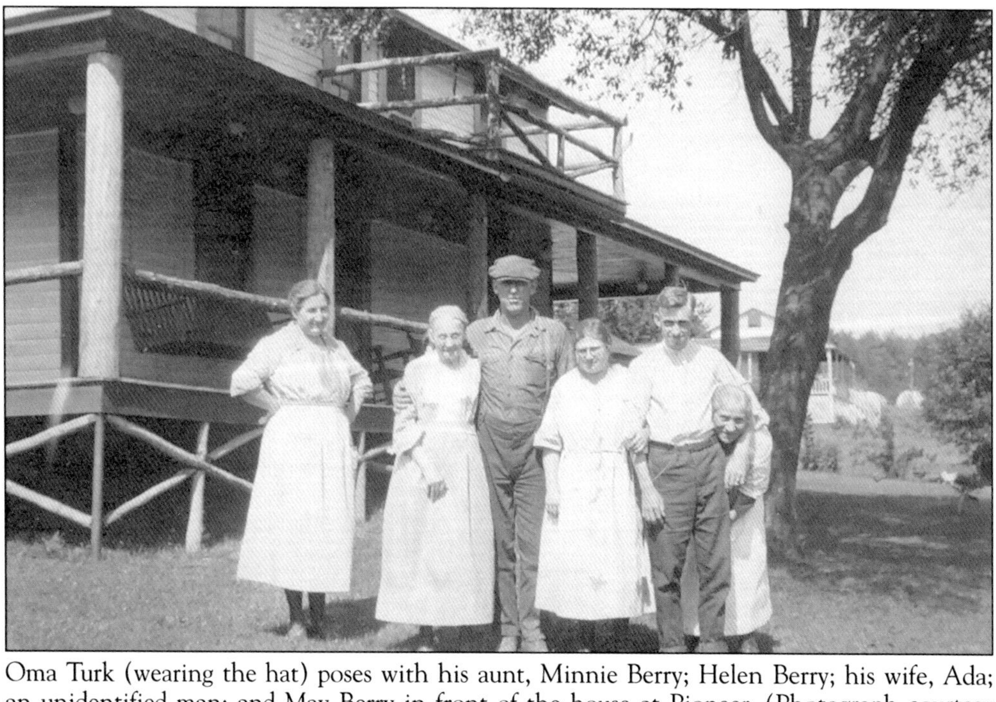

Oma Turk (wearing the hat) poses with his aunt, Minnie Berry; Helen Berry; his wife, Ada; an unidentified man; and May Berry in front of the house at Pioneer. (Photograph courtesy Dick Turk.)

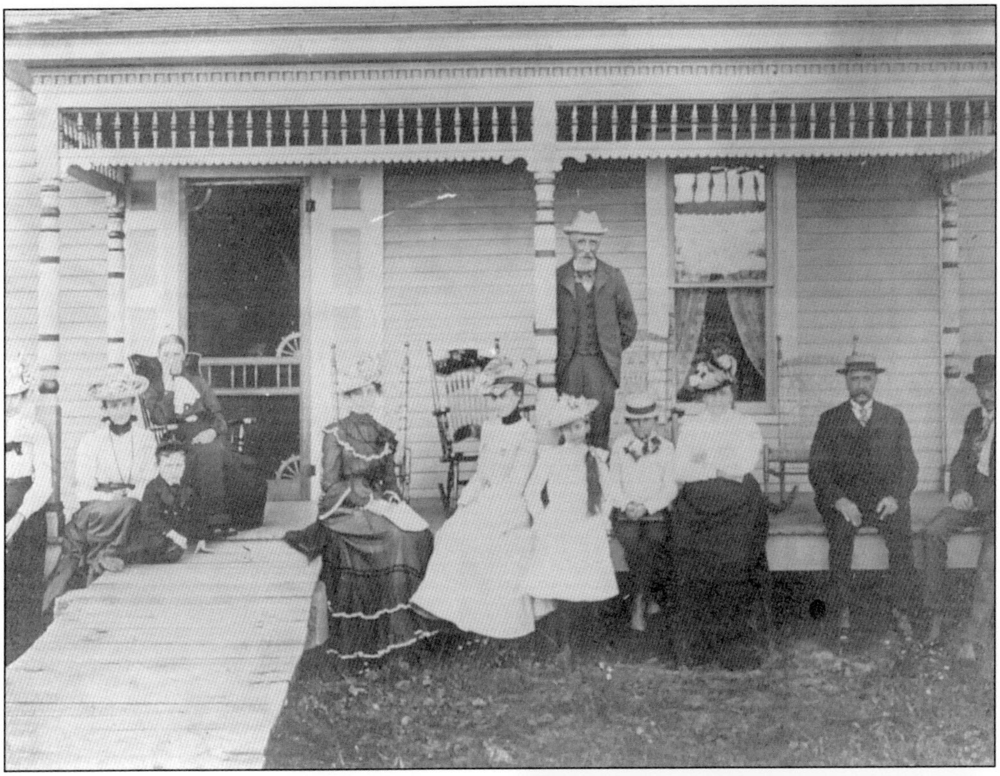

The Russell brothers had emigrated from Canada to Cornplanter Township before the oil excitement and settled the area now known as Russell Corners. Initially, they farmed and then worked as teamsters once the oil boom began. In 1895, they bought the property where the present house sits in Plumer from S.C.T. Dodd. Dodd achieved much notoriety as John D. Rockefeller's attorney. Identified in front of the Russell house in Plumer, *c.* 1900, are Emma Russell, Jane Russell, Alice Russell, Mary Robinson, ? Binder, L. Binder, Alex Russell, Elizabeth Russell, John Russell, and Jean Russell. (Photograph courtesy the Russell family.)

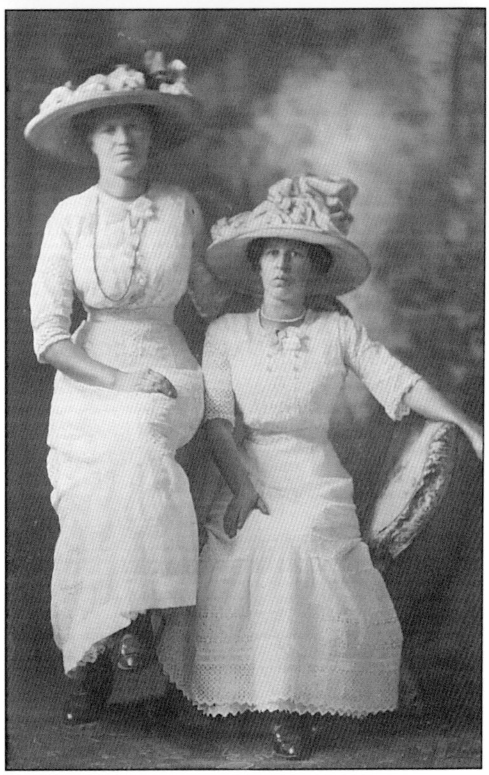

Flo and Maggie Haupt, *c.* 1905, were the first daughters of William Haupt, the Humboldt refinery stone mason. (Photograph courtesy the Russell family.)

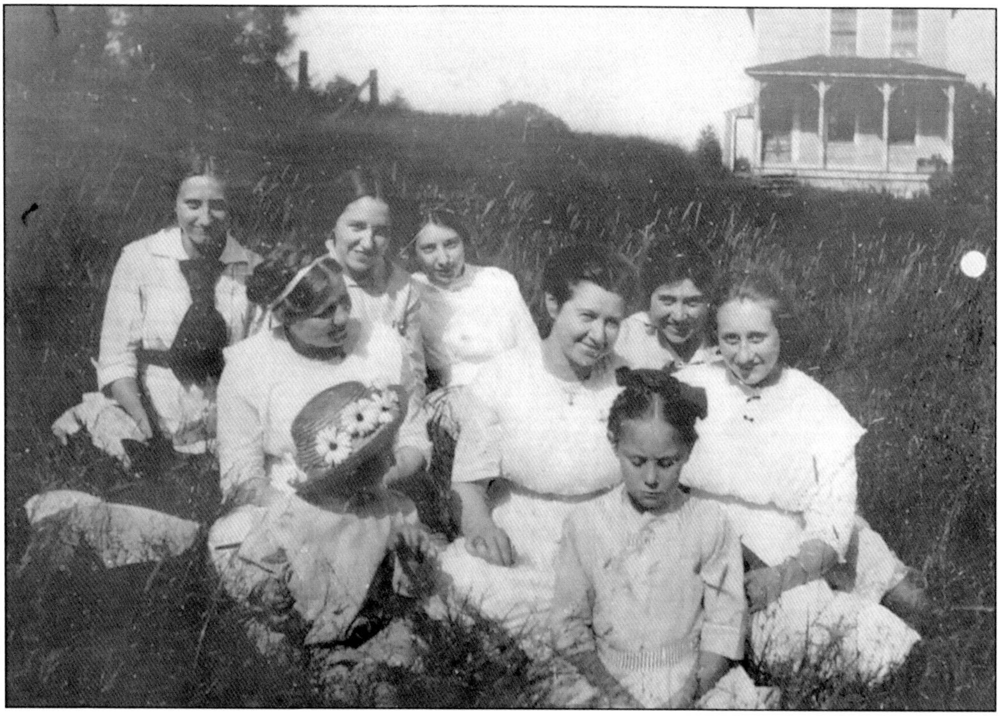

The daughters of William Haupt pose in front of the Haupt homestead, c. 1900. (Photograph courtesy Bill Grove.)

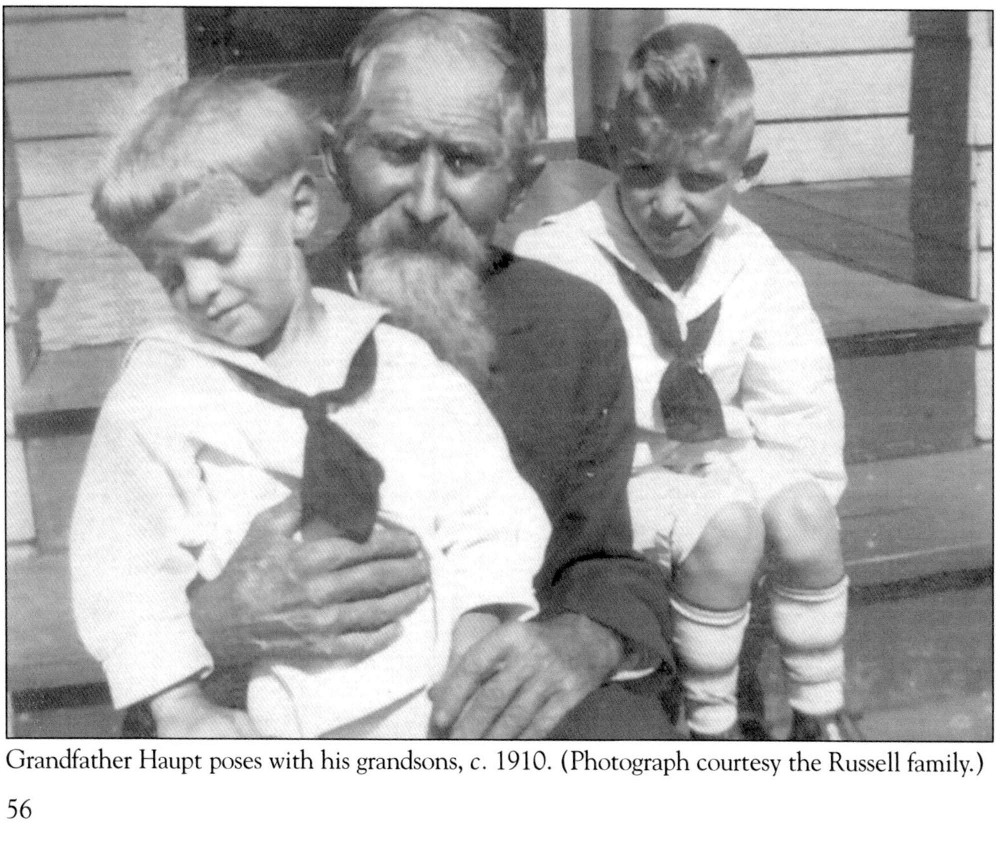

Grandfather Haupt poses with his grandsons, c. 1910. (Photograph courtesy the Russell family.)

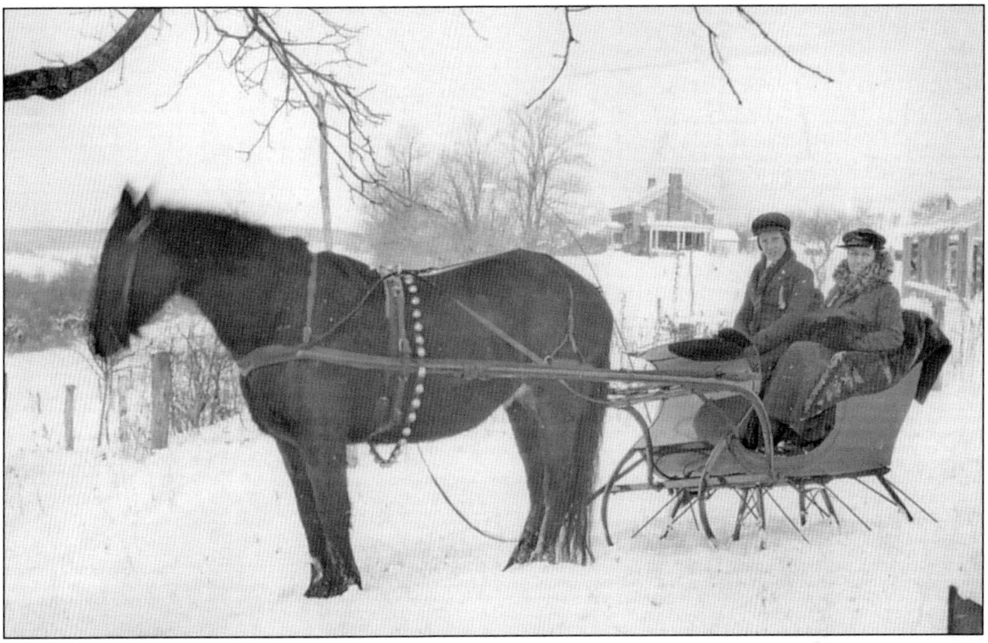

Herbert Huber takes a sleigh ride near the Old Stone House with his grandmother, *c.* 1913. (Photograph courtesy Bill Huber.)

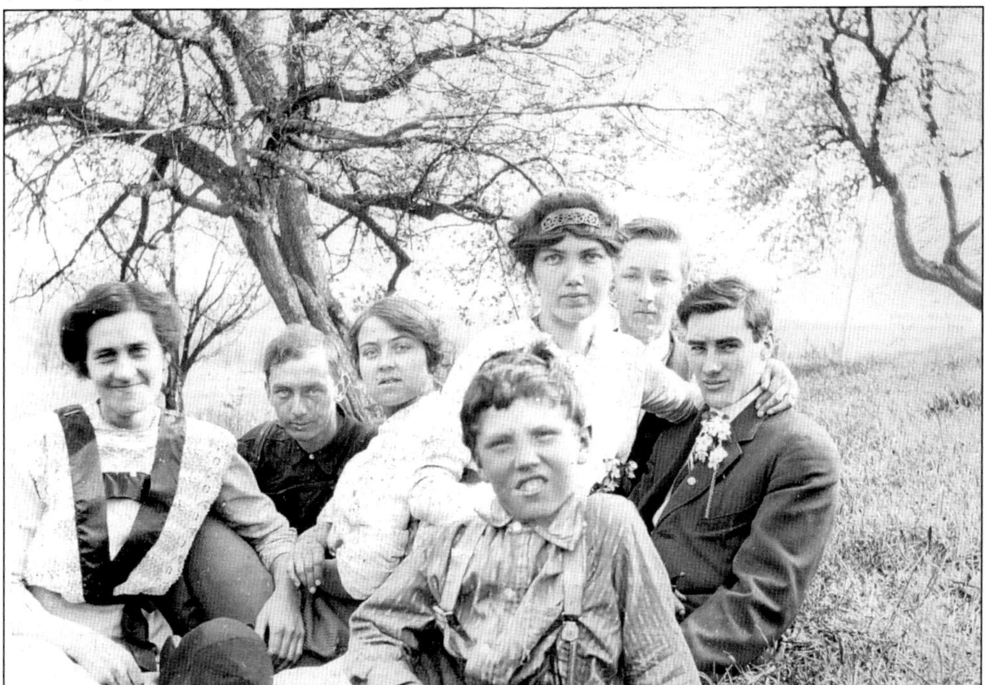

Viola Ensle and Henry McDaniels wed in the orchard on the Ensle farm on Bankston road, a mile south of Plumer, *c.* 1915. The young boy in the foreground is Viola's cousin, Herbert Huber. The boy between the two girls is Kelly Brecht, grandson of Christian Brecht. Christian started the Brecht Brewery in Plumer in the 1860s and later moved the brewery to Franklin, Pennsylvania. (Photograph courtesy Bill Huber.)

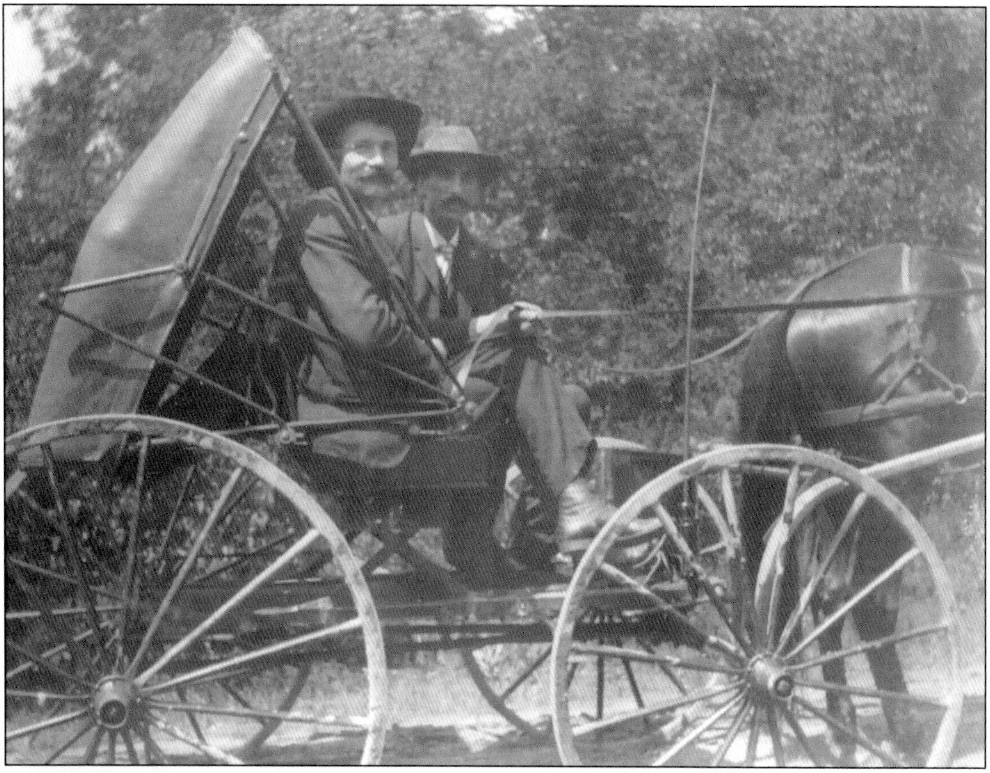

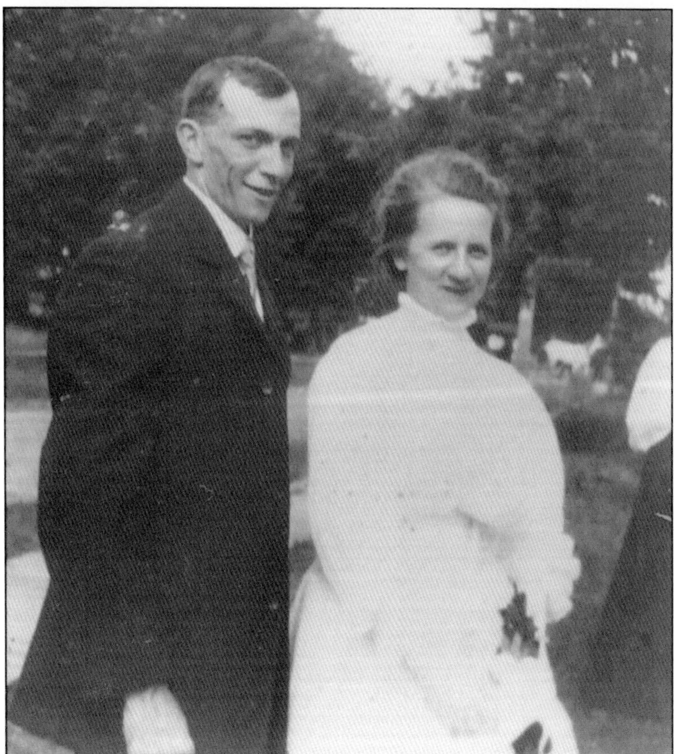

Henny Huber and Perry Irwin pose in their Sunday best. Both gentlemen listed their occupation as oil well drillers. Henny was notorious for his mischievous pranks. Unfortunately, one prank put him behind bars—he blew up one family member's home. Perry Irwin was known more for his trout fishing than for his oil drilling. (Photograph courtesy Dick Turk.)

Oma"Gobbler" Turk is shown with a friend of his new bride, Ada Berry. Ada was the daughter of former Senator Peter Berry. (Photograph courtesy Dick Turk.)

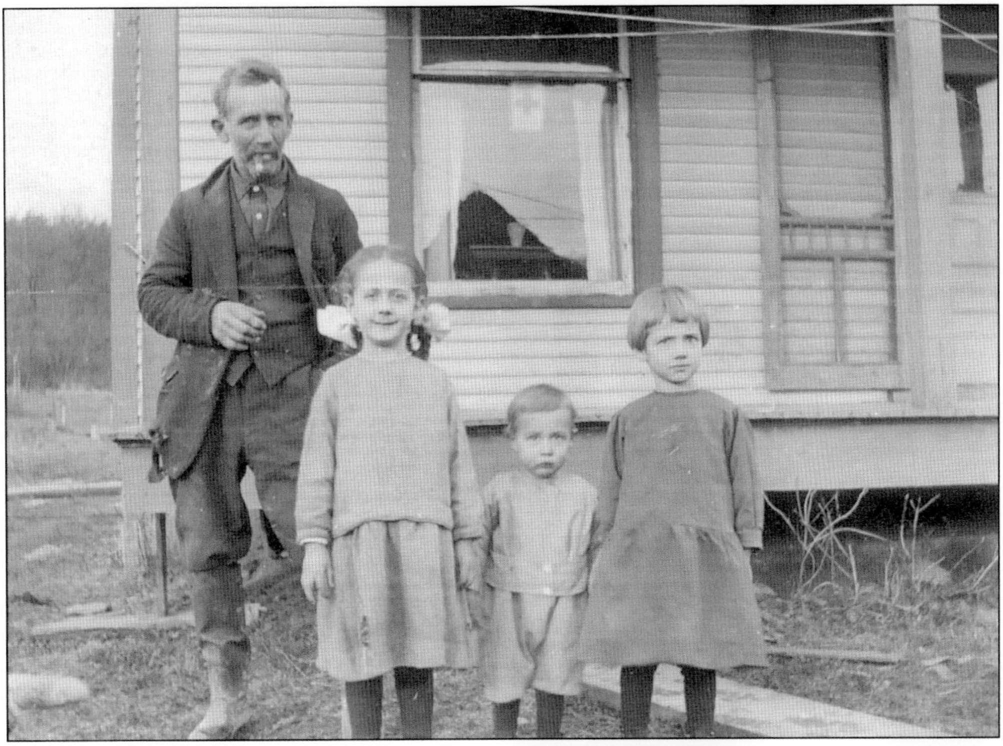

Grandfather Fred Ensle poses with his grandchildren—Milli, Chuck, and Alice—outside the Ensle homestead on Eagle Rock Road. (Photograph courtesy Kay Ensle.)

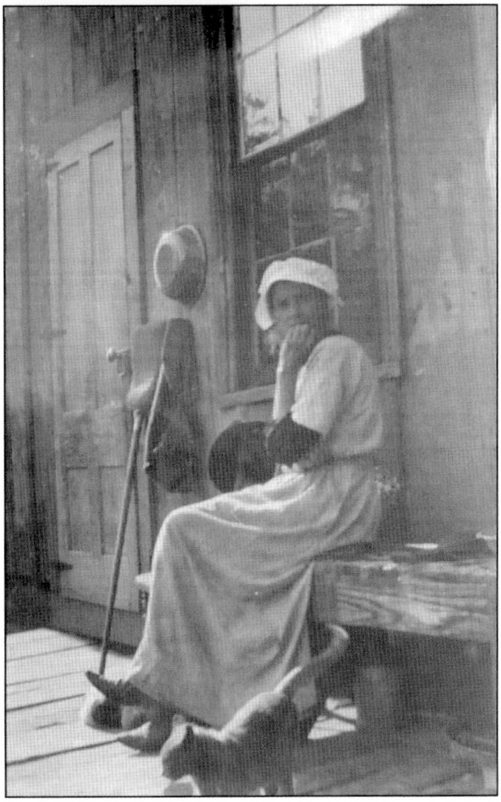

One of the Haupt daughters appears on their porch, c. 1905. (Photograph courtesy Bill Grove.)

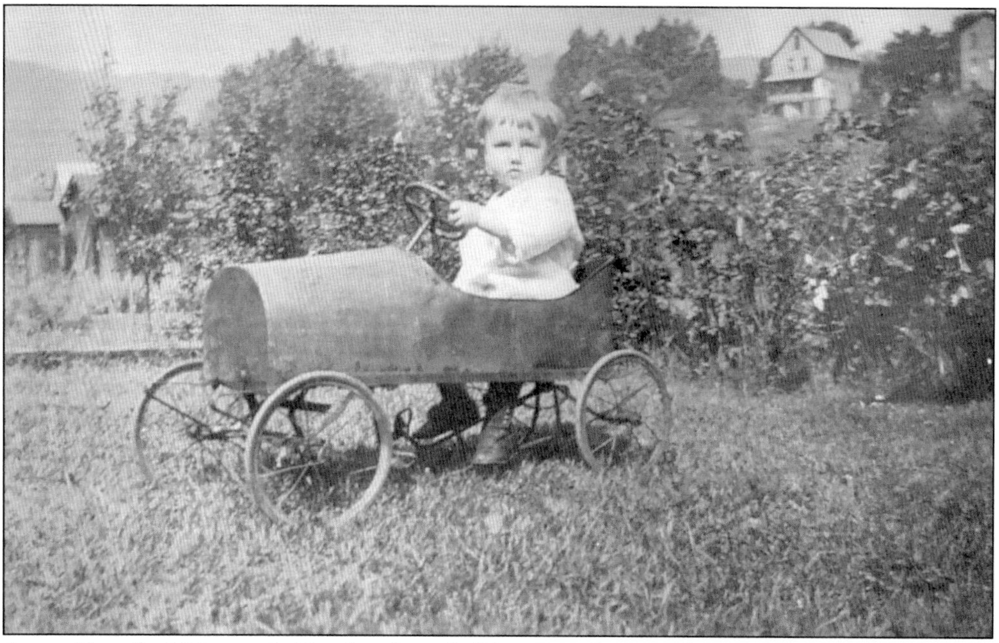

An unidentified Haupt child rides through Plumer in his peddle car, *c*. 1915. (Photograph courtesy Bill Grove.)

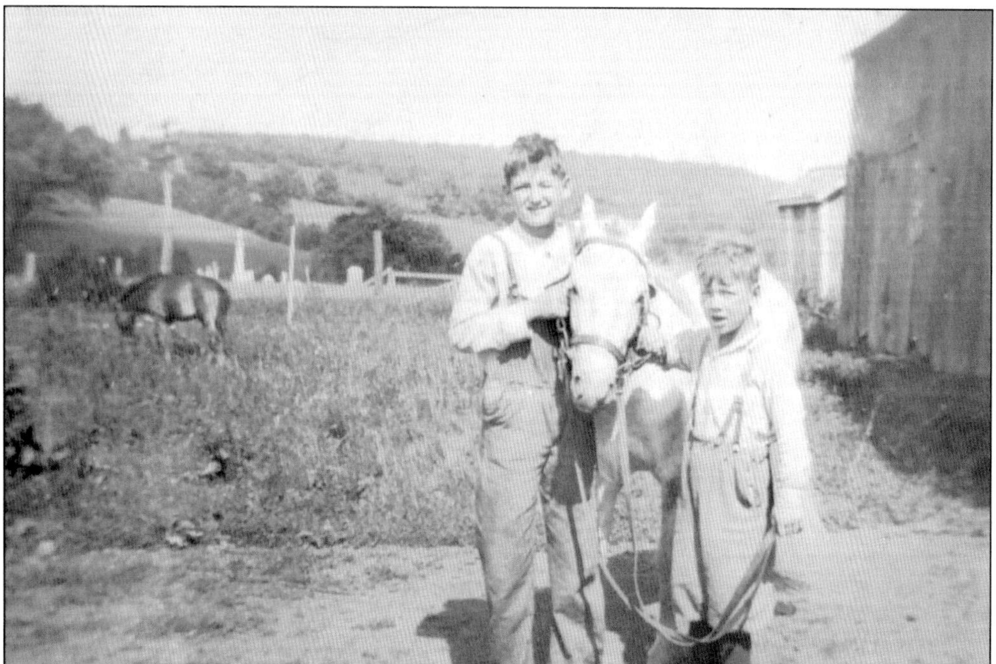

Jack and Dick Turk, sons of Oma and Ada Turk, pose *c*. 1920 with their pony, Babe. (Photograph courtesy Dick Turk.)

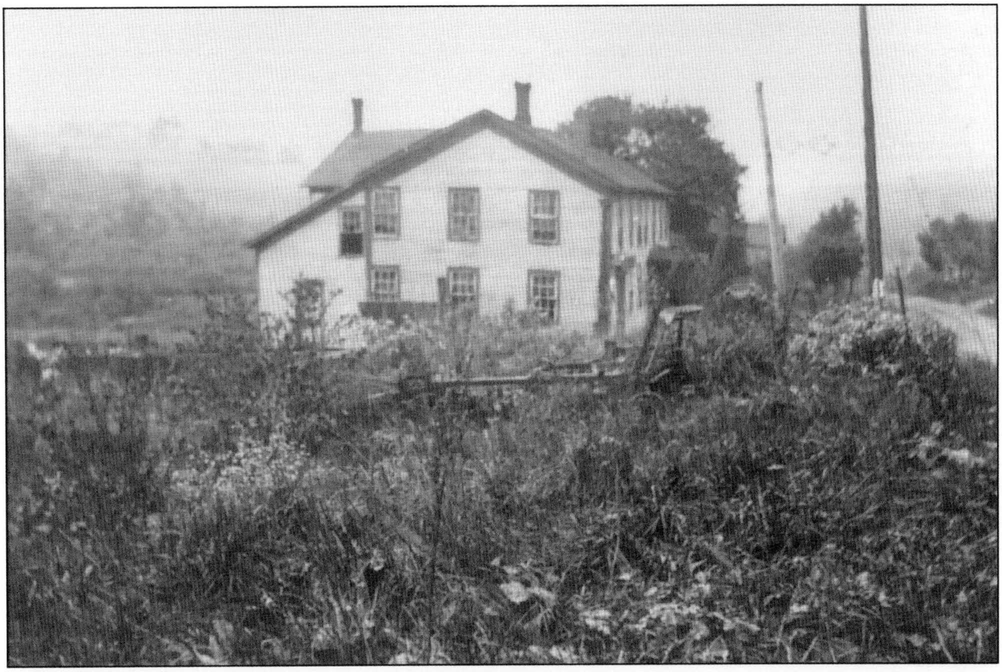

Dick Turk recalls riding his pony through the front door of the former Prather house, past the angry innkeeper, Sam Nelson, and out the back door that was held open by a friend. (Photograph courtesy Dick Turk.)

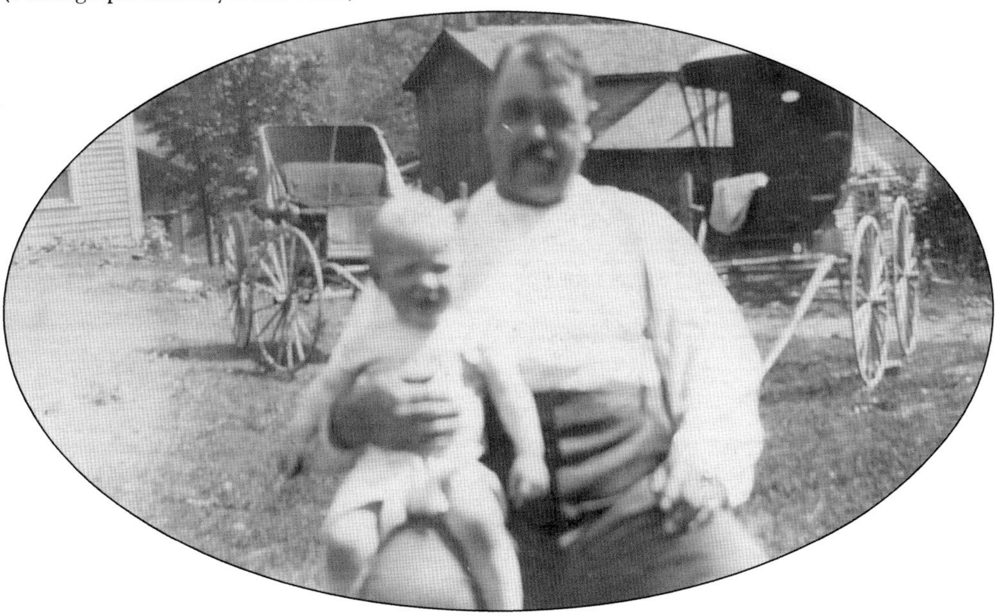

This photograph of George Campbell and Dick Turk on his knee was taken *c.* 1913. George was a carpenter and rig builder whose house still stands in Plumer. It is the second house on west side of Route 227, past Eagle Rock Road. Campbell, along with Oma Turk, built the replica and performed in *The World's Struggle for Oil* (see chapter 7). Campbell left an endowment to build a belfry and furnish a new bell for the Presbyterian church of Plumer. (Photograph courtesy Dick Turk.)

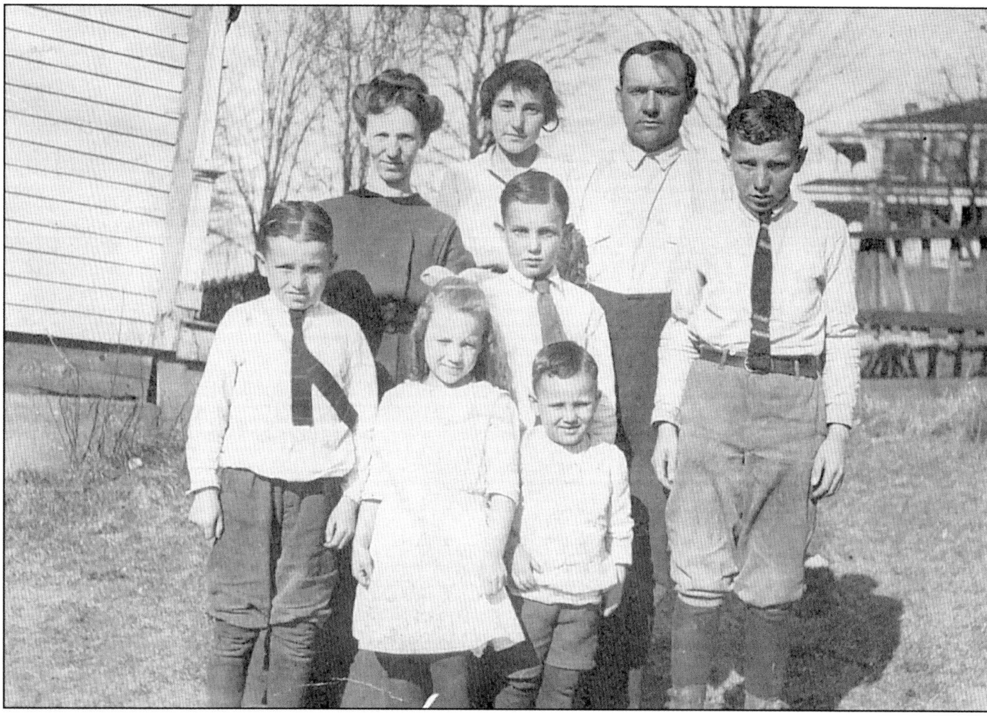

Willis Stephens, shown here with his family, moved to Plumer in 1912. (Photograph courtesy Roxanne Hitchcock.)

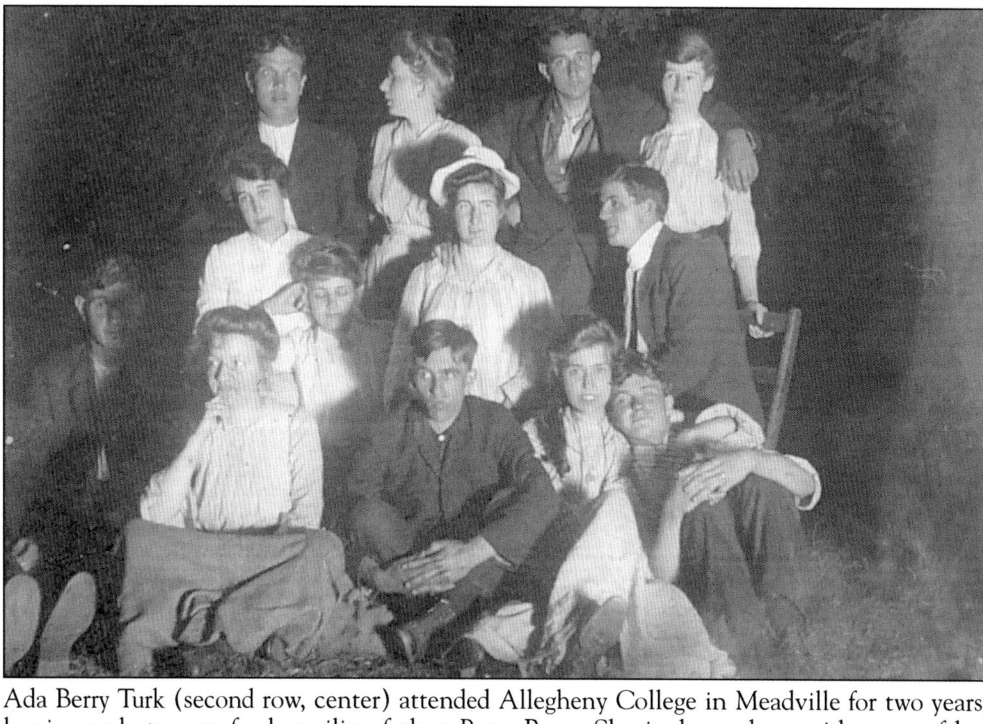

Ada Berry Turk (second row, center) attended Allegheny College in Meadville for two years, leaving early to care for her ailing father, Peter Berry. She is shown here with some of her college friends. (Photograph courtesy Dick Turk.)

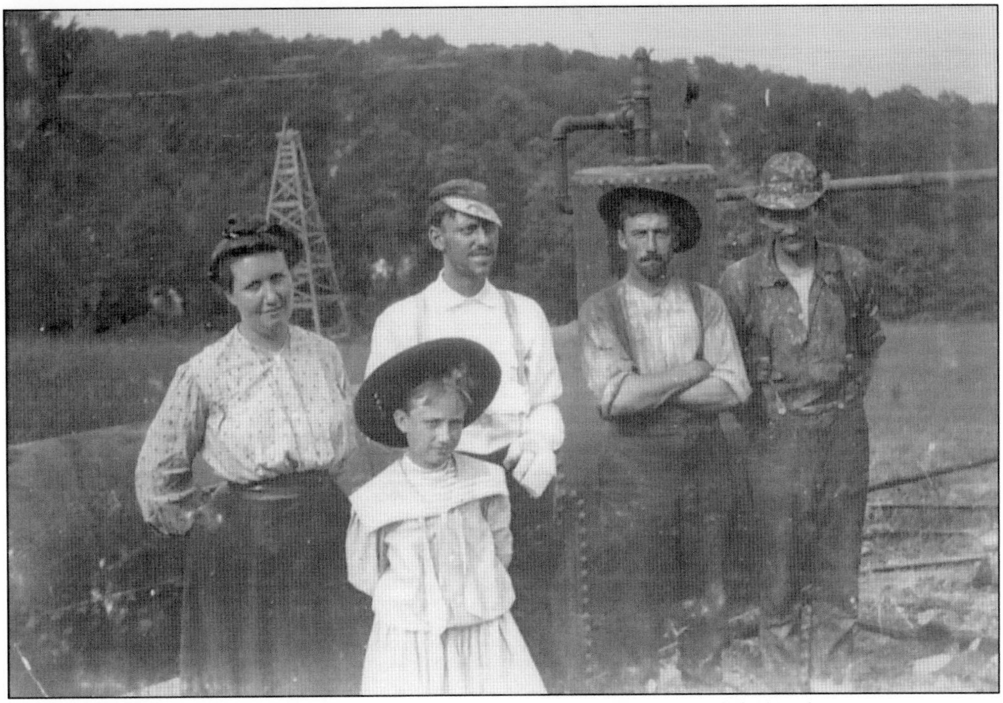

Oma Turk, first man on left, had just shot one of his wells. Oma delighted in spattering any onlookers with mud by placing them downwind while he shot his wells. He kept an open account at Goldstein's Clothing Store in Oil City. (Photograph courtesy Dick Turk.)

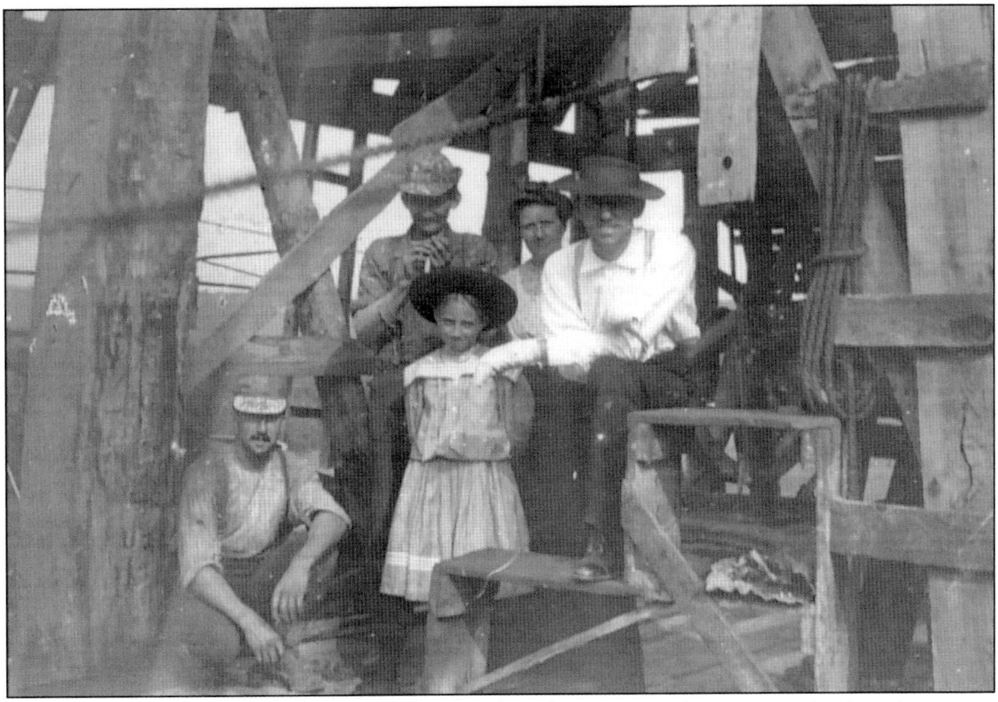

Oma Turk is shown with bandages on his hands as he recovers from a near fatal explosion on one of his rigs. (Photograph courtesy Dick Turk.)

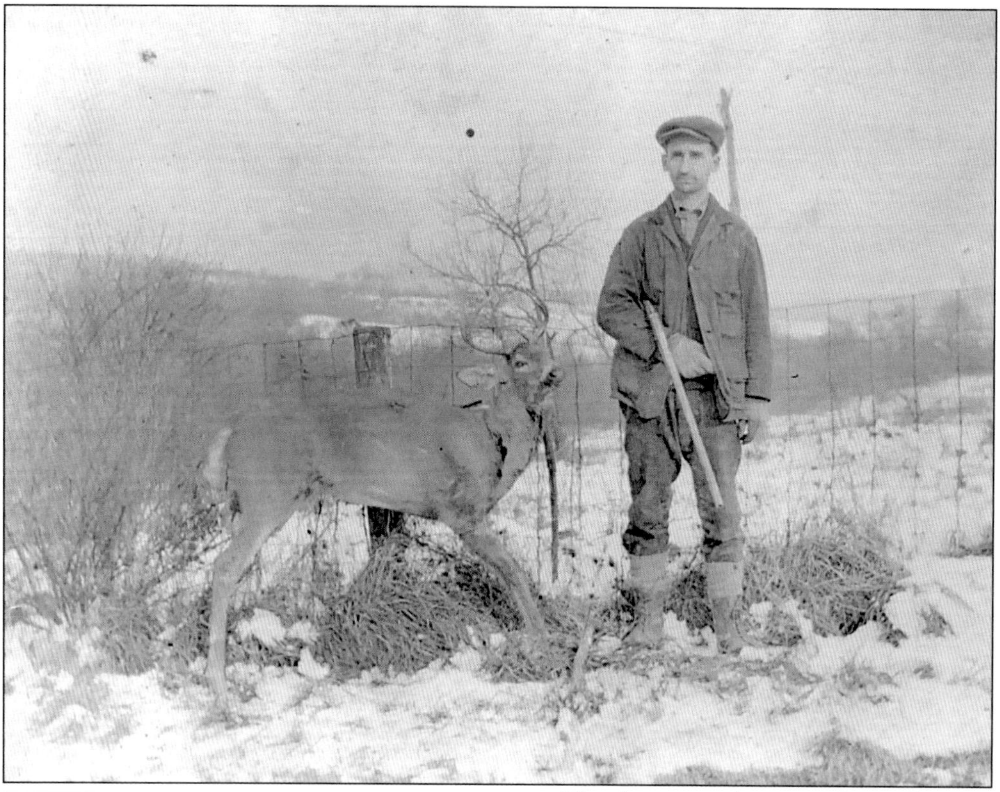

The deer around western Pennsylvania had been almost hunted out by 1900. Charlie Ensle is shown above with the first buck taken after the state had restocked the game lands, c. 1920. (Photograph courtesy Kay Ensle.)

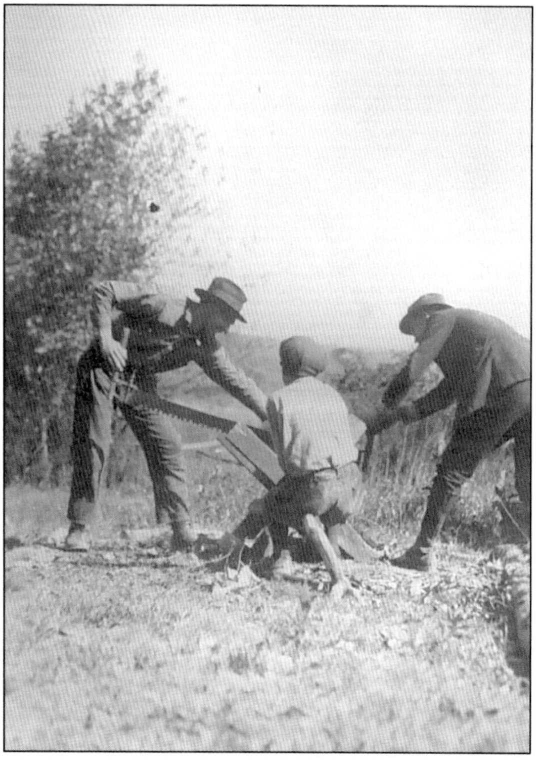

The Haupt boys are sawing wood, c. 1925. (Photograph courtesy the Russell family.)

Norm McCormick owned the Plumer Store from the late 1890s through the early 1920s. Dick Turk remembers delivering kerosene to his store with a horse and wagon. The Plumer Store is located one-quarter mile south of Eagle Rock Road on the west side of Route 227 in Plumer. (Photograph courtesy of Dick Turk.)

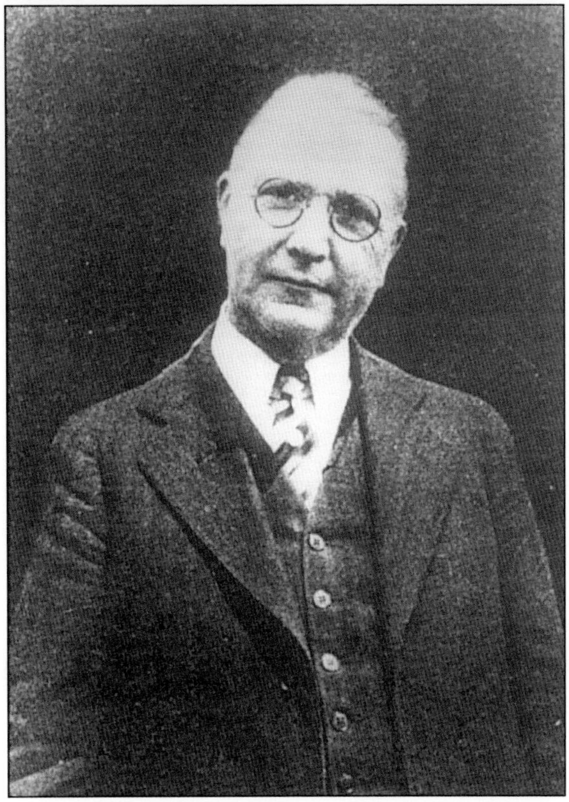

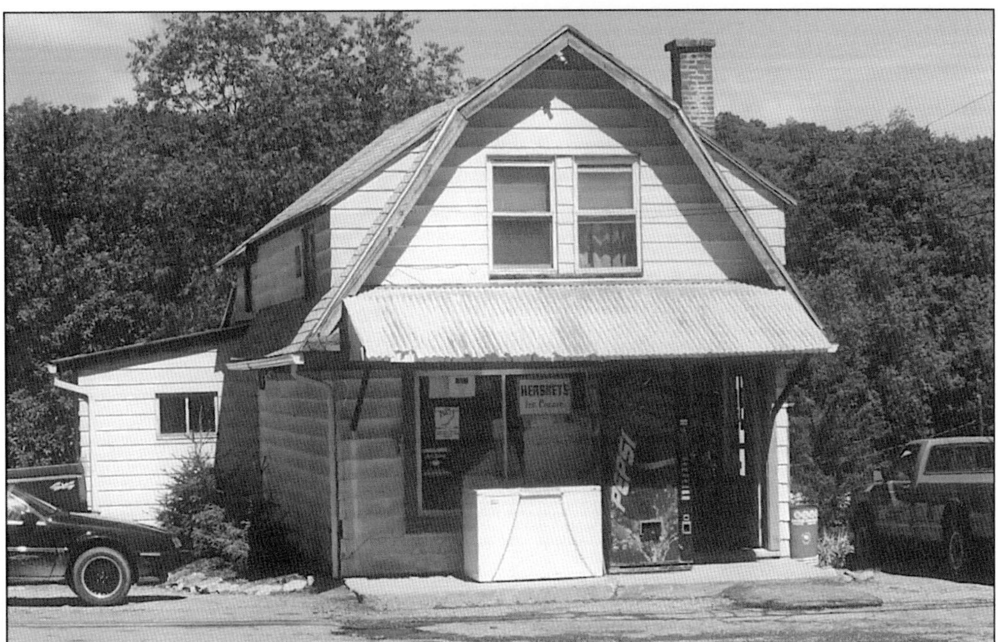

The store has been a constant in the landscape of Plumer. It is seen here at the end of the 20th century. (Photographed by Jim Stoudt.)

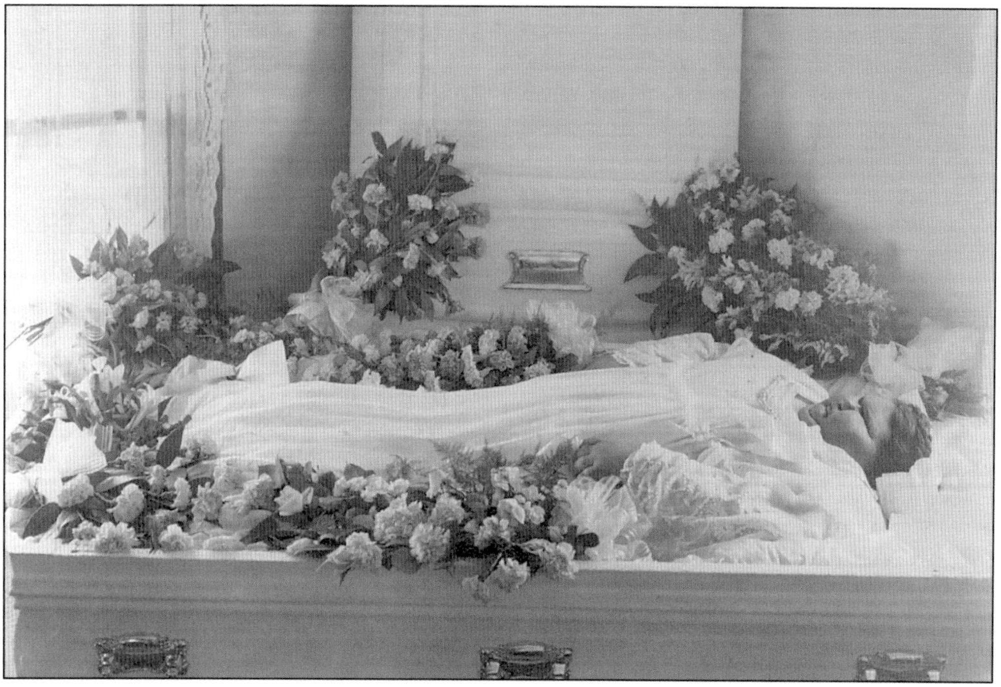

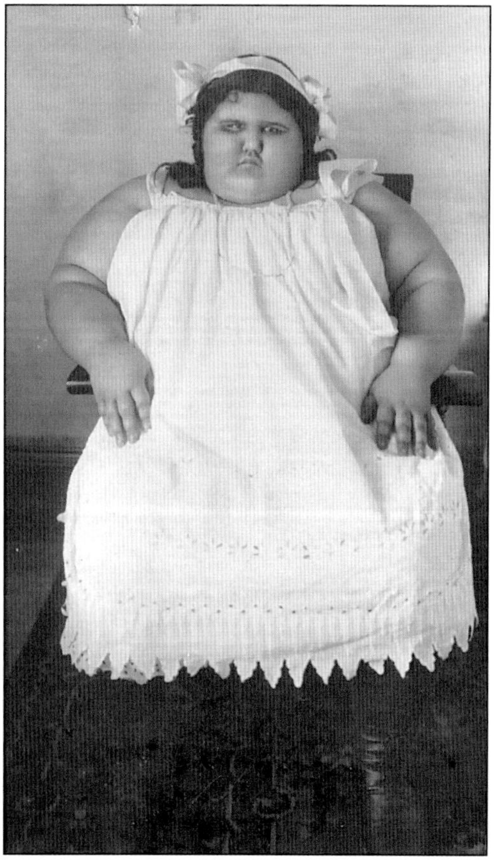

Emma Snyder was laid to rest in 1912 at the age of 12. Born in Plumer in 1900, Emma grew to more than 450 pounds by the age of 10. Emma was so embarrassed by the ridicule of her peers that she withdrew from school at age 11 and joined a sideshow that traveled throughout America. The night before she was to leave on her second tour, she fell ill with pneumonia and died the following morning. (Photograph courtesy the Russell family.)

Six

Life on the Leases

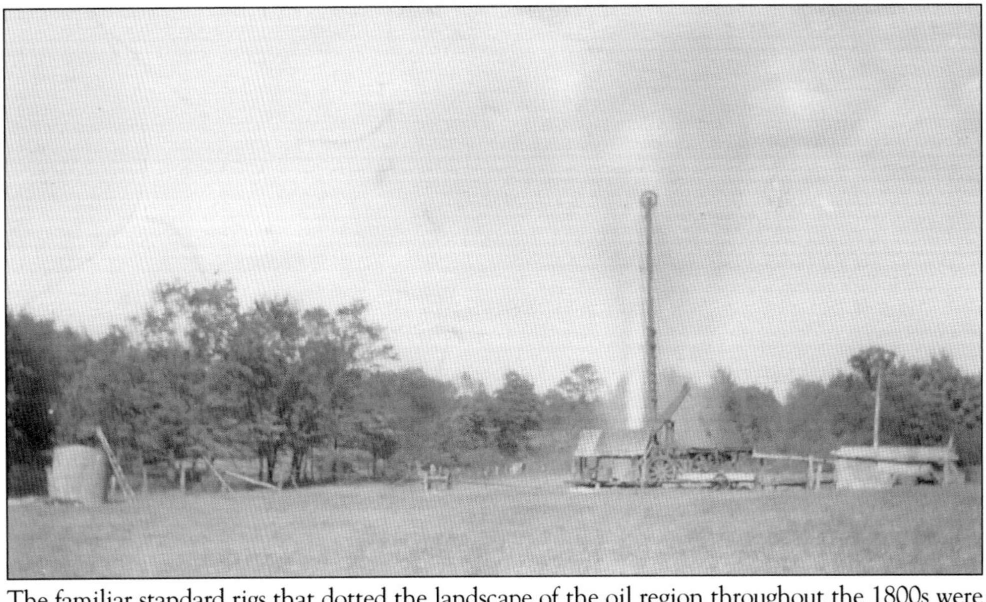

The familiar standard rigs that dotted the landscape of the oil region throughout the 1800s were replaced by 1915 with a new breed of drilling machines. Here, a Wolf rig is being shot with nitroglycerin near Plumer. The rigs were still powered by steam. Other drilling machines can still be seen abandoned throughout the forest of Venango County. (Photograph courtesy Bill Huber.)

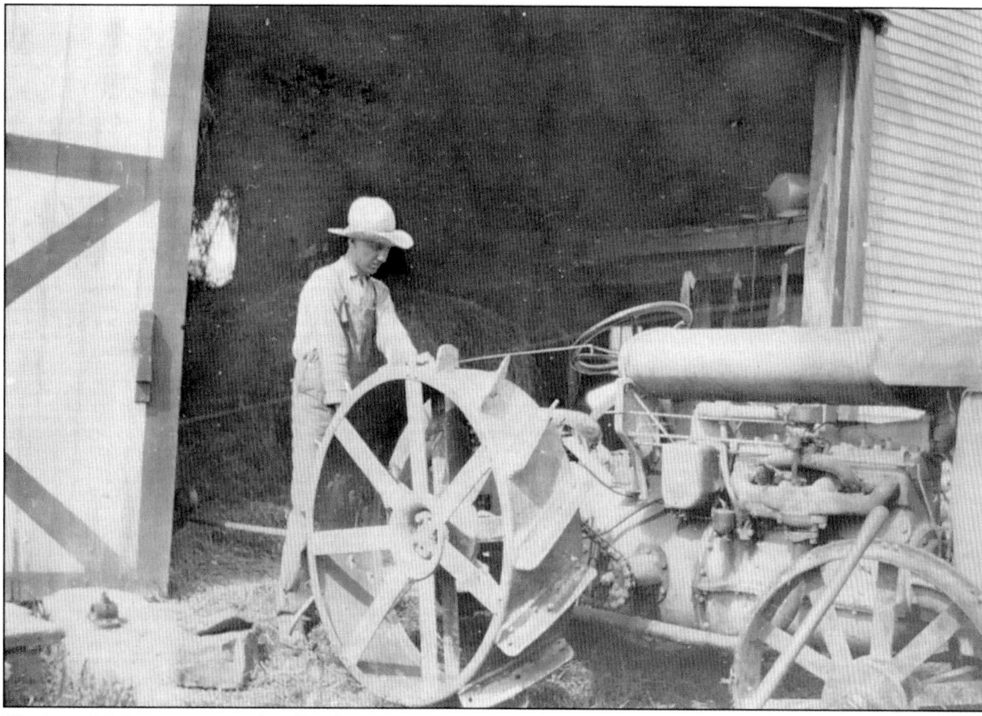

Herbert Huber prepares his Fordson tractor for a day of work on the leases. The Fordson, with its metal wheels, was ideally suited for the rough terrain and muddy conditions of the oil fields. (Photograph courtesy Bill Huber.)

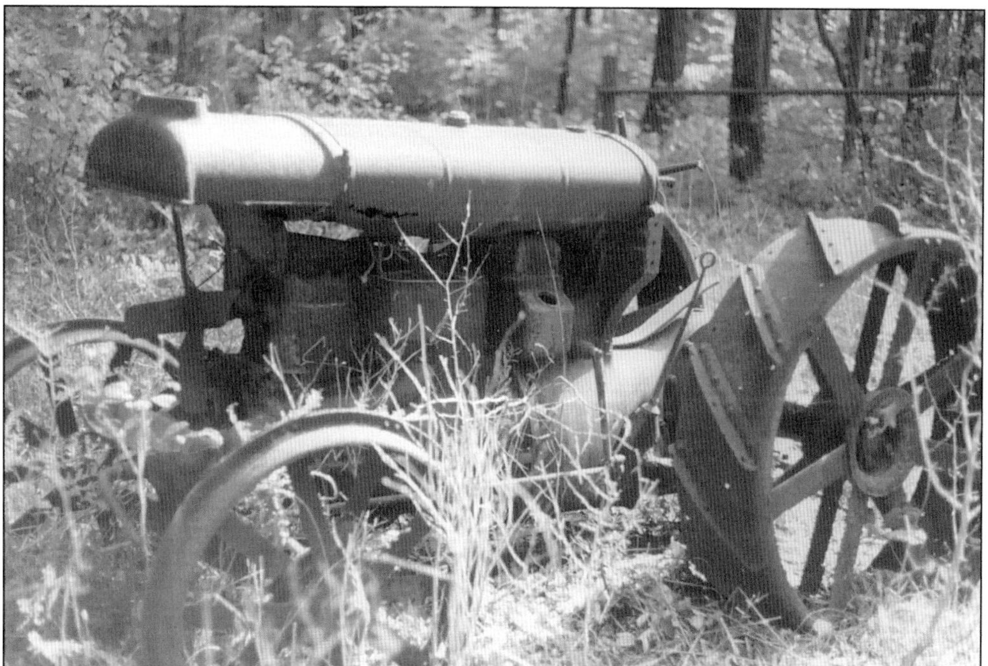

This Fordson tractor was abandoned in a field near the Oleopolis Road. (Photographed by Jim Stoudt.)

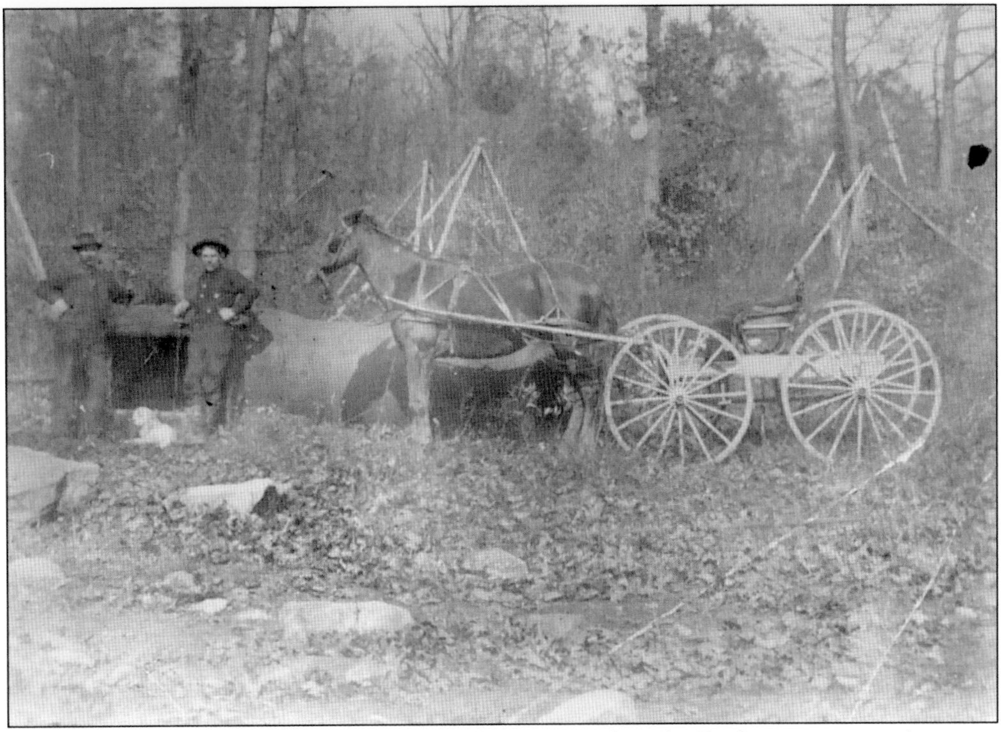

Oma Turk's crew works their team. Oma Turk never purchased a Fordson tractor, preferring to use his three teams of horses to work the rigs. (Photograph courtesy Dick Turk.)

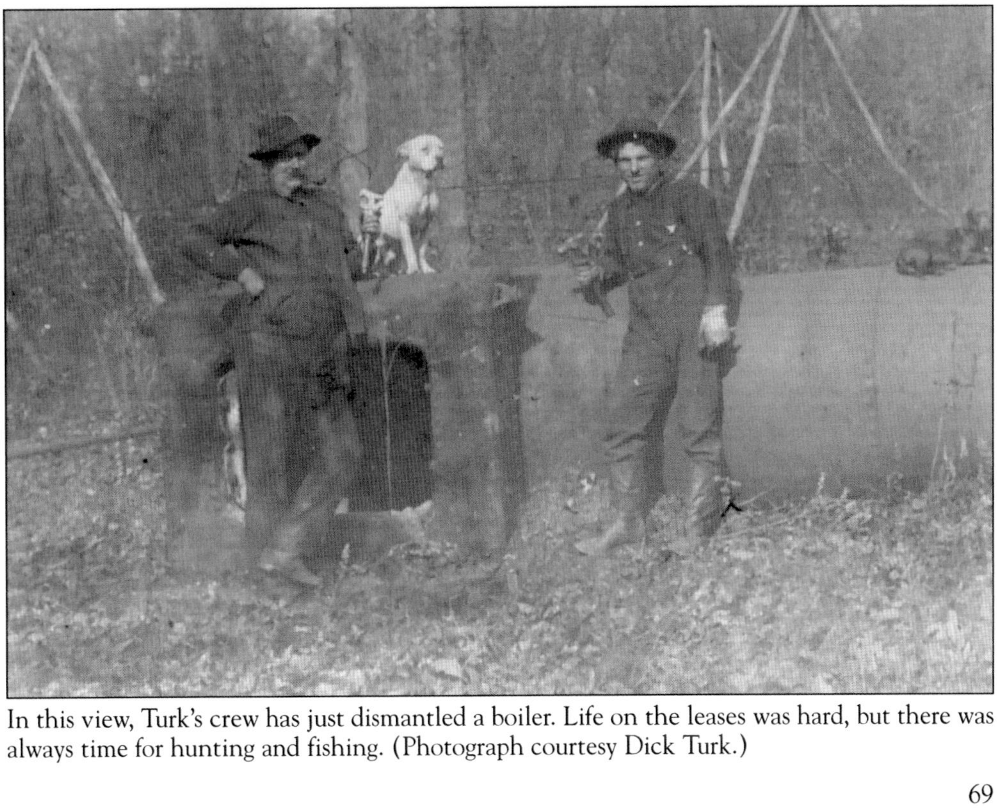

In this view, Turk's crew has just dismantled a boiler. Life on the leases was hard, but there was always time for hunting and fishing. (Photograph courtesy Dick Turk.)

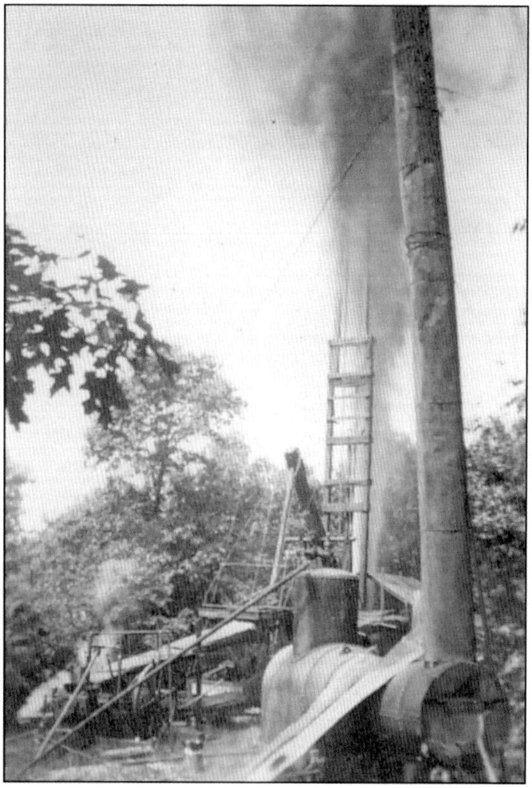

The life expectancy of a well could be extended by shooting nitroglycerin down the casing. A torpedo filled with the volatile substance was lowered to the bottom of the well, where it was ignited. The pressure would clear the well of built-up paraffin and loosen any pockets of crude below the surface. Many dry holes were made productive after they were shot. (Photograph courtesy Bill Huber.)

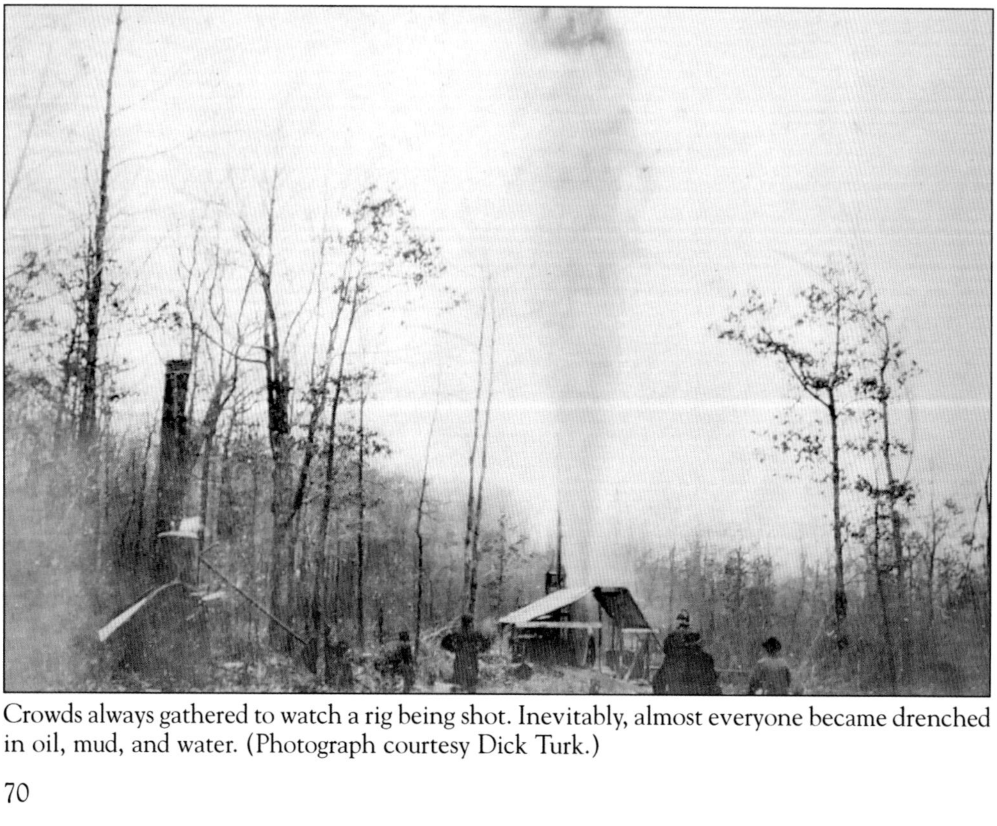

Crowds always gathered to watch a rig being shot. Inevitably, almost everyone became drenched in oil, mud, and water. (Photograph courtesy Dick Turk.)

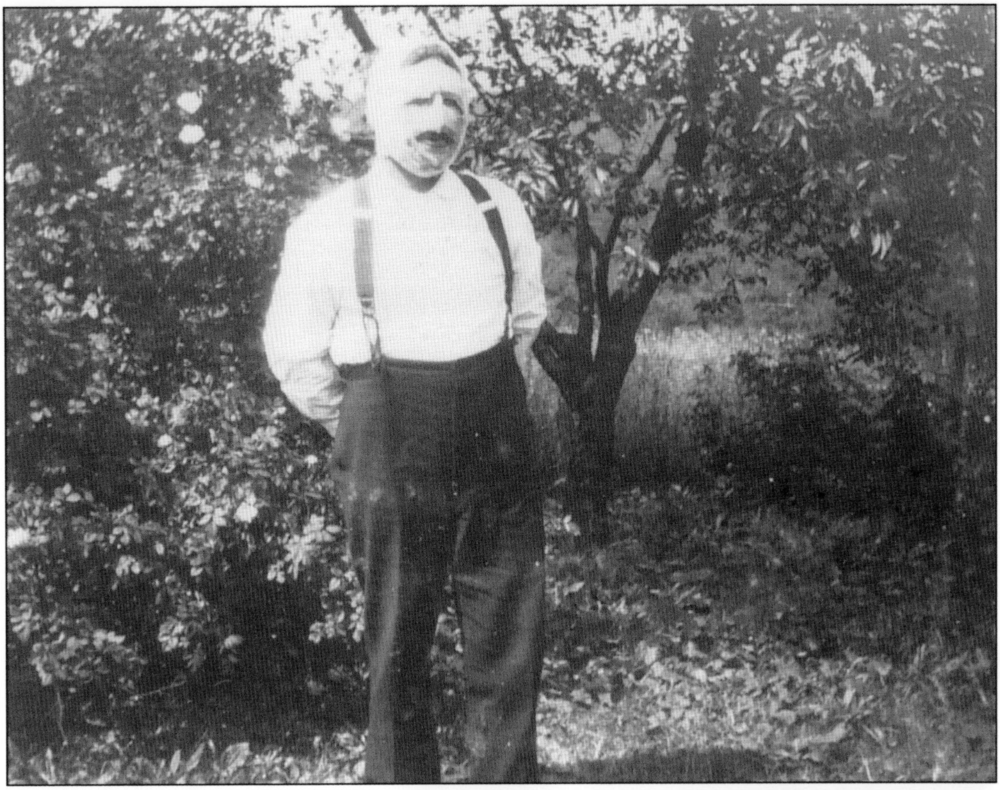

Oma "Gobbler" Turk was seriously injured when a boiler exploded on one of his rigs. His son, Dick, remembers that when they removed the bandages, there was little scarring. Gobbler had dodged another bullet. Dick says no one could cuss like his father. (Photograph courtesy Dick Turk.)

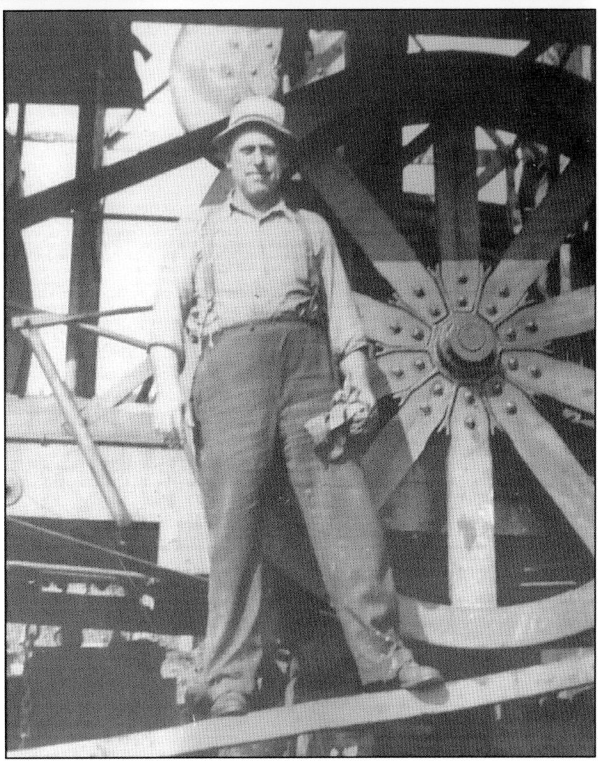

As tough a man as Oma Turk was to work for, he will always be remembered as a generous man. In 1929, after the banks failed in Oil City, he cashed in all his insurance policies to help his neighbors and friends. (Photograph courtesy Dick Turk.)

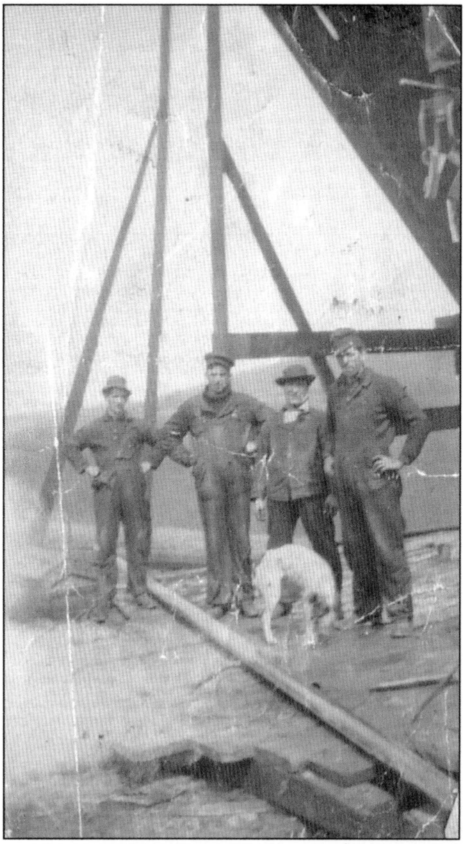

The Warrant drilling crew was known throughout the oil fields as one the toughest and best to be found. (Photograph courtesy Bill Huber.)

Charlie Ensle cuts rough timber to be used on an oil lease, *c.* 1920s. This lumber mill is one of many scattered throughout the oil region. (Photograph courtesy Kay Ensle.)

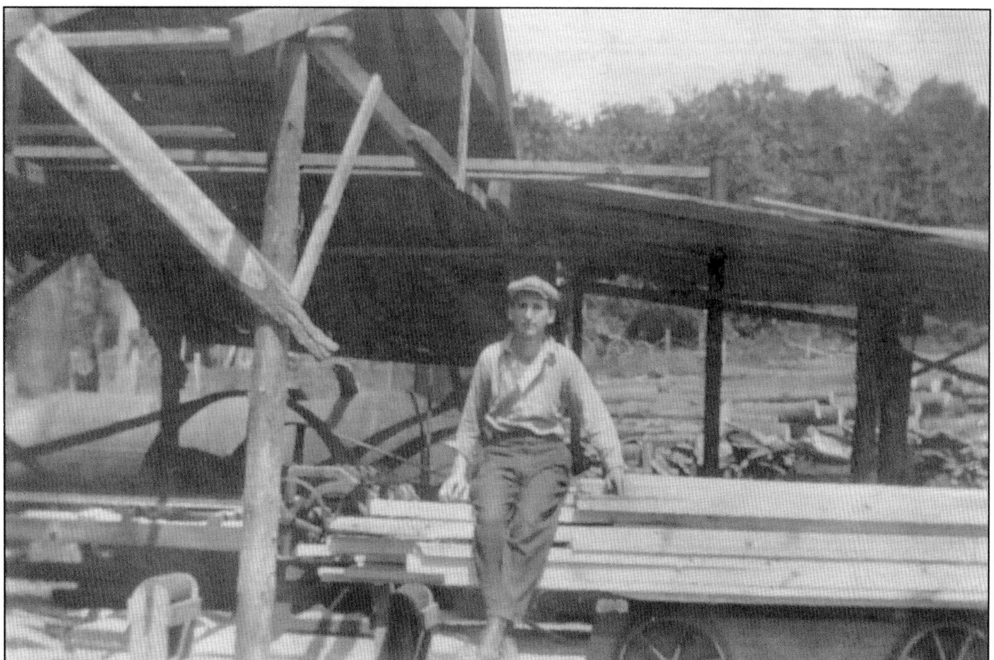

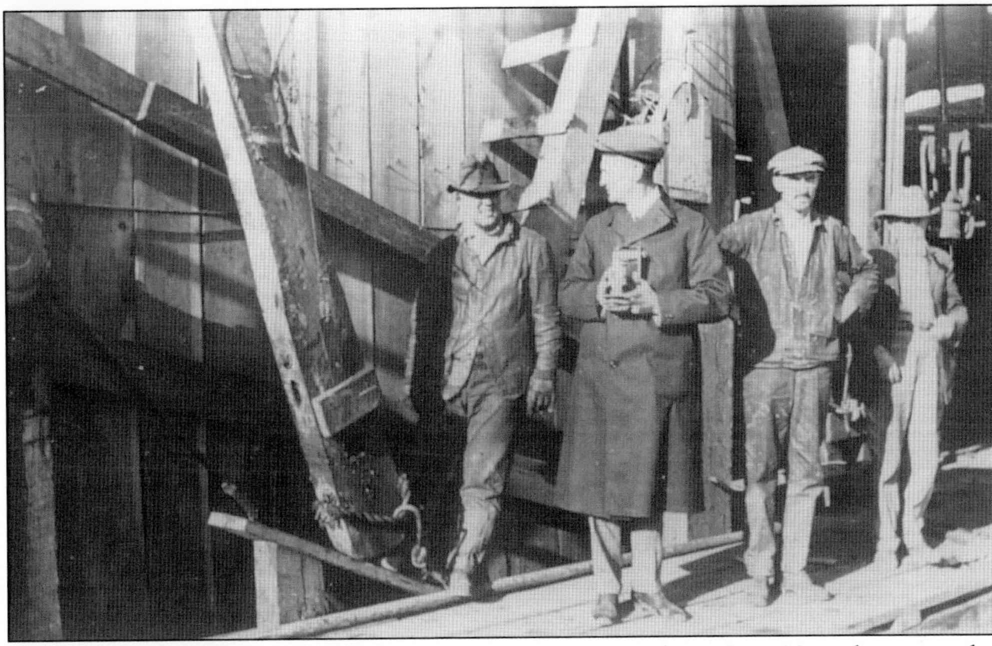

Perry Irwin, second from the right, can be seen on a rig on Cherry Run. Note the man to his left with the box camera.

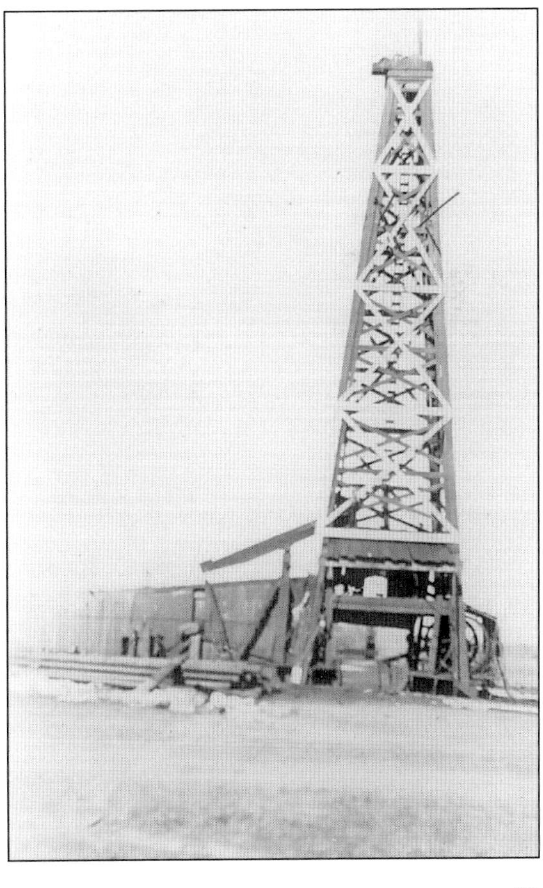

One of the last standard rigs built on Cherry Run was photographed here, c. 1920. The standard rig had changed little from the first derrick erected in 1859 by Colonel Drake and his driller, Uncle Billy Smith.

Phones:—MAIN OFFICE, Bell 128-J, Pet. 1740-1—RESIDENCE, Bell 237-r-1, Pet. 1740-2 or 916-H
—CLINTONVILLE OFFICE, C. P. Whitman's Residence.

W. W. BOWERS

(Successor to A. Harper)

OIL AND GAS WELL SHOOTER

AND MANUFACTURER OF
NITRO-GLYCERINE

OIL CITY, PENN'A.

Main Office—Room 2, Smart & Silberberg Bldg., 212 Centre St.

All Work Done at Well Owner's Risk

W.W. Bowers and the Allansons were competitors in well shooting. The life of a shooter could often times be measured in months or even days. Most shooters were calm, with an almost cavalier attitude when approaching a well. Many shooters would supplement their salary by moonlighting independently at night. (Photograph courtesy Bill Huber.)

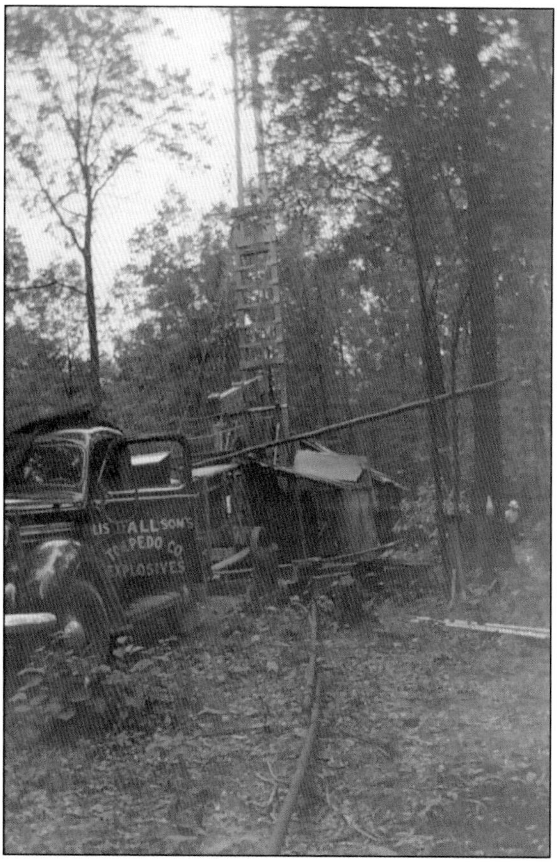

This truck is typical of the nitroglycerin trucks used throughout the 1930s and 1940s. (Photograph courtesy Bill Huber.)

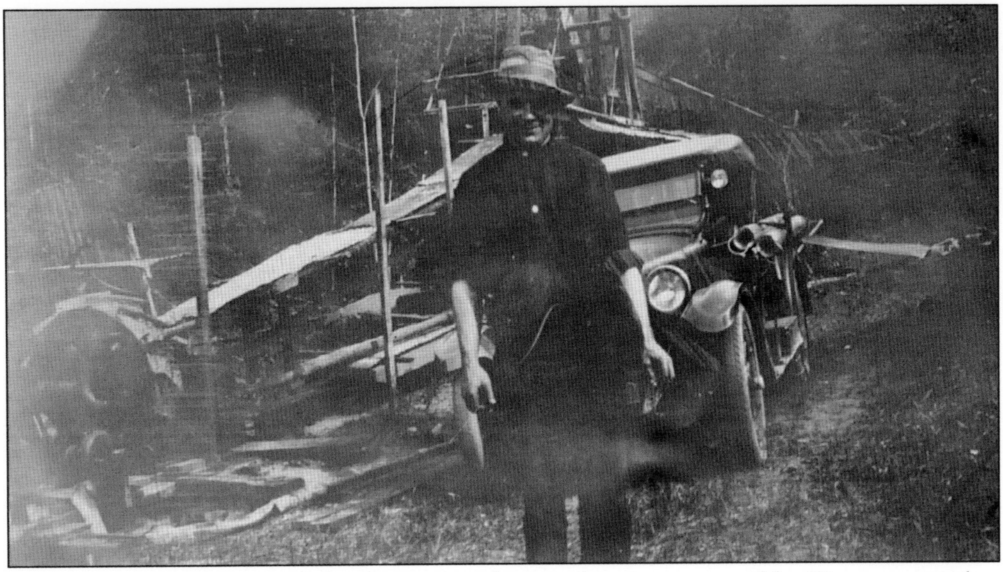

Eddie Kinnear is shown with his fancy nitroglycerin-shooting convertible. Kinnear started to shoot wells in the late 1920s; he shot one of his last wells for young Bill Huber (below, left) in the mid-1950s. (Photograph courtesy Bill Huber.)

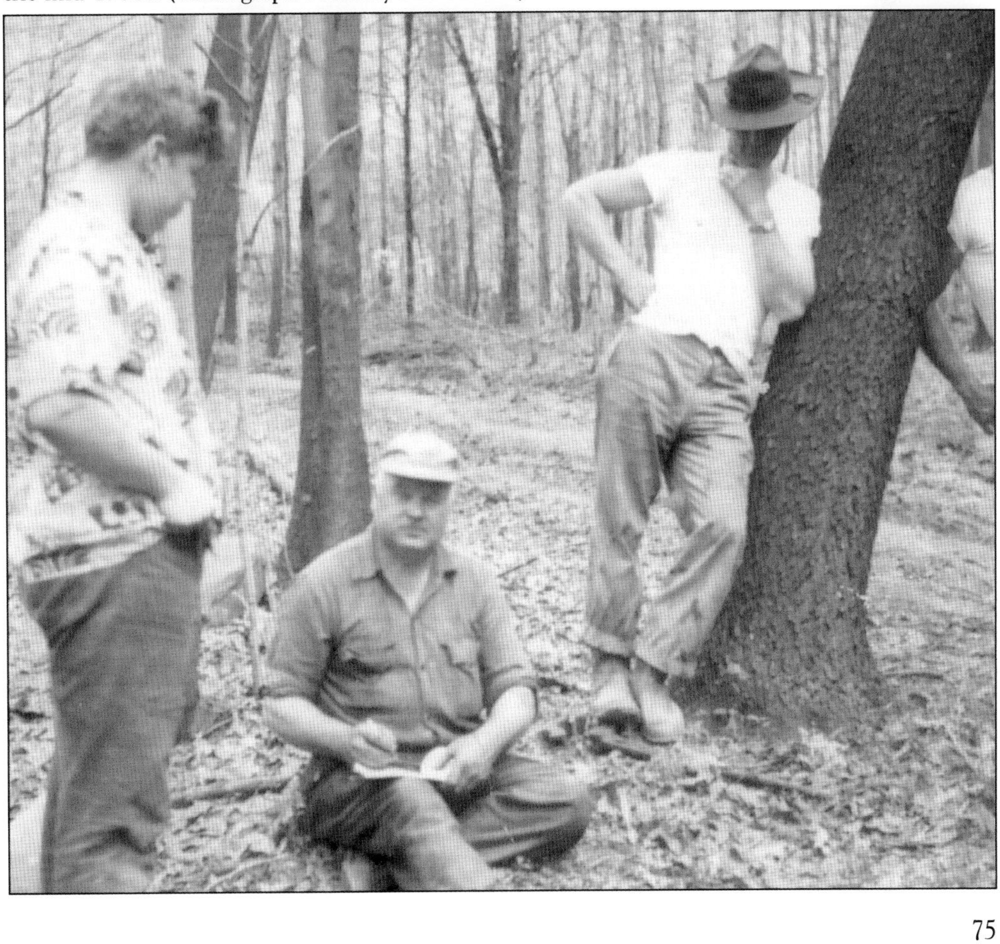

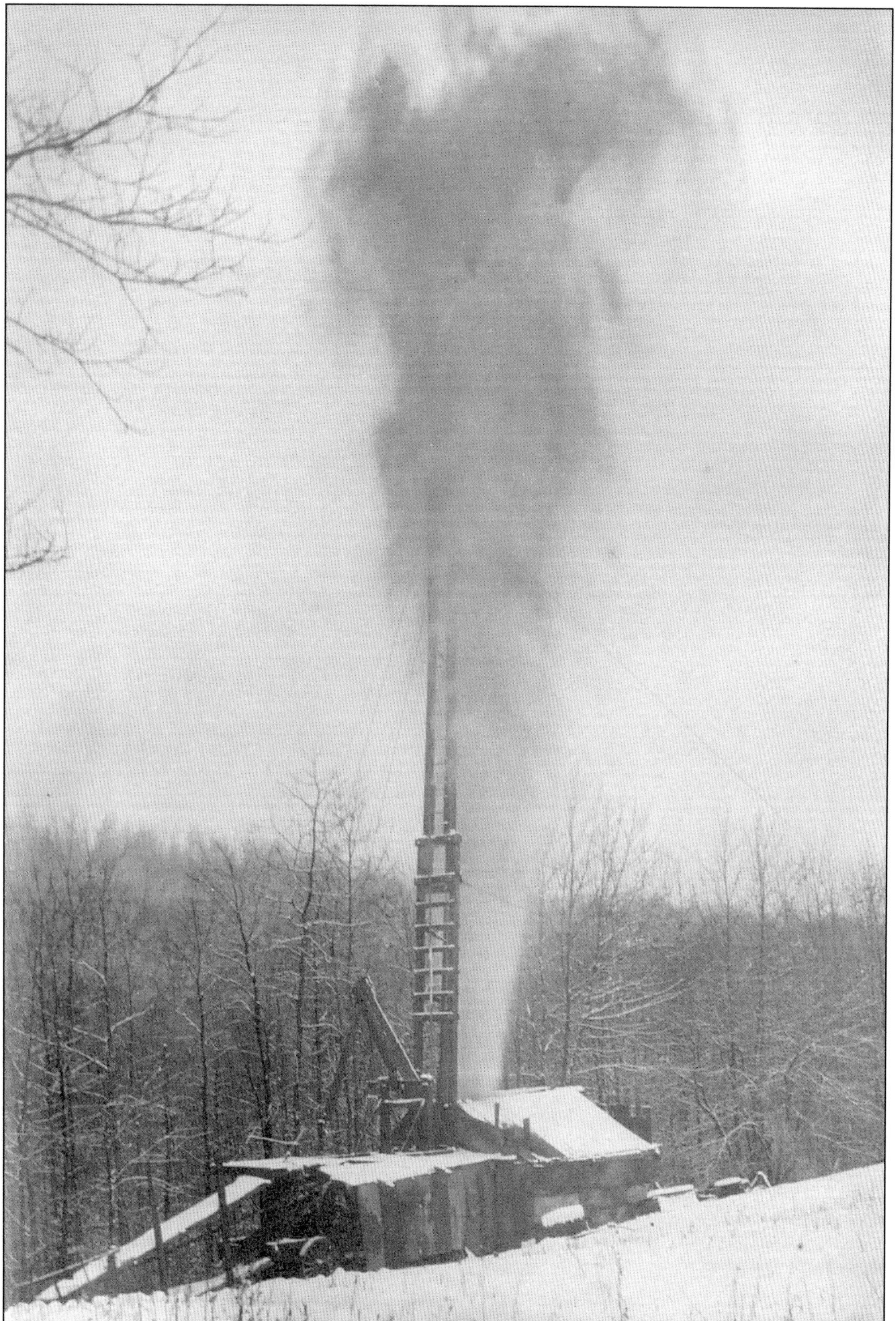

The snow was almost undisturbed when this Wolf rig was shot on the McFate farm, *c.* 1920s. (Photograph courtesy Dick Turk.)

Seven

BEERS CAMP
THE WORLD'S STRUGGLE FOR OIL

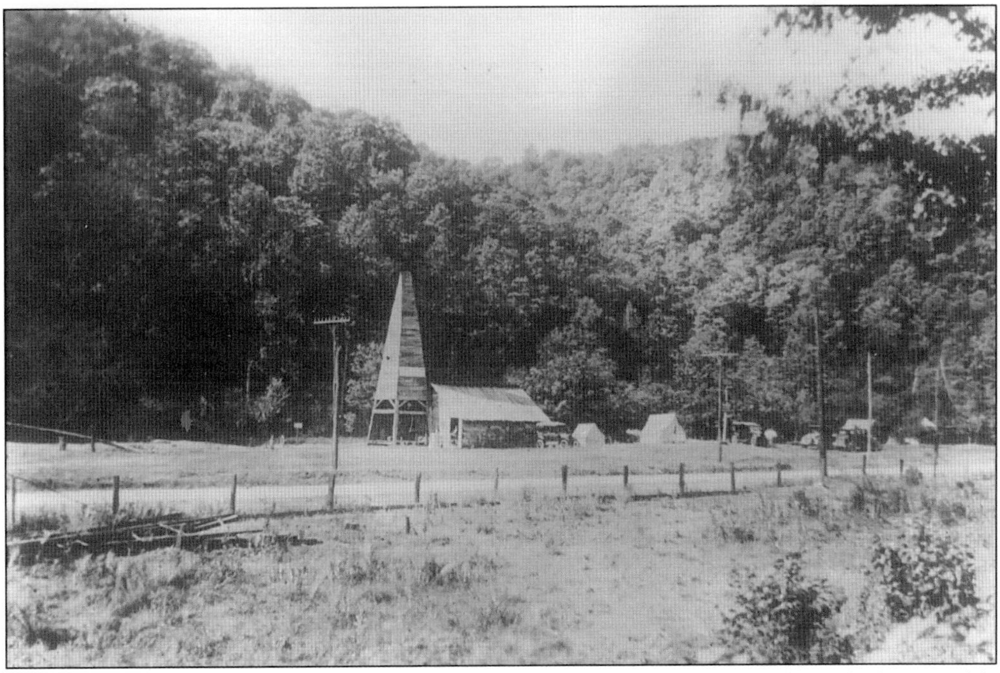

In the spring of 1922, the Sinclair Oil Company approached Edwin Bell to find a suitable location to shoot a feature film entitled *The World's Struggle for Oil*, a chronicle of the history of the oil industry. After receiving opposition from the Daughters of the American Revolution, who owned the original site of the Drake Well near Titusville, they instead chose the area along Cherry Run between Plumer and Rouseville owned by Percy Beers. The Beers family had long been involved as oil producers along Cherry Run and its tributary, Moody Run. After the film was completed in the summer of 1922, the family property was converted into a resort commonly known as Beers Camp. (Photograph courtesy the Venango Historical Society.)

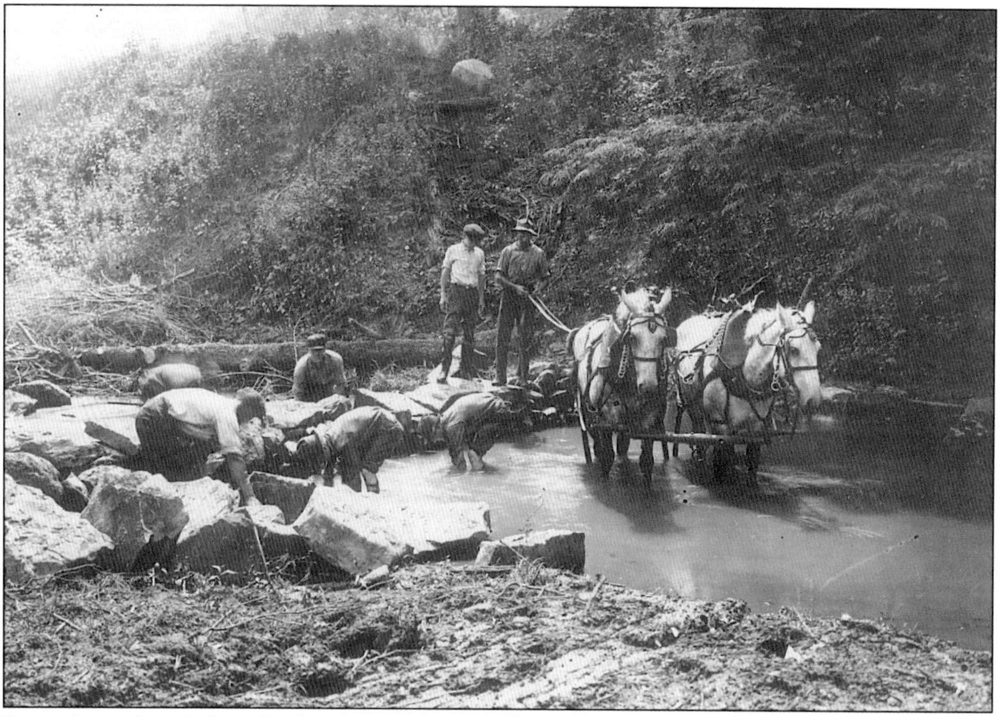

Percy Beers hired Oma Turk, George Campbell, and Bill Fornof from Plumer to build the replica of the Drake Well. Bob Branon and Ted Foster of the Rouseville Drilling Company are seen with their team damming Cherry Run to create a pond that would be used for filming the pond freshet scenes. (Photograph courtesy Dick Turk.)

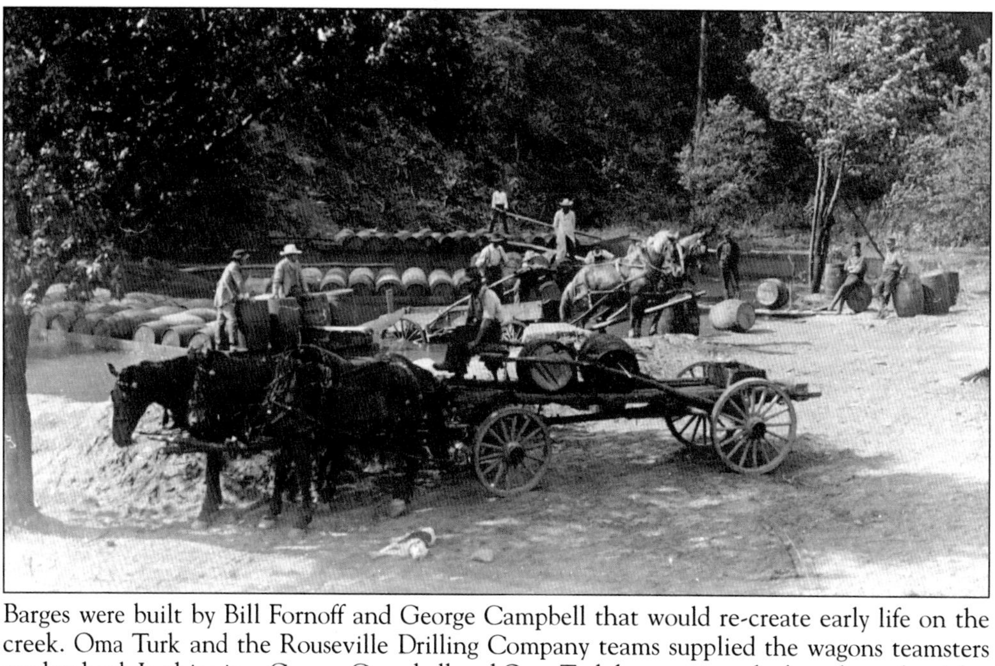

Barges were built by Bill Fornoff and George Campbell that would re-create early life on the creek. Oma Turk and the Rouseville Drilling Company teams supplied the wagons teamsters used to haul. In this view, George Campbell and Oma Turk lean against the barrels on the right. (Photograph courtesy the Drake Well Museum.)

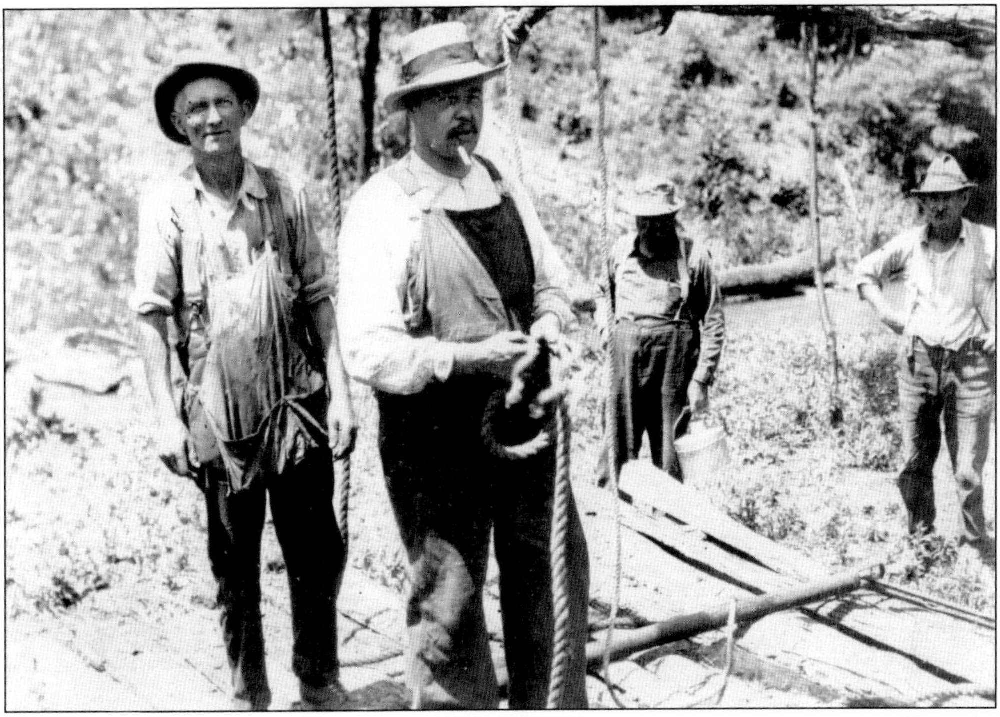

George Campbell, an excellent rig builder, designed the spring pole rig used in the film. The majority of labor used to construct the sets was provided by Oma Turk's crew. (Photograph courtesy Dick Turk.)

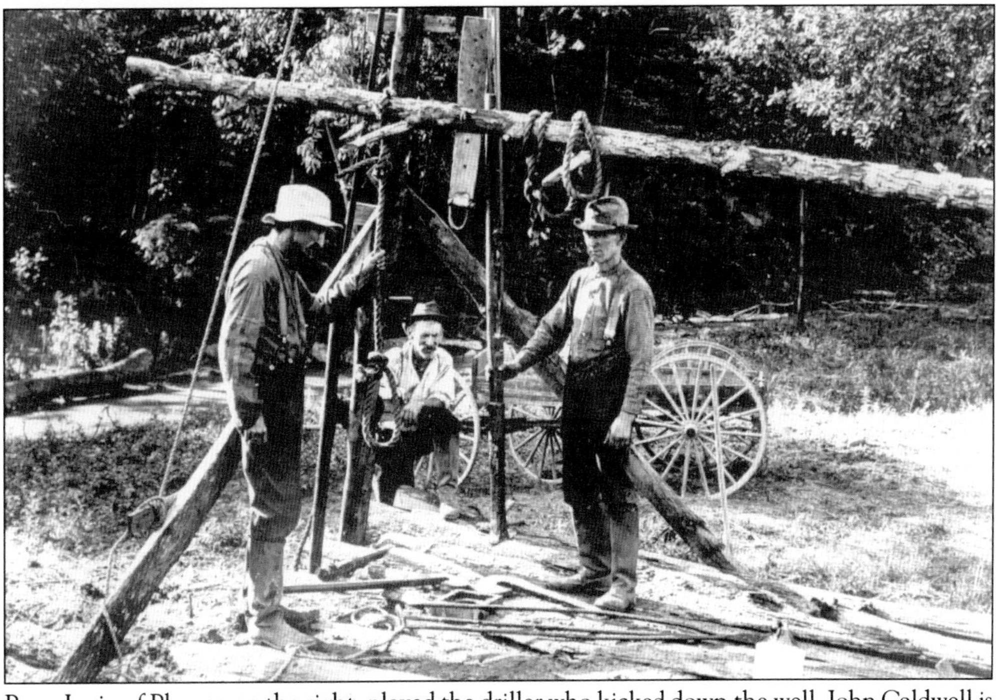

Perry Irwin of Plumer, on the right, played the driller who kicked down the well. John Caldwell is kneeling in the center under the spring pole. (Photograph courtesy the Drake Well Museum.)

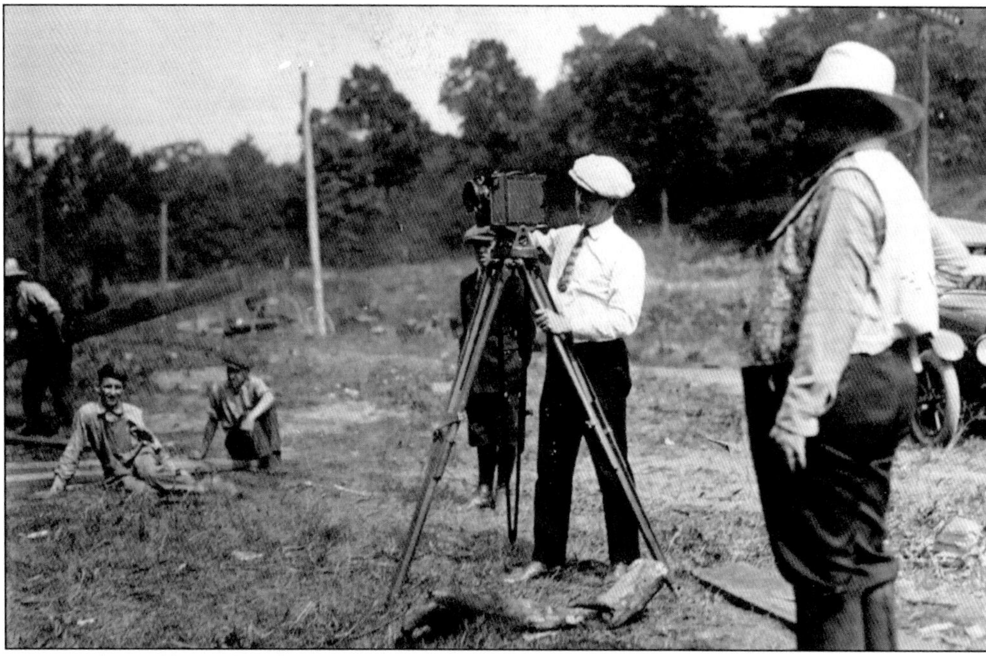

H.C. Butler, a film maker from New York, was hired to shoot the film. He is seen preparing the camera. Walter Beers, the brother of Percy Beers, is seen in the foreground, observing the shoot. (Photograph courtesy the Drake Well Museum.)

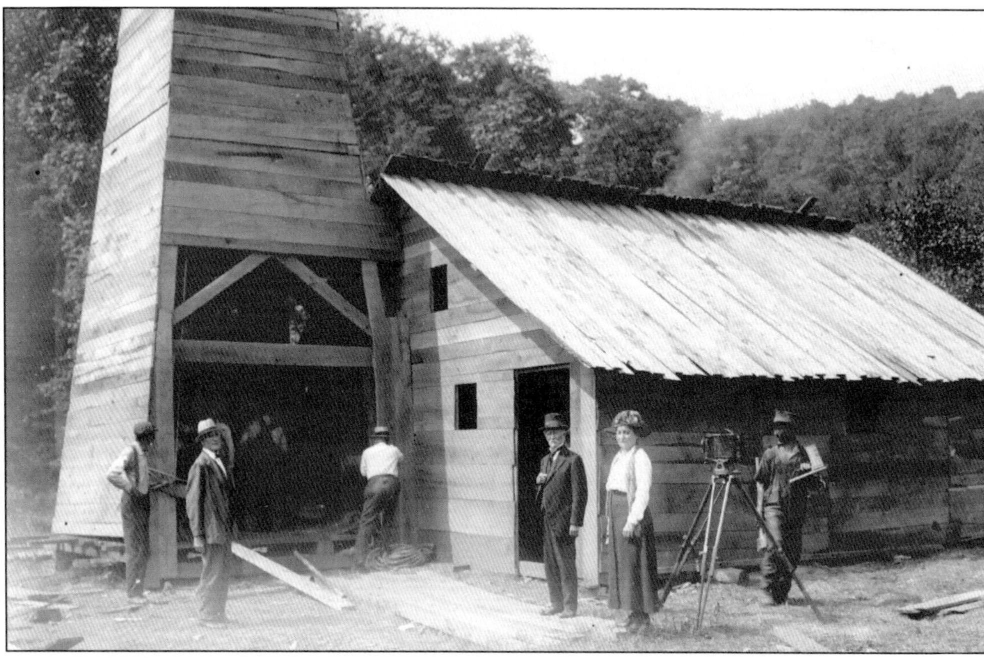

Sam Smith, the son of Uncle Billy Smith who drilled the original Drake Well in 1859, is the man in the suit on the left. Sam was 16 when he helped his father sink the first well. Edwin C. Bell, the man on the right in the suit and hat, created the first Drake Memorial Museum in 1913; his wife, Jessie, is to his right. Bell and Smith served as technical consultants to the filmmakers. (Photograph courtesy Joe and Jerri Saunders.)

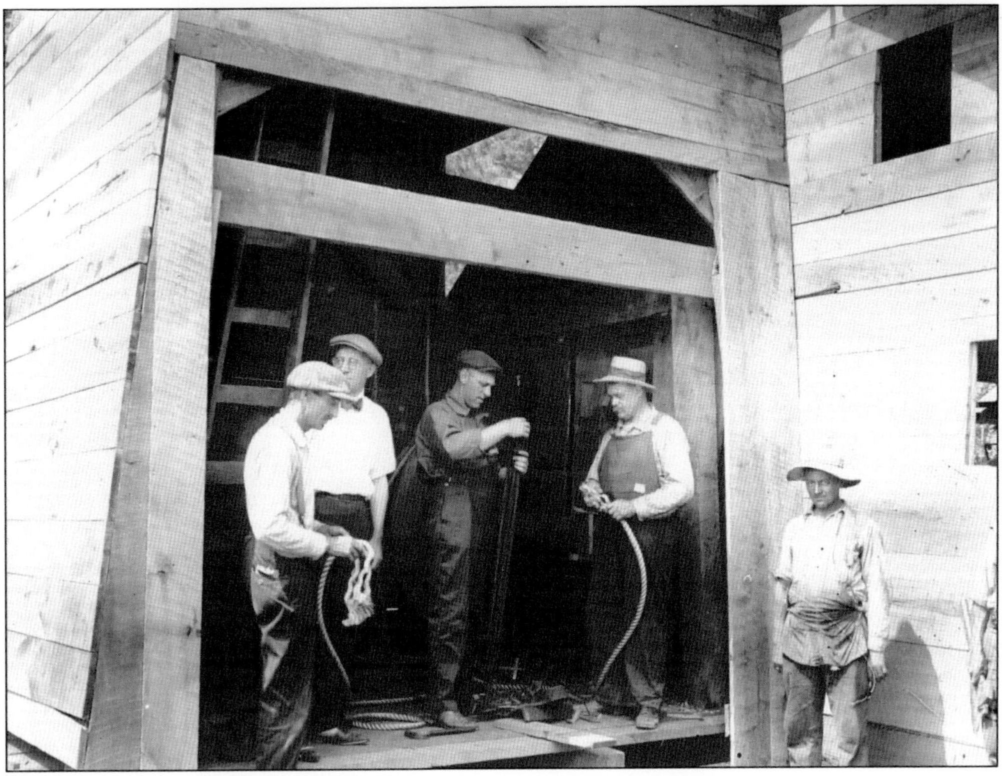

Perry Irwin, H.C. Butler, Oma Turk, George Campbell, and Kelly Brecht are shown in the replica of the well. (Photograph courtesy Joe and Jerri Saunders.)

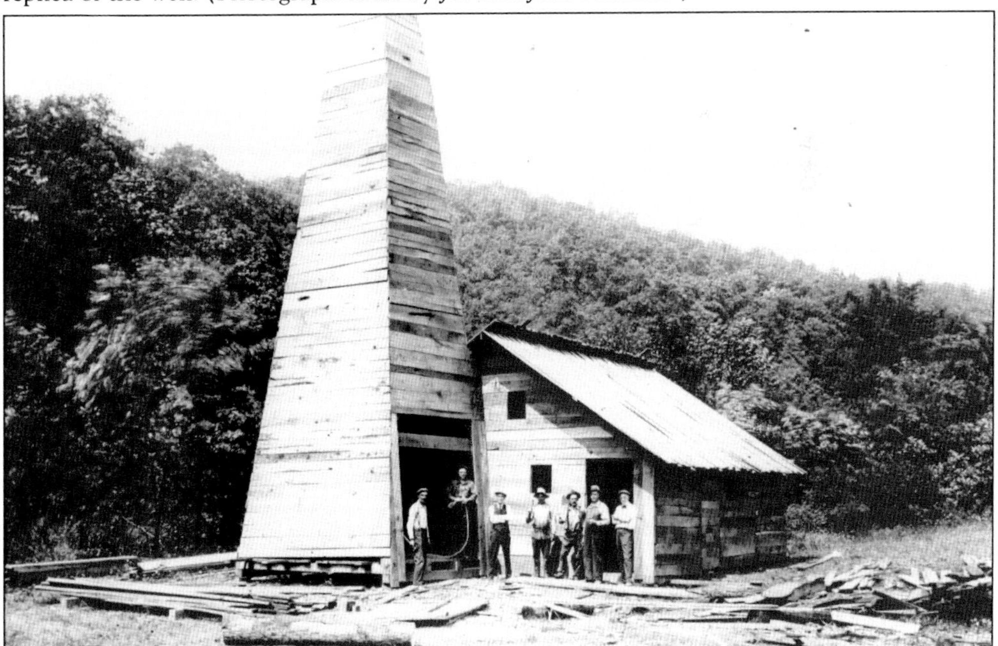

The construction crew poses for this shot the day the replica was completed. (Photograph courtesy the Drake Well Museum.)

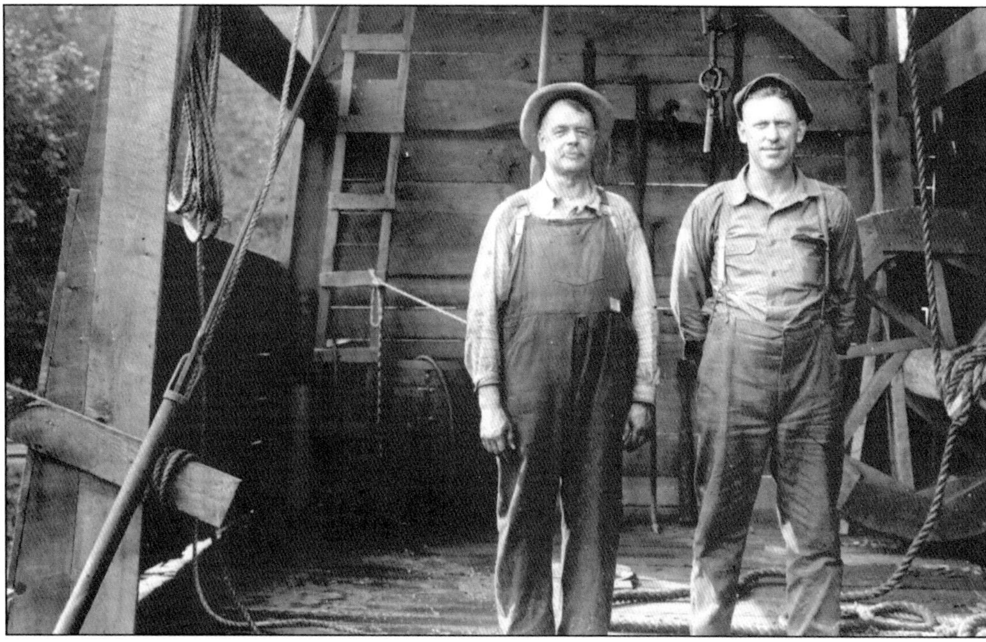

George Campbell and Oma Turk pose inside the replica of the well. The tools used for the shoot were some of the original tools used by Edwin Drake and Billy Smith at the original well. (Photograph courtesy Dick Turk.)

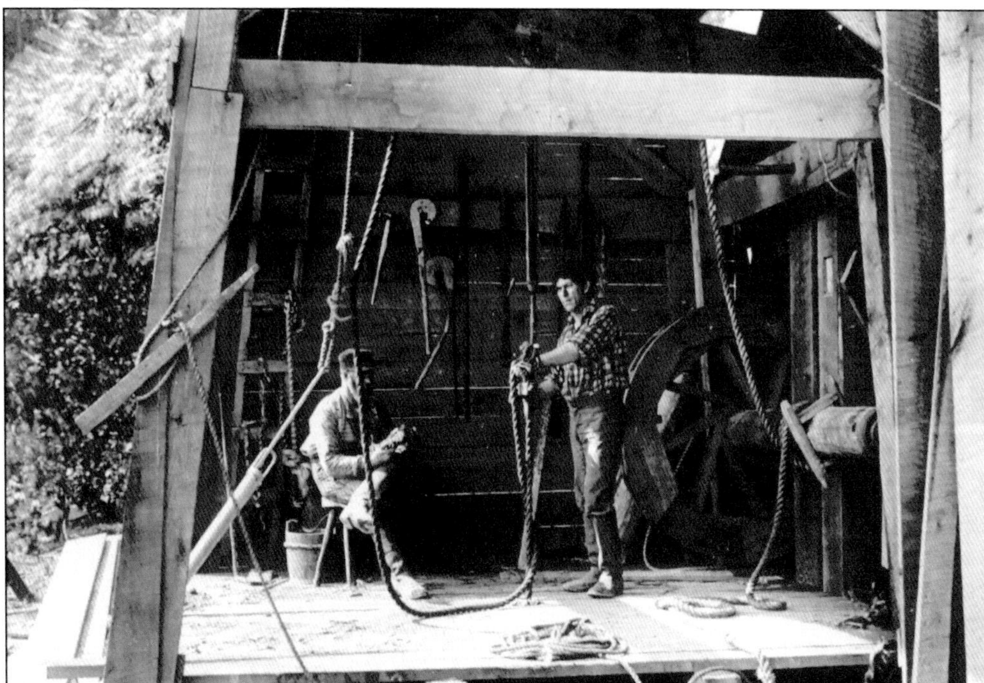

George Campbell and Oma Turk were asked to portray Uncle Billy and Sam Smith in the scenes that re-created Drakes's first successful attempt. George, to the left, played Uncle Billy; Oma portrayed Sam Smith. With their combined expertise in drilling and building rigs, the film was as authentic as possible. (Photograph courtesy the Drake Well Museum.)

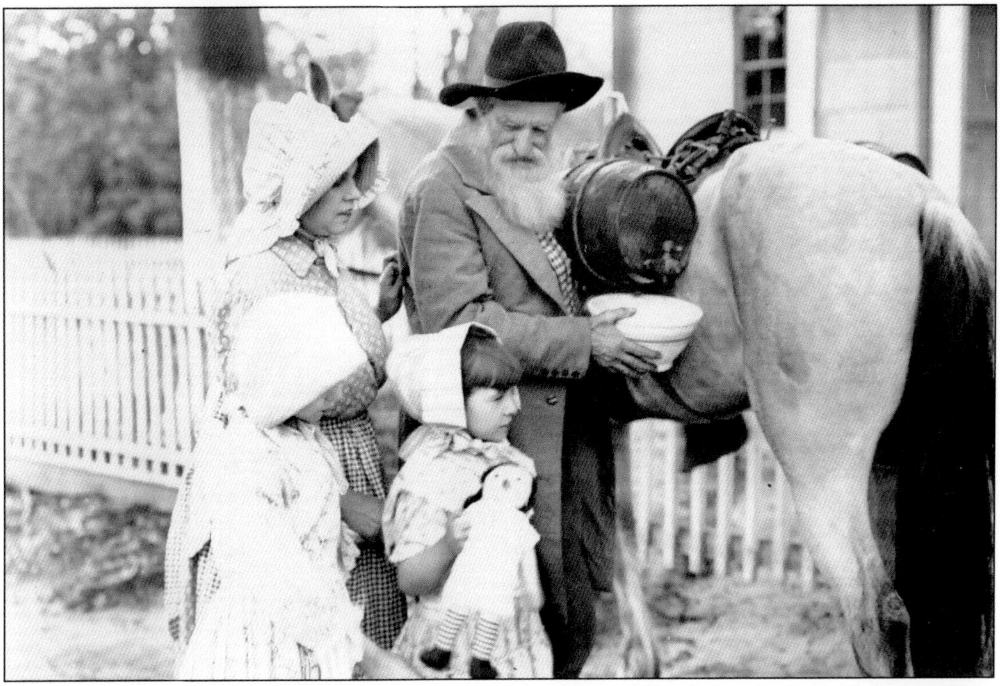

This scene from the film portrays a Seneca snake oil peddler. Long before oil was used as a lubricant and a fuel, it was sold as a medicinal with special healing powers. (Photograph courtesy Dick Turk.)

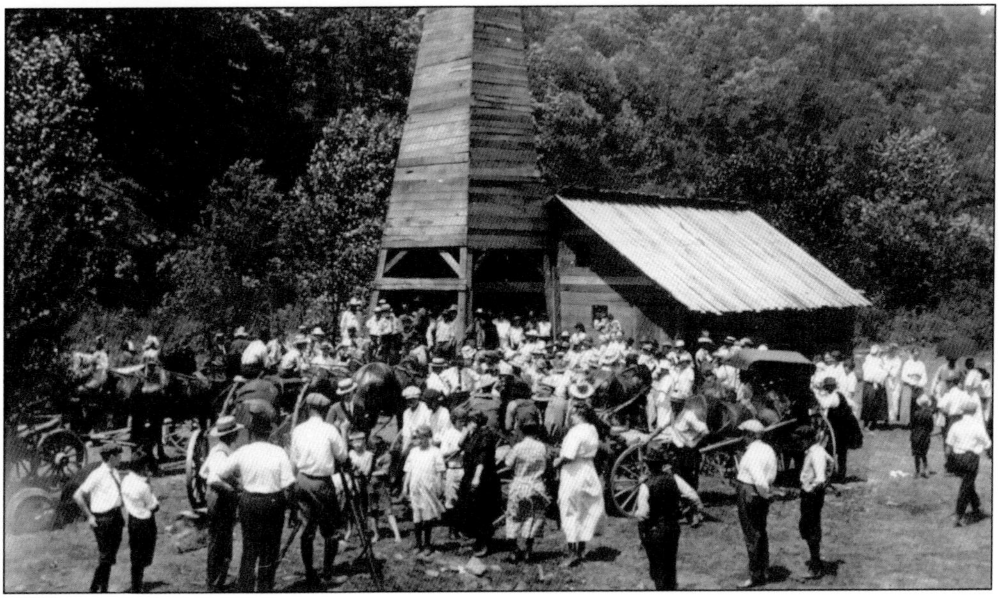

Edwin Bell created the Drake Day Association in 1913 to honor Edwin Drake and to raise funds to build a museum in his name. The organization held its annual meeting at Beers Camp on August 26, 1922. The guests were encouraged to wear a period costume and create the crowd scenes for the film. Dick Turk, then eight or nine years old, is the son of Oma Turk. Riding in the wagon on the left, he wears a large white hat and is turned toward the camera. (Photograph courtesy Dick Turk.)

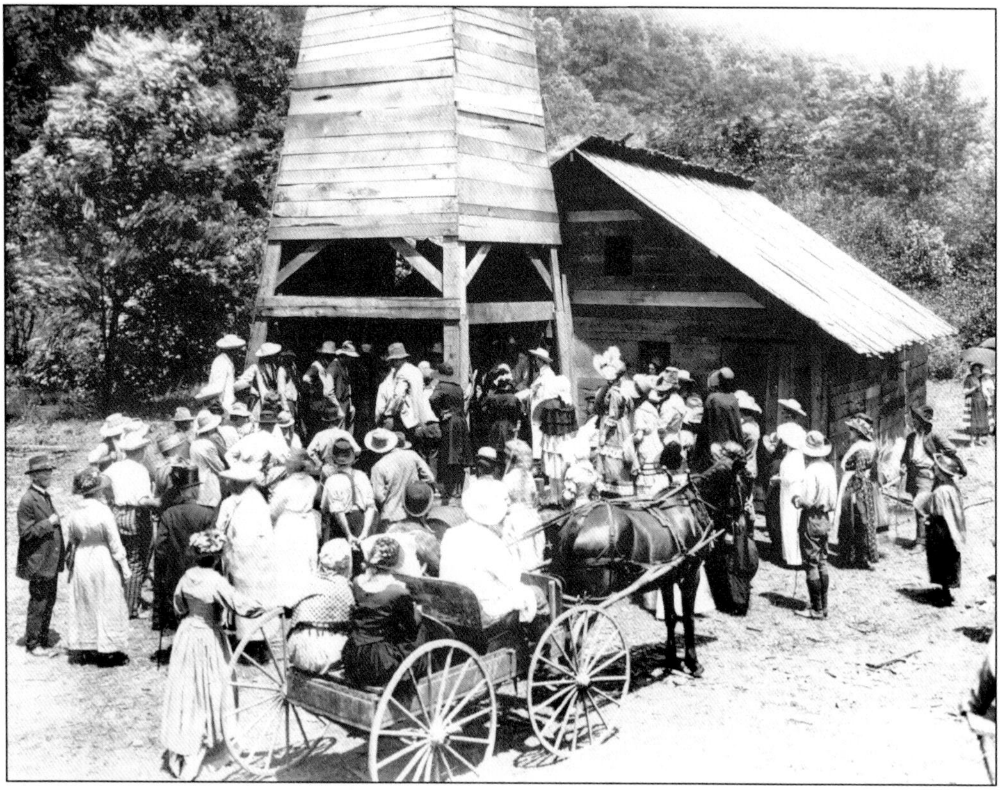

J.P. Russell of Plumer portrayed Drake that clear August day, as more than 1,000 people attended the festivities. (Photograph courtesy the Drake Well Museum.)

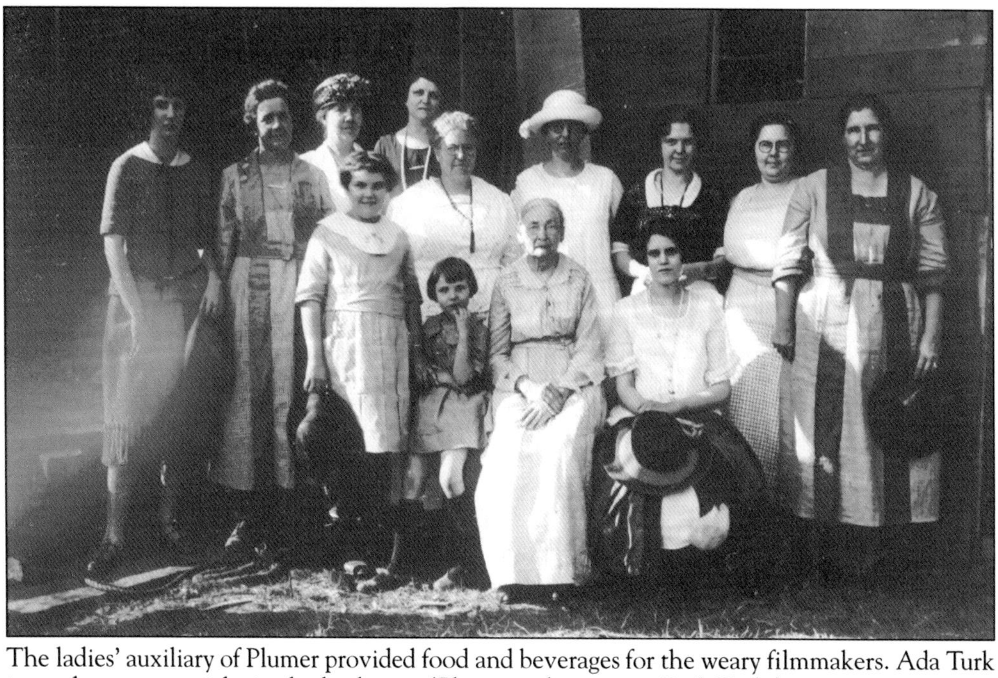

The ladies' auxiliary of Plumer provided food and beverages for the weary filmmakers. Ada Turk is on the extreme right in the back row. (Photograph courtesy Dick Turk.)

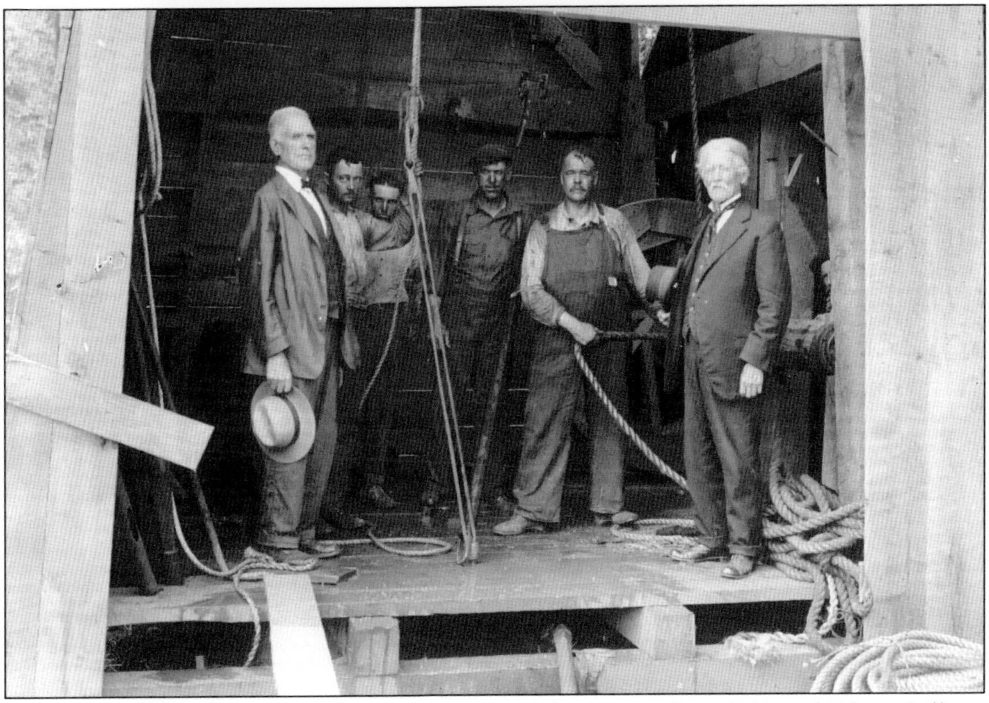

Sam Smith, Kelly Brecht, Dutch Stevens, Oma Turk, George Campbell, and Edwin Bell are shown here. (Photograph courtesy Dick Turk.)

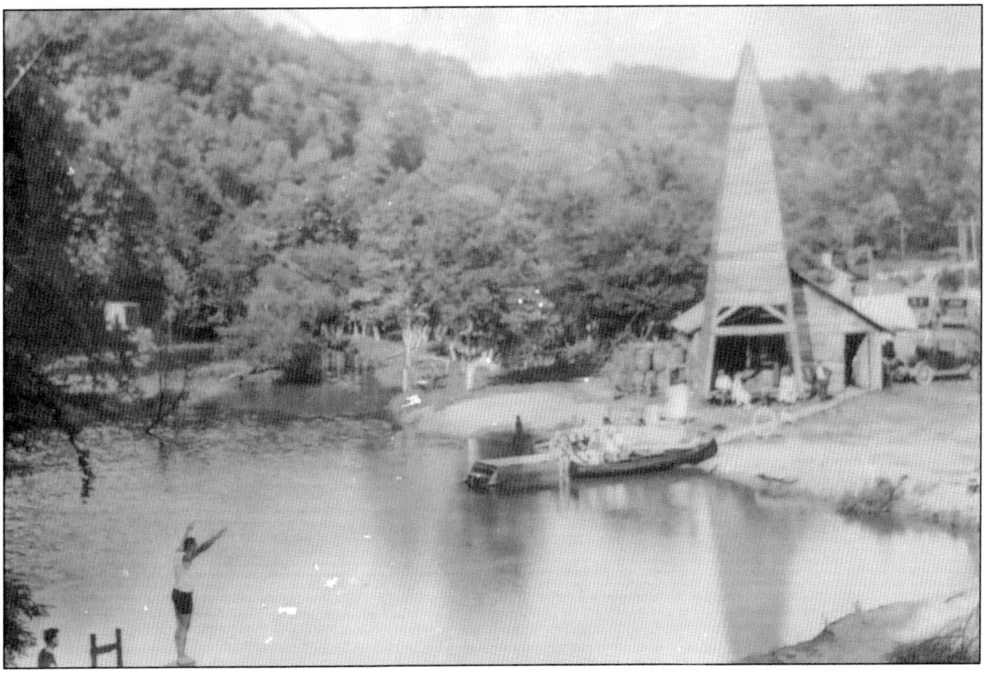

Beers Camp became a popular resort with a somewhat shady reputation. The pond was deepened and a platform for diving was added. The replica of the Drake Well was converted into a barbecue restaurant with a pavilion added for dancing and large parties. (Photograph courtesy the Oil City Genealogical Society.)

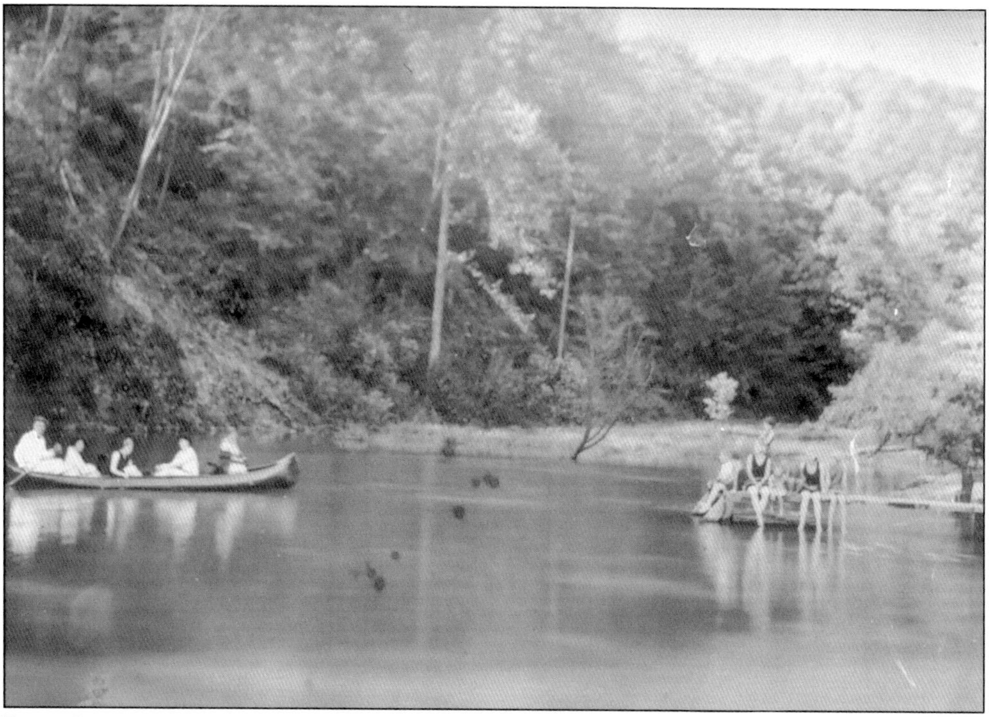

Beers Camp was to remain a great place to swim, canoe, and picnic until it was purchased by Pennzoil before World War II. (Photograph courtesy the Oil City Genealogical Society.)

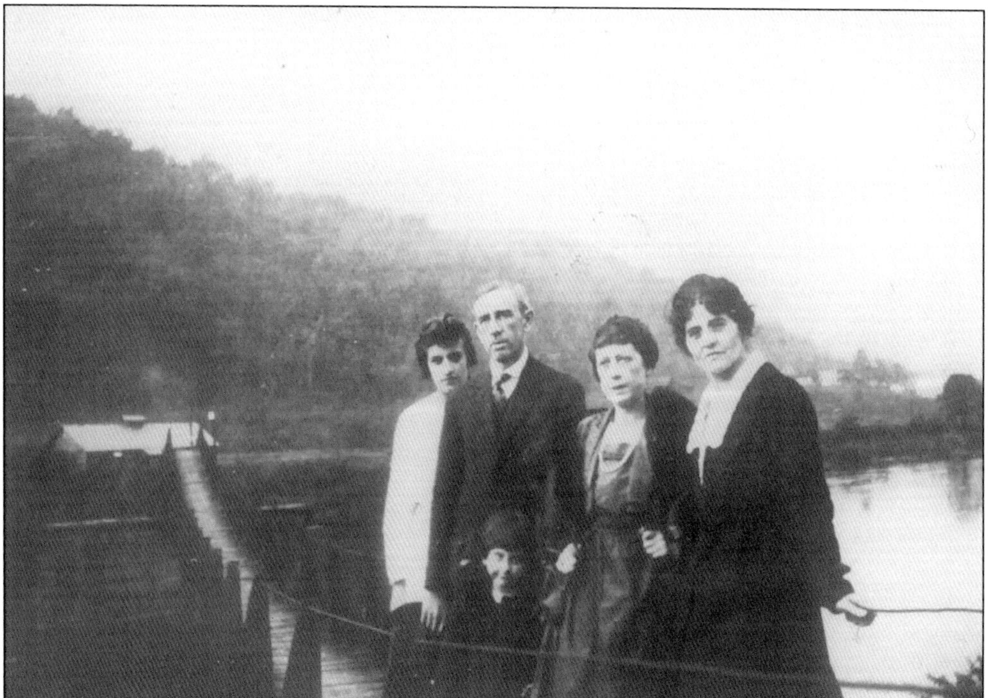

The Beers family crosses a rope-and-cable suspension bridge near their home in Rouseville. (Photograph courtesy the Venango Historical Society.)

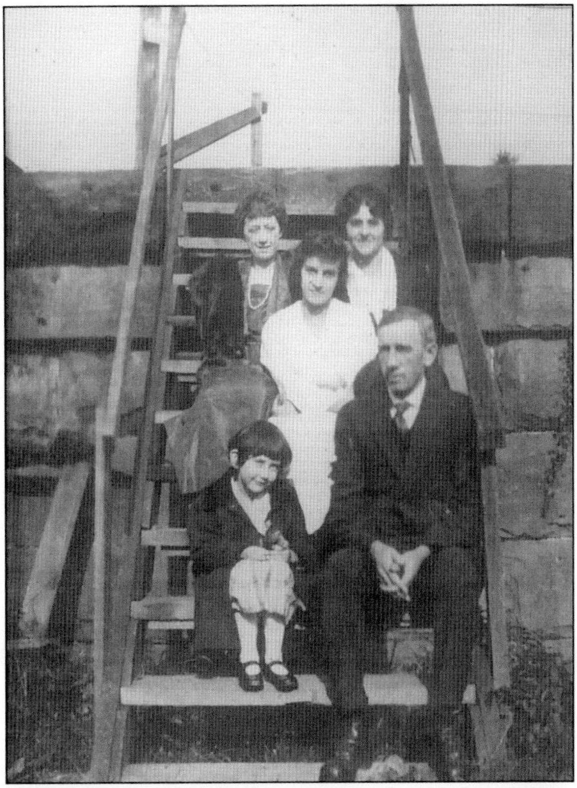

The Beers family can be seen at the base of the suspension bridge. The family had great success as oil producers from the early 1860s. (Photograph courtesy the Venango Historical Society.)

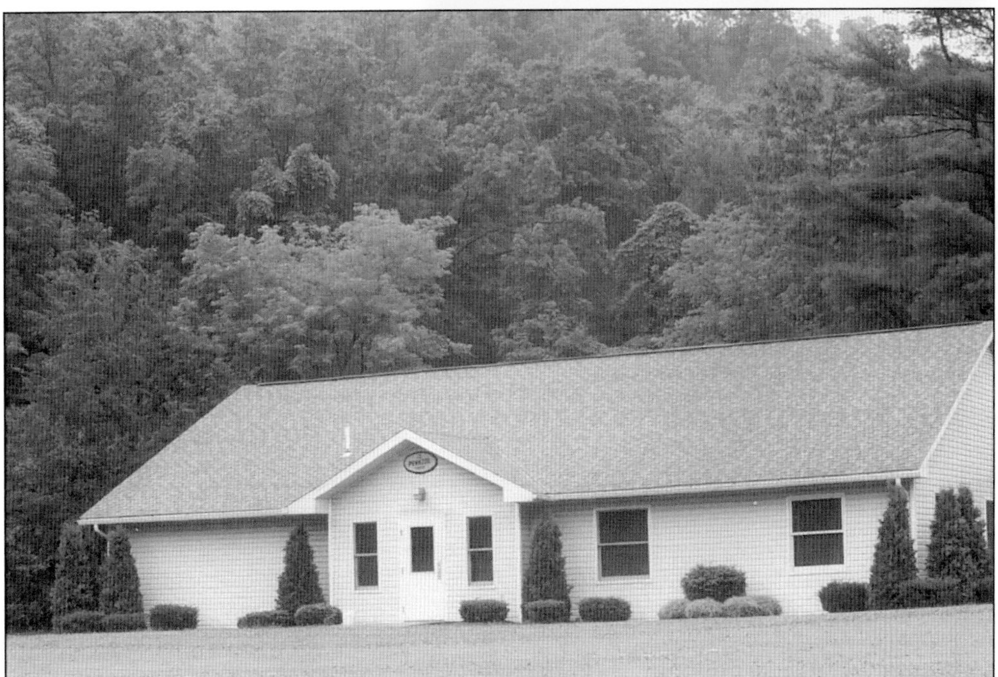

This contemporary photograph shows the Pennzoil truck depot that was built on the site of Beers Camp. (Photograph by Jim Stoudt.)

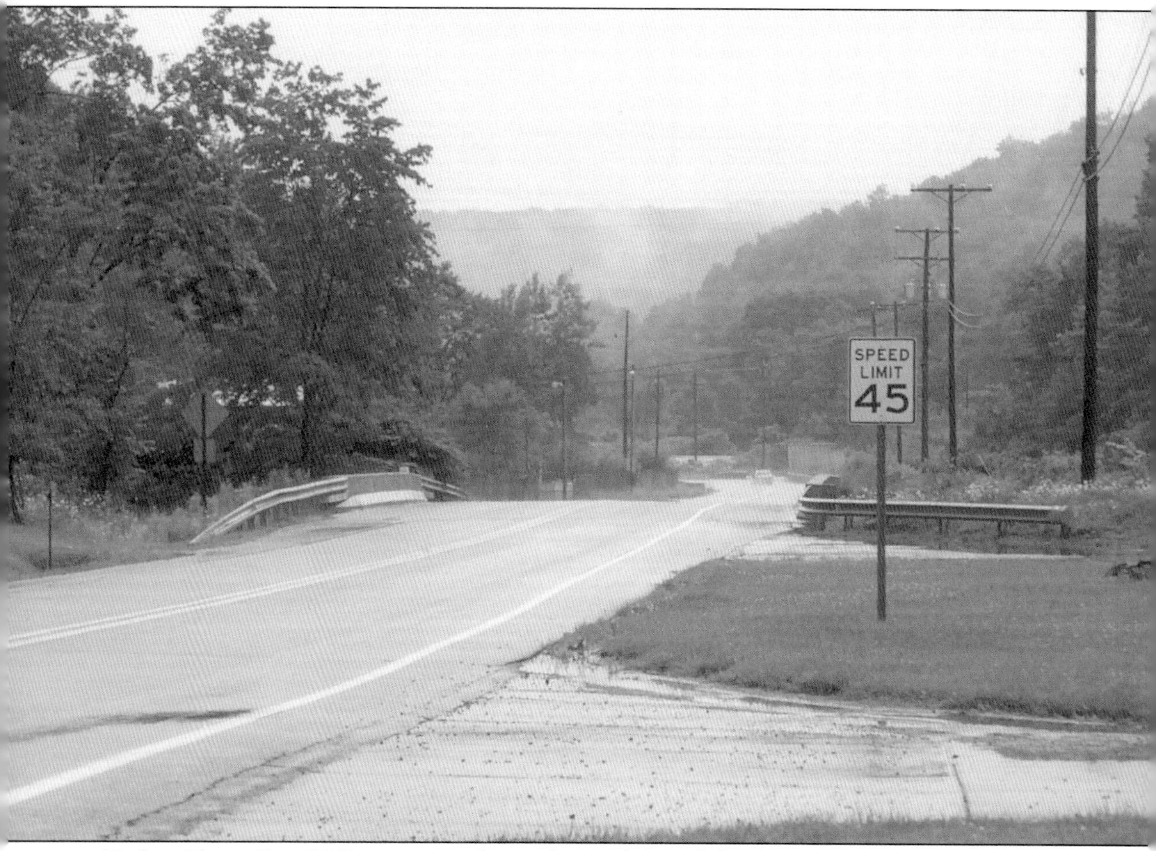

Today, Cherry Run Valley appears almost deserted. It is difficult to imagine the frantic activity that enveloped the valley in the 1860s. (Photograph by Jim Stoudt.)

Eight

Plumer Families

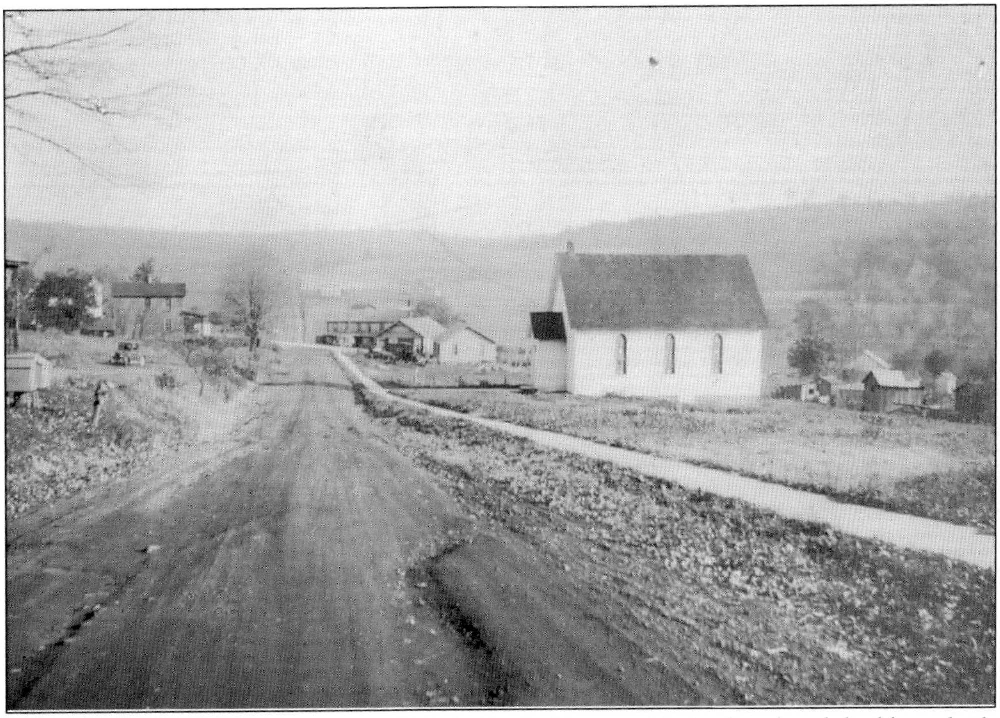

This view of Plumer looks east toward Eagle Rock. The new Methodist church had been built in 1914; the old church, originally built in 1865, was dismantled. Toward the upper right side, the old Prather store can be seen a few years before it burned down. The sidewalks were installed in 1924.

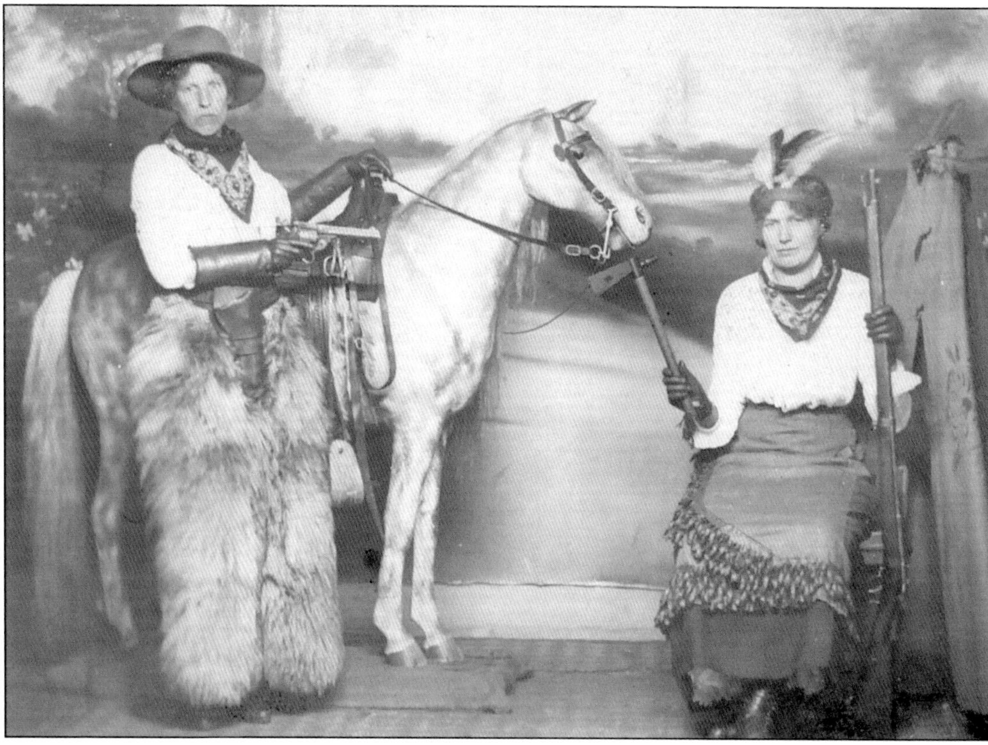

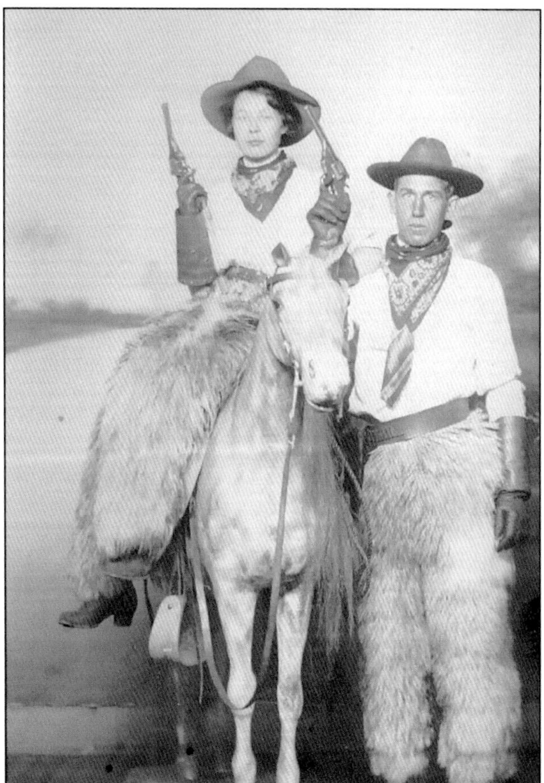

Above, Maggie and Flo Haupt of Plumer pose at an amusement park photograph shop in the early 1920s. At left, Nellie Haupt, Sam Nelson's sister, and her husband, Bill, enjoy themselves on the same trip. (Photographs courtesy the Russells.)

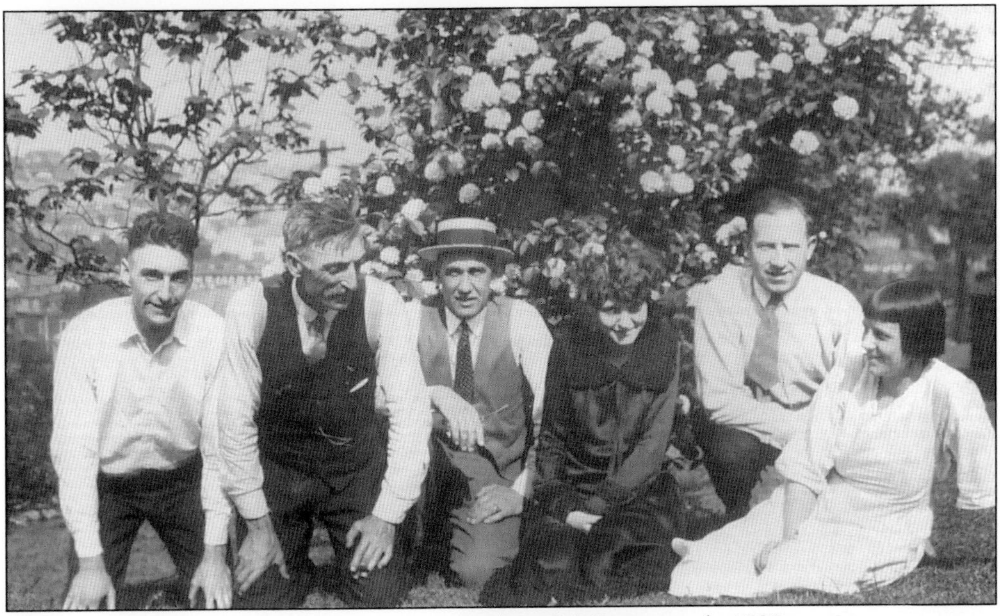

The Haupts and Irwins get away to Hasson park at Oil City, *c.* early 1930s.

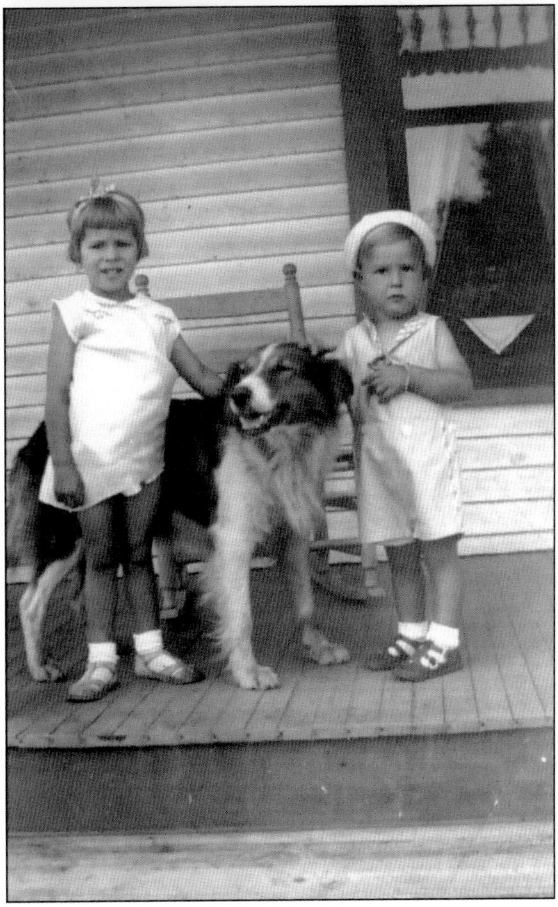

June and John Russell can be seen with their dog, Jack, on their porch, *c.* 1930. (Photograph courtesy of June Russell Pearson.)

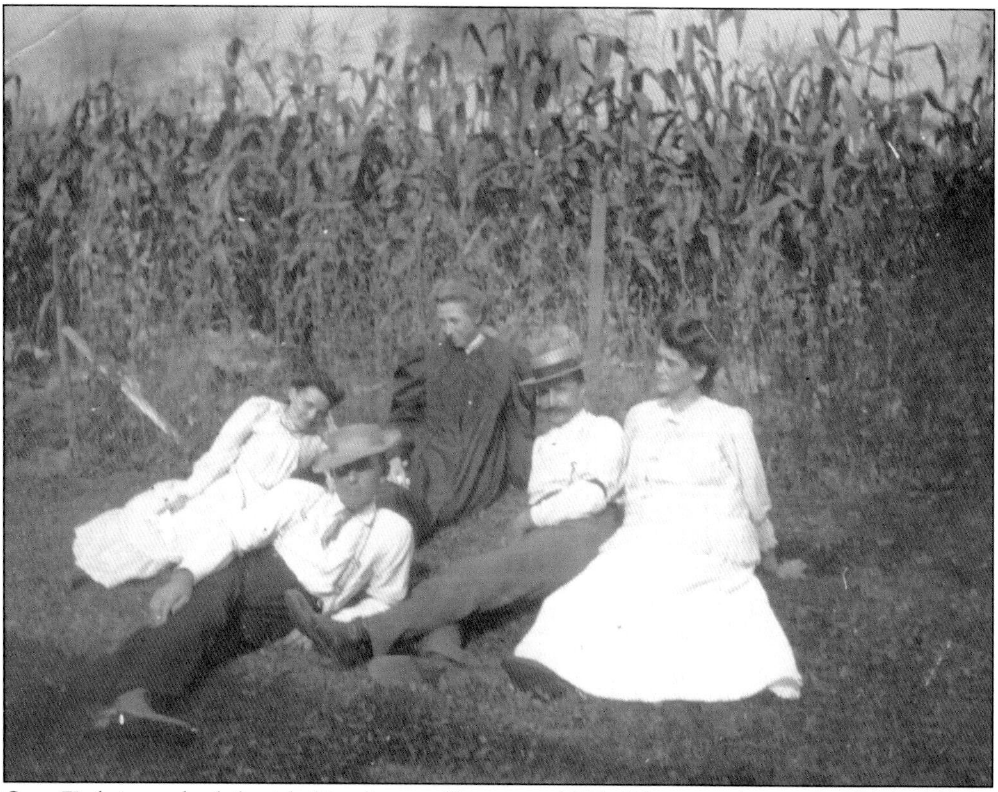

Oma Turk is on the left with friends near Plumer, *c.* 1905. (Photograph courtesy Dick Turk.)

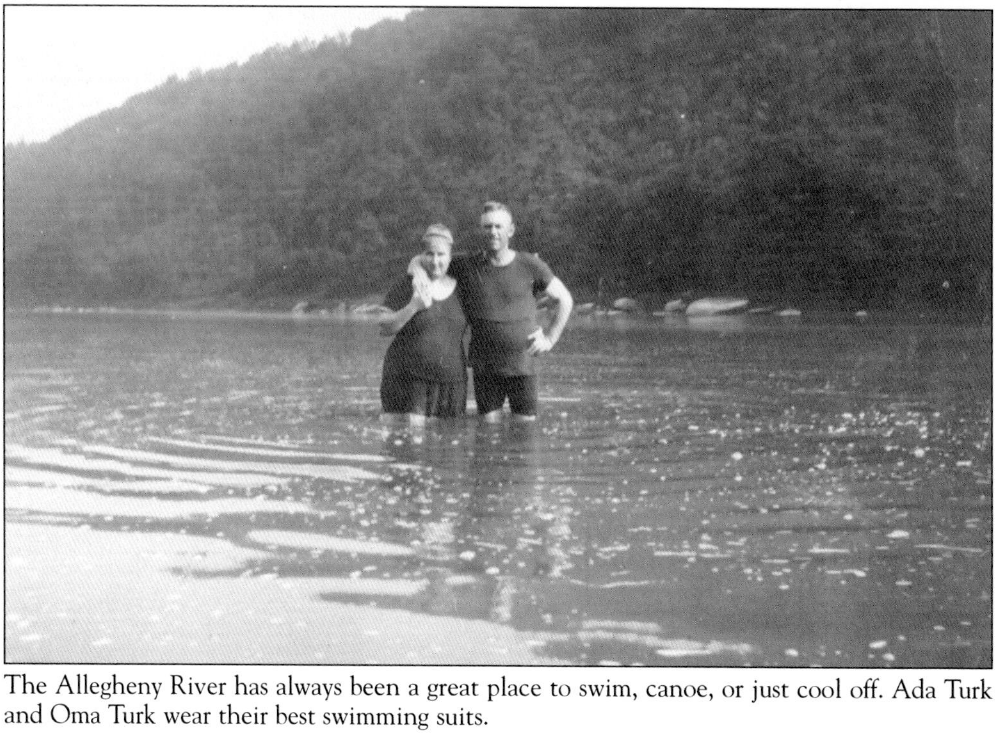

The Allegheny River has always been a great place to swim, canoe, or just cool off. Ada Turk and Oma Turk wear their best swimming suits.

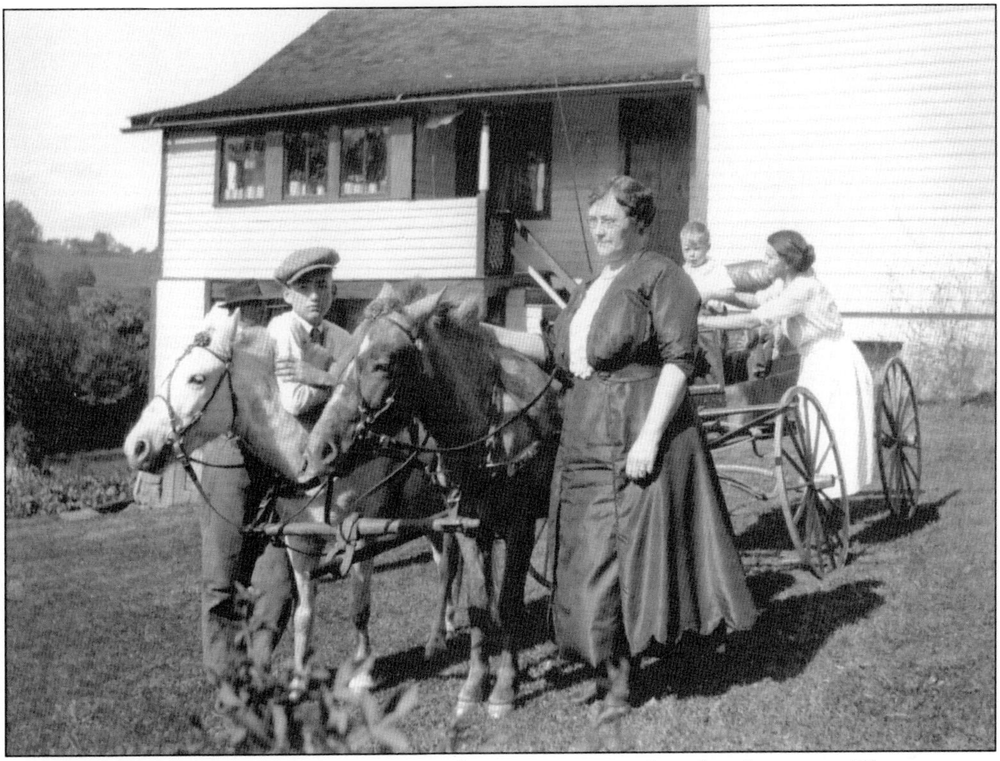

Jack Turk, by the horse, and his cousin, in the wagon, get ready to head to town. They are seen with their aunt Lib and Viola Turk at the Turk homestead in Plumer, c. 1920. (Photograph courtesy Dick Turk.)

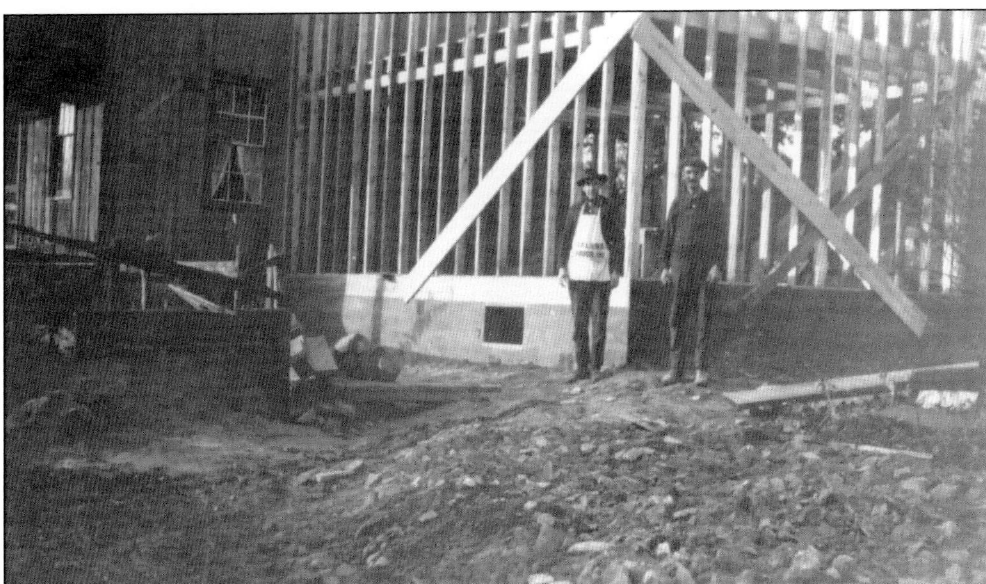

Bill Haupt and Perry Irwin build an addition to the original Haupt homestead, c. 1928. (Photograph courtesy the Russells.)

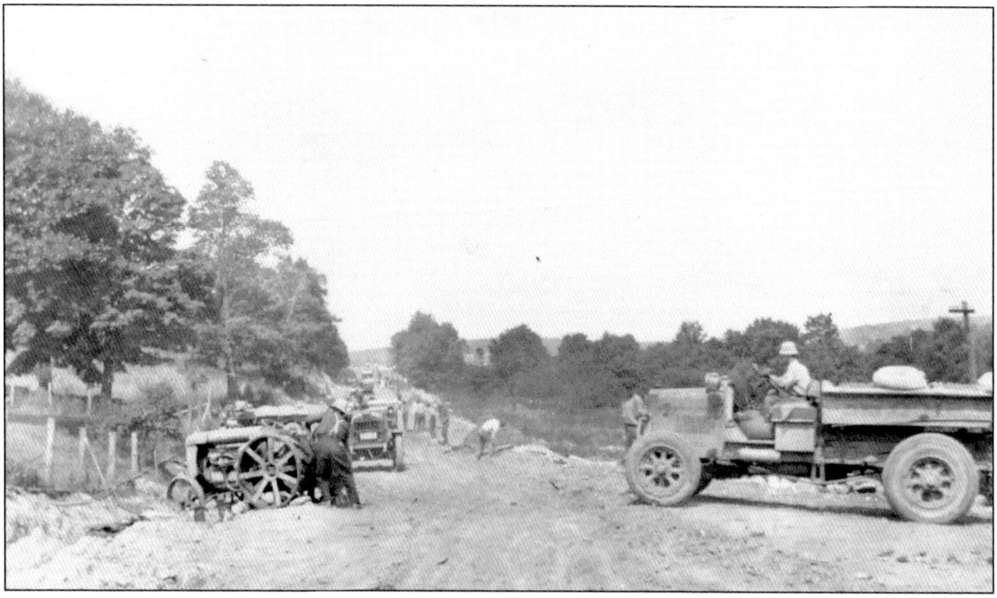

Herbert Huber uses his Fordson tractor to help prepare the regrading of Highway 227 from Plumer to Rouseville, *c.* 1922. (Photograph courtesy of Bill Huber.)

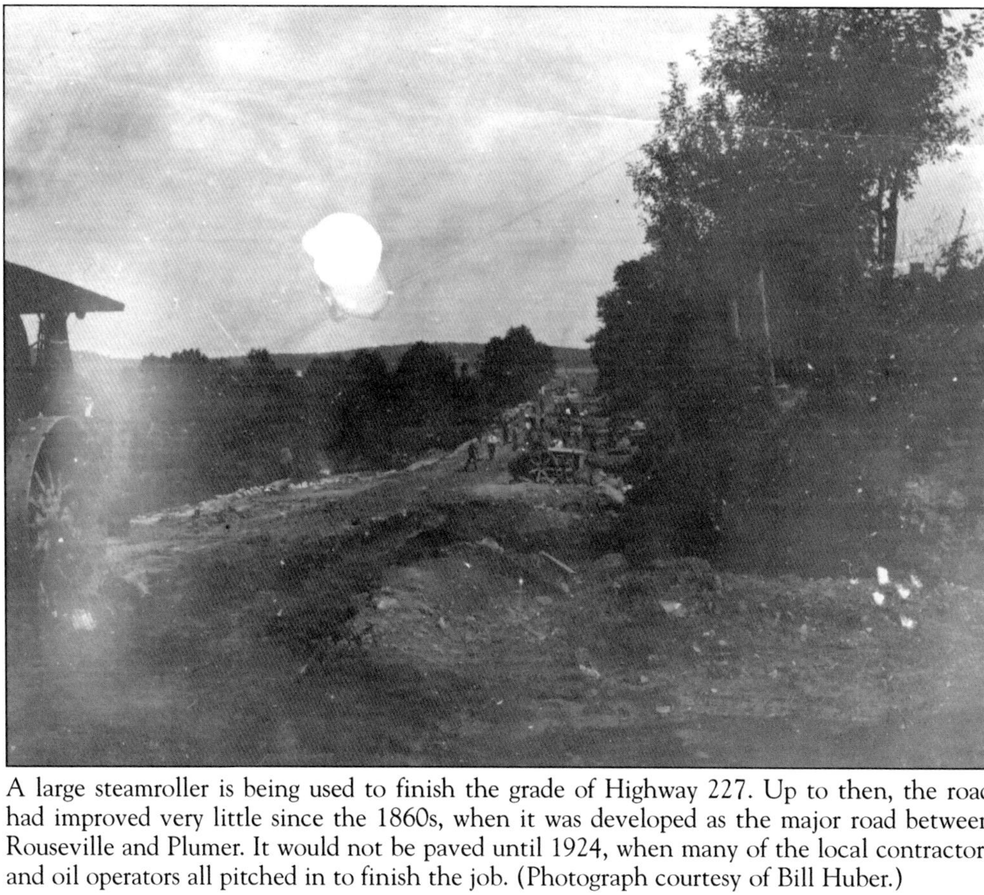

A large steamroller is being used to finish the grade of Highway 227. Up to then, the road had improved very little since the 1860s, when it was developed as the major road between Rouseville and Plumer. It would not be paved until 1924, when many of the local contractors and oil operators all pitched in to finish the job. (Photograph courtesy of Bill Huber.)

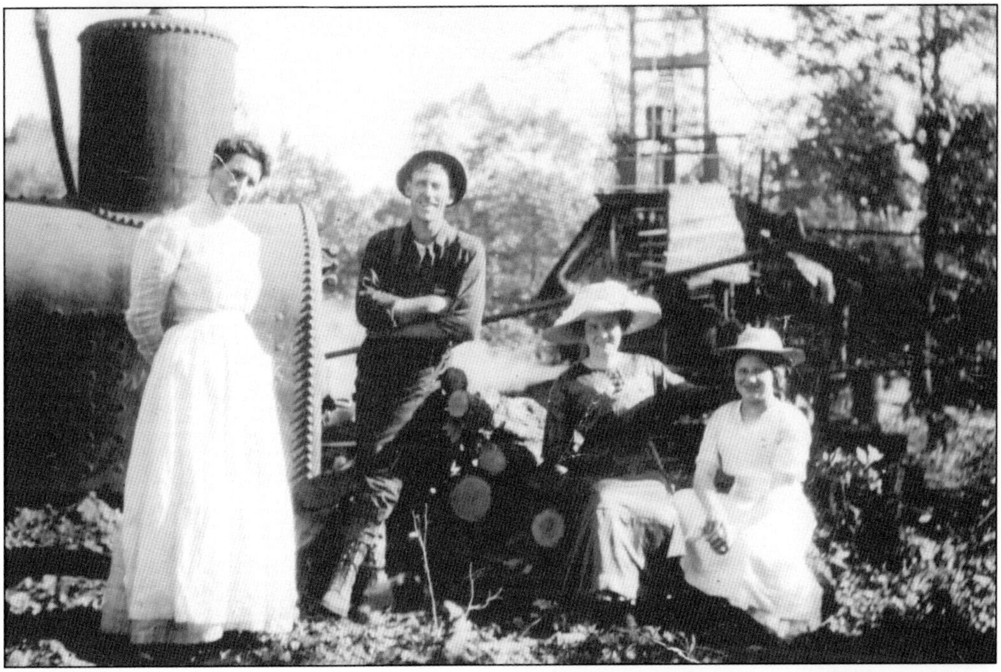

Oma Turk founded the Pioneer gas works near Petroleum Centre before World War I. He and Ada Turk relax with her cousins near the gas works, *c.* 1920. In 1918, with gasoline prices high, Turk's partner refused an offer of $1 million. They eventually sold the entire works for $4,000. Such are the fortunes of oil men. (Photograph courtesy Dick Turk.)

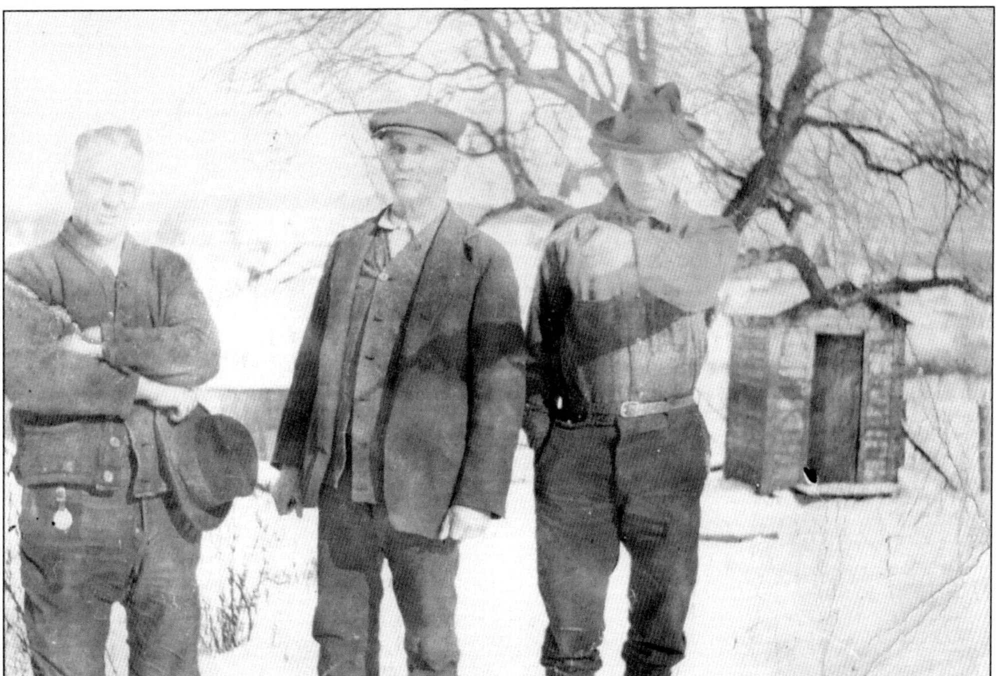

Max and Frank Smith, shown with their son, Hiram Smith (right), were drillers for the Hubers and Ensles. (Photograph courtesy Bill Huber.)

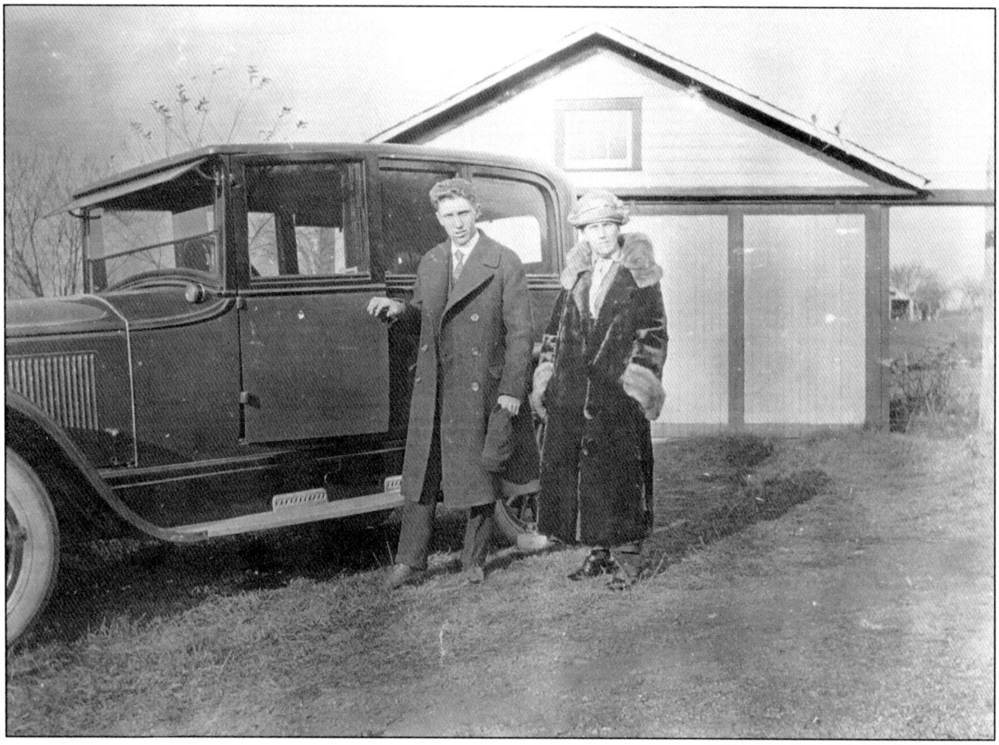

Herbert Huber poses with his grandmother Ensle outside their garage on the old Humboldt refinery grounds, *c.* 1928. (Photograph courtesy Bill Huber.)

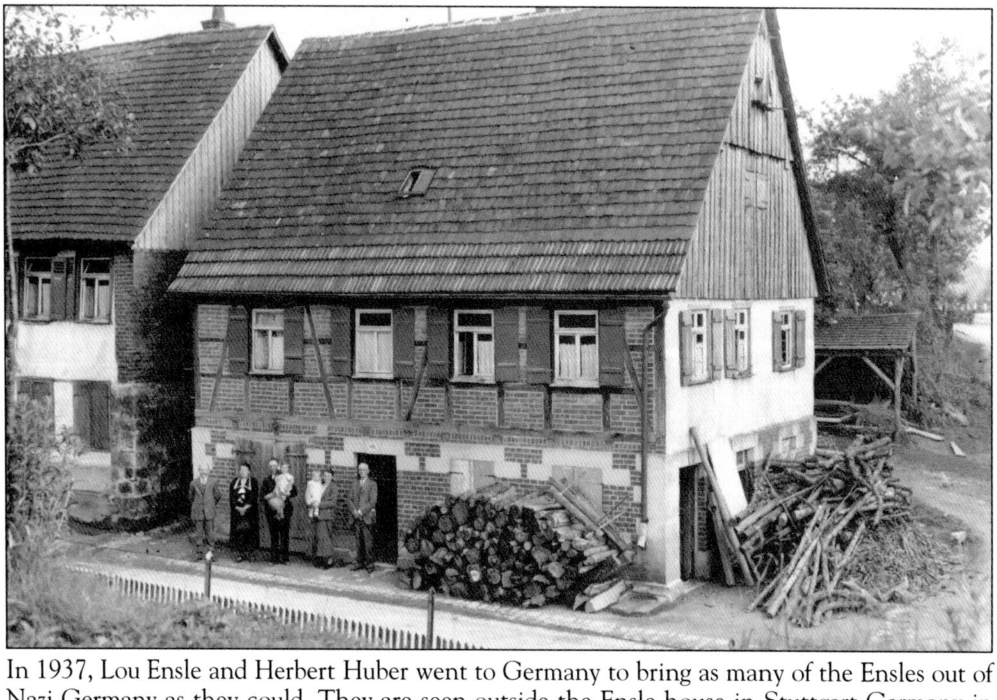

In 1937, Lou Ensle and Herbert Huber went to Germany to bring as many of the Ensles out of Nazi Germany as they could. They are seen outside the Ensle house in Stuttgart Germany in 1937. The Ensles settled around Pittsburgh. (Photograph courtesy Bill Huber.)

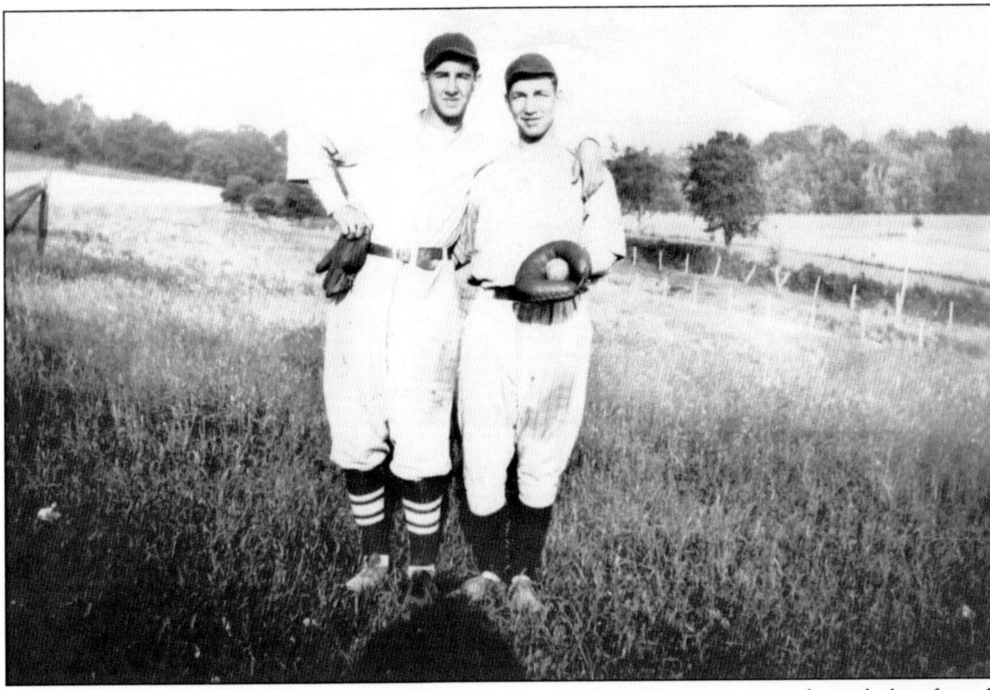

Dick Turk, one of the best catchers to come out of the oil region, stands with his friend, Chuck Dillemuth (left). Dick would go on to play for the Pennzoil team, where he would play until a collision at home plate almost cost him his life. Dick barnstormed against the likes of the Wanner brothers from Pittsburgh and Satchel Paige of the old Negro League. Before his injury, Dick was offered contracts to play for the Pirates and the Yankees. (Photograph courtesy Dick Turk.)

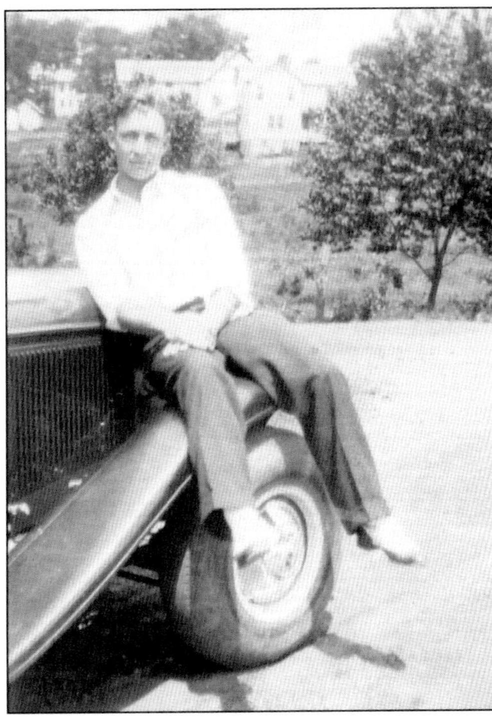

Dick Turk poses on the hood of his Plymouth coupe, c. 1932. Dick claims that he kept a bat in the rumble seat to keep the girls away. (Photograph courtesy Dick Turk.)

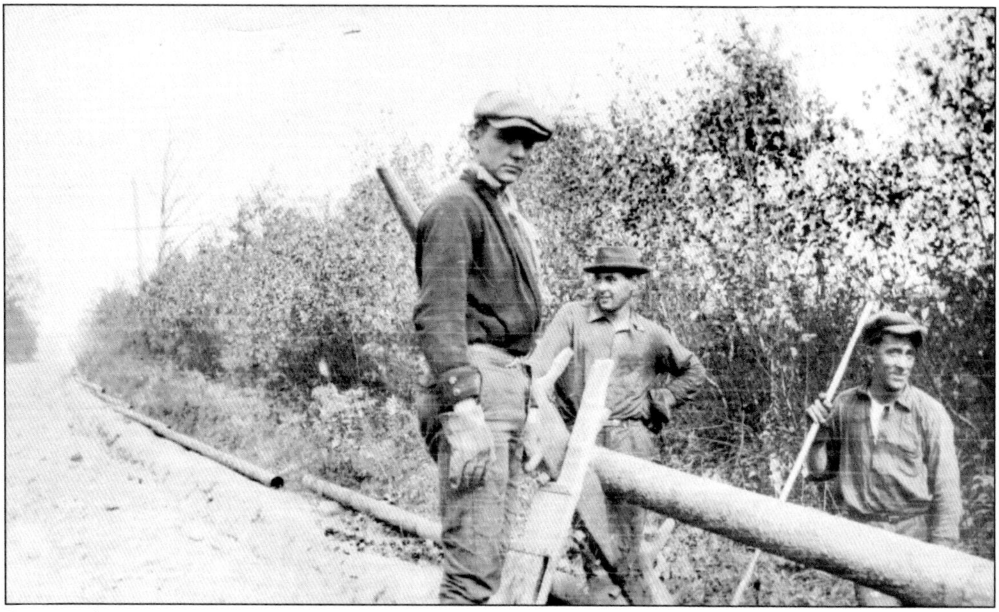

During the Great Depression, work was very scarce in the valley. Boyd Stephens lays water pipe for the WPA on the road from Plumer to Pleasantville. Many families lost everything they had. (Photographs courtesy Lois Horner.)

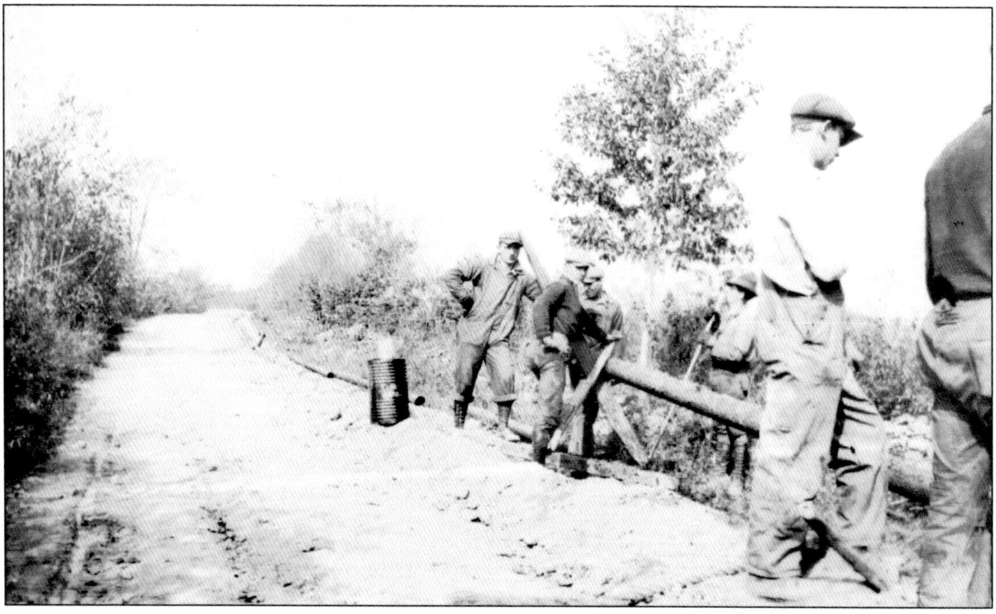

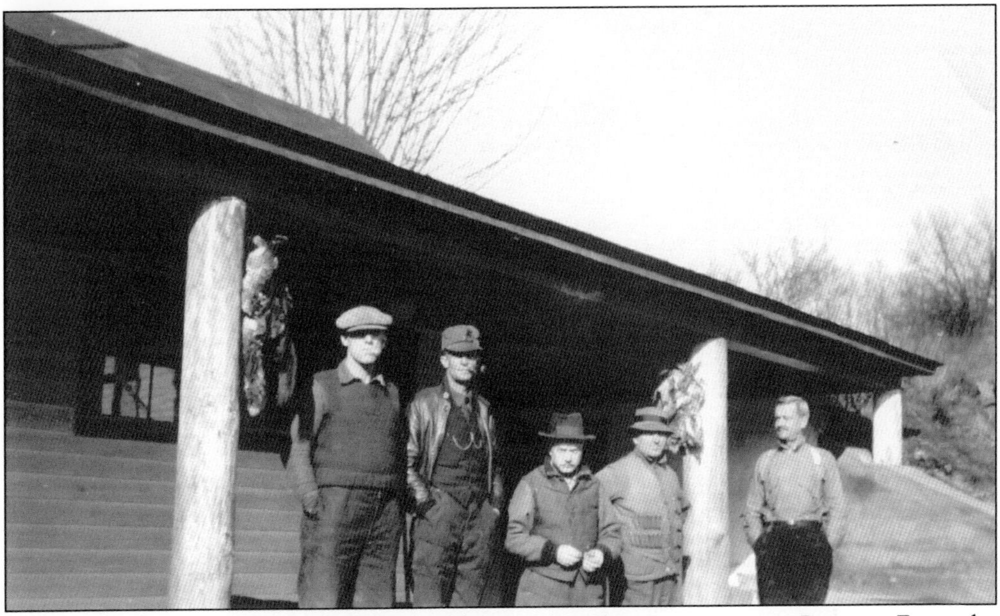

Oma Turk is seen with his hunting buddies at their hunting camp at Pioneer. From the game hanging off the porch rail, it looks like they had a good day. Shown are Oma Turk, Charlie York, Charlie Smith, Fred Slieman, and an unidentified man. (Photograph courtesy Dick Turk.)

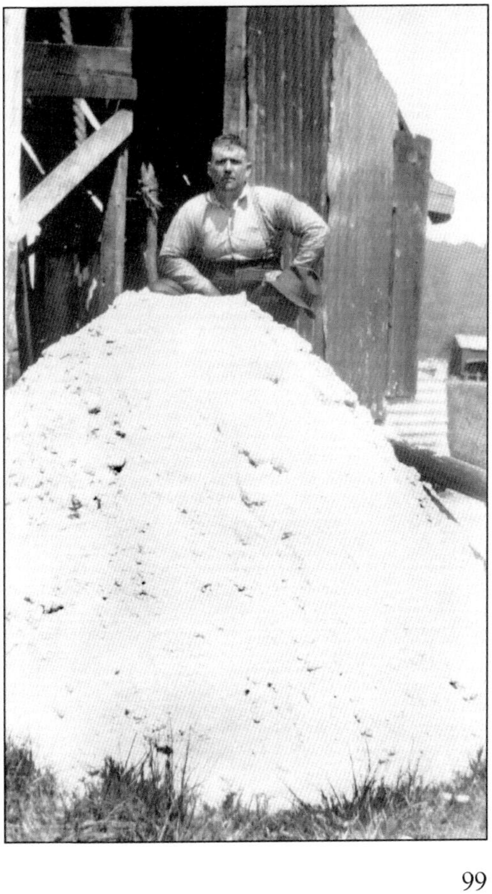

Willis Stephens on top of a sawdust pile at Cubbons sawmill, *c.* 1930s. (Photograph courtesy Lois Horner.)

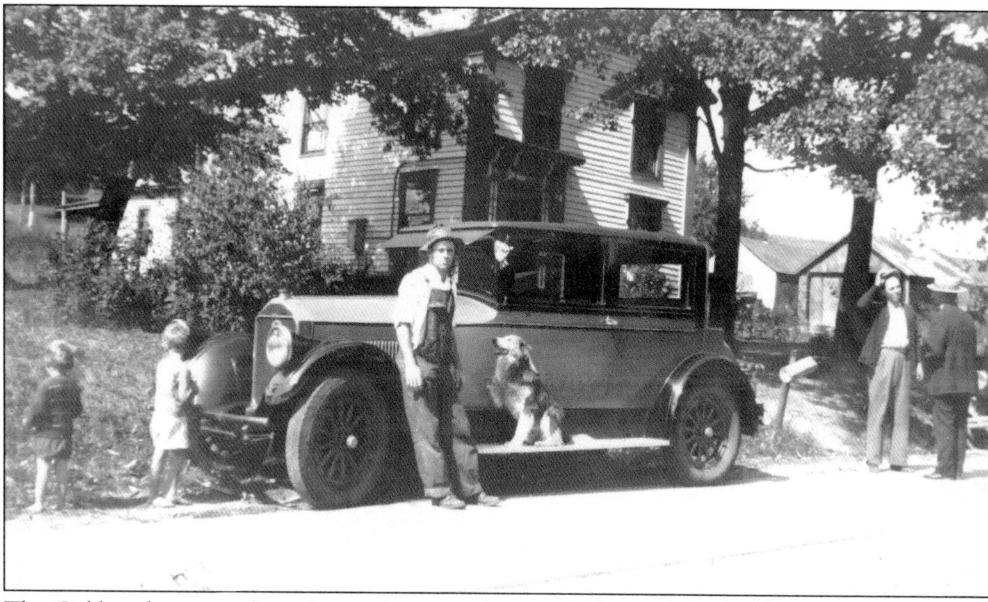

The Cubbon homestead was located just northwest of Plumer. The Cubbons were engaged in oil since their days at Pithole. They would expand into the lumber business, which is owned by John Cubbon today. (Photograph courtesy Kenny and Carol Cubbon.)

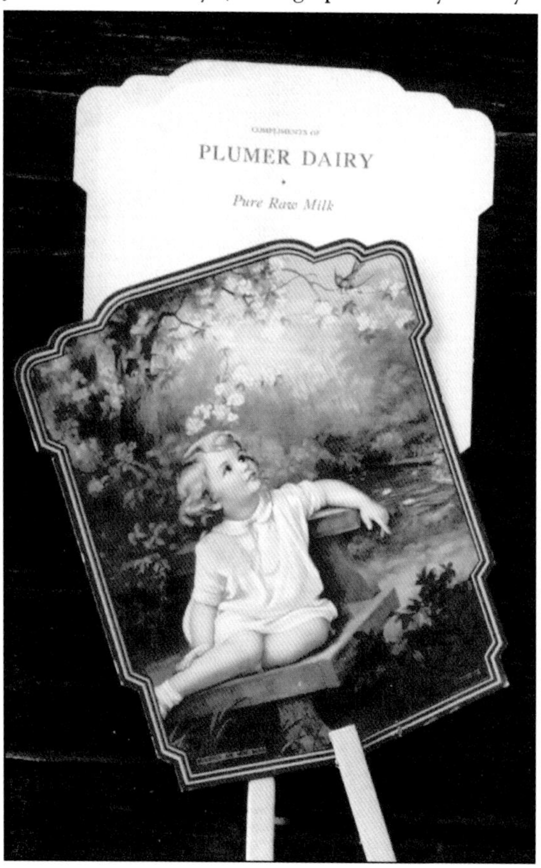

The Plumer Dairy was started by Charlie Busch and John Shaffer, who leased the land and barn from the Cubbons. Dick Turk's first job was delivering milk for the dairy from the back of an old Model T Ford. His last stop was the Oil Well Supply in Oil City, where the men would drink the milk right from the bottles, then put the empties right back in the wooden milk crate. The dairy was last run by Kenny Cubbon's father, Art, before World War II. (Photographed by Jim Stoudt.)

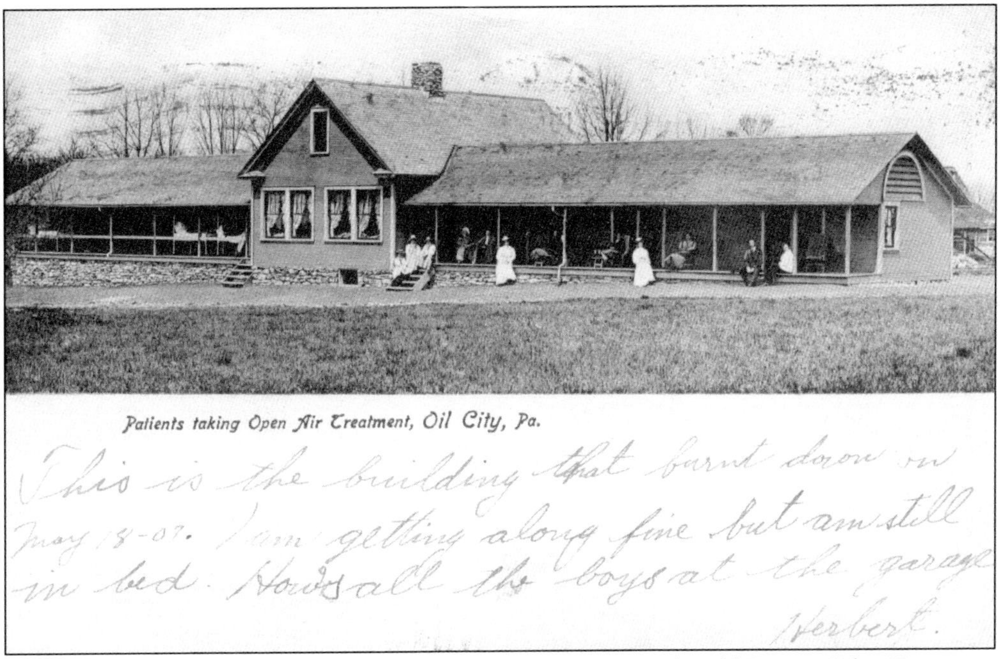

Patients taking Open Air Treatment, Oil City, Pa.

The Grandview Sanitarium was just a mile south of Plumer on the old Warren Pike. Treatment was often quite primitive and was often worse than the disease itself. The patients below have been moved outside to freeze the tubercle bacillus in the minus 28-degree weather. Notice their beds and rooms have been moved outside. (Photograph courtesy of John and Margie Hummel.)

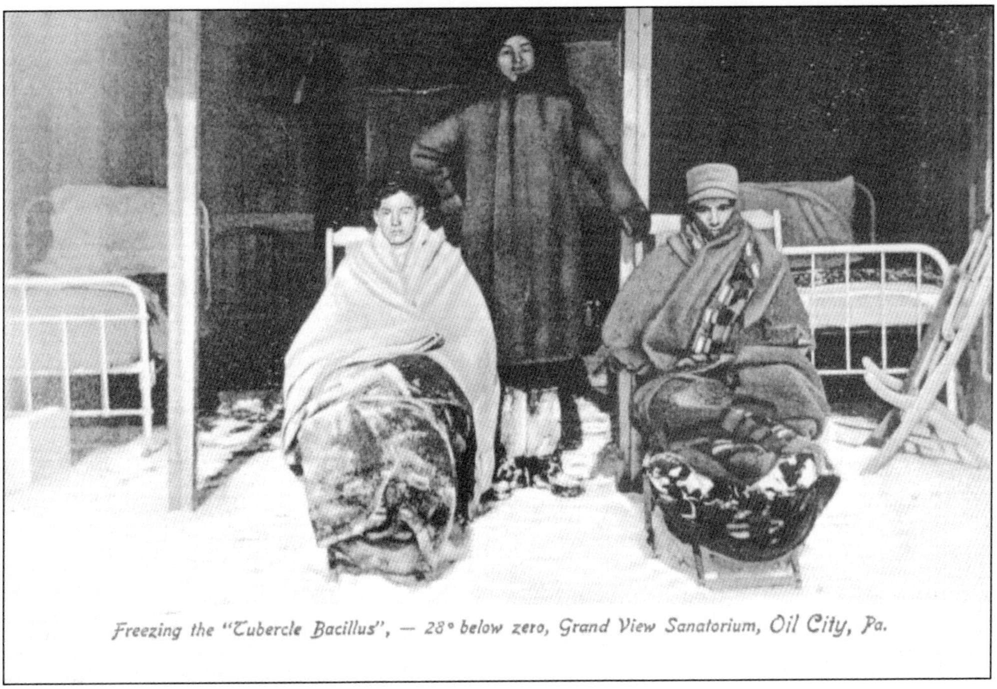

Freezing the "Tubercle Bacillus", — 28° below zero, Grand View Sanatorium, Oil City, Pa.

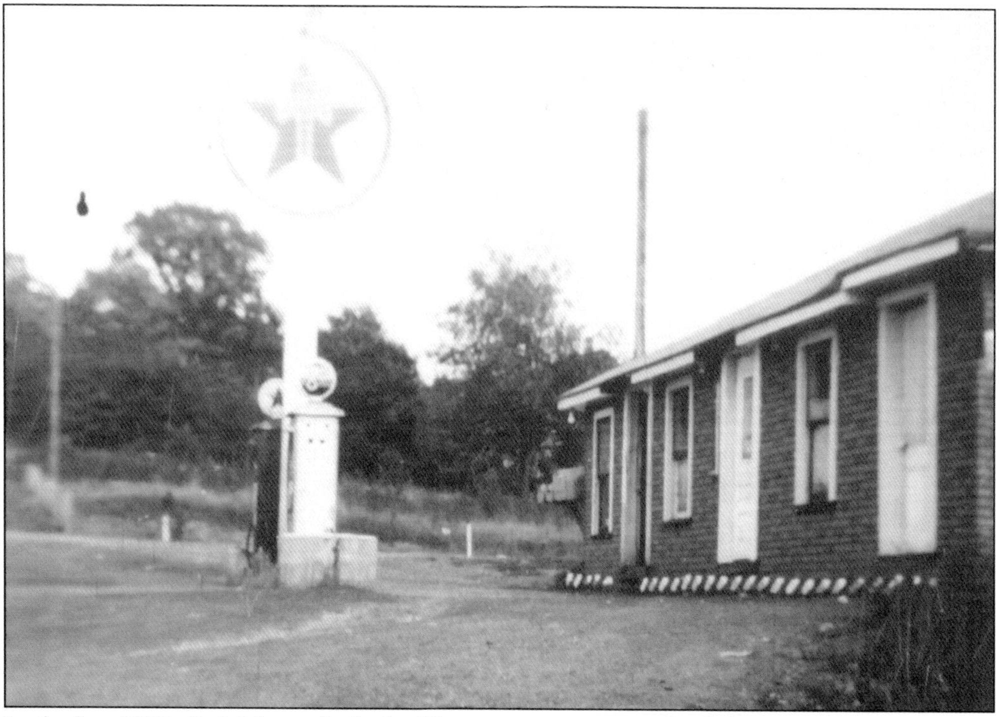

In the late 1930s, Jack Horner built this Texaco station just north of Plumer on Highway 227 at Burnt House Hill. Jack ran the station until the mid-1950s. (Photograph courtesy Jack Horner.)

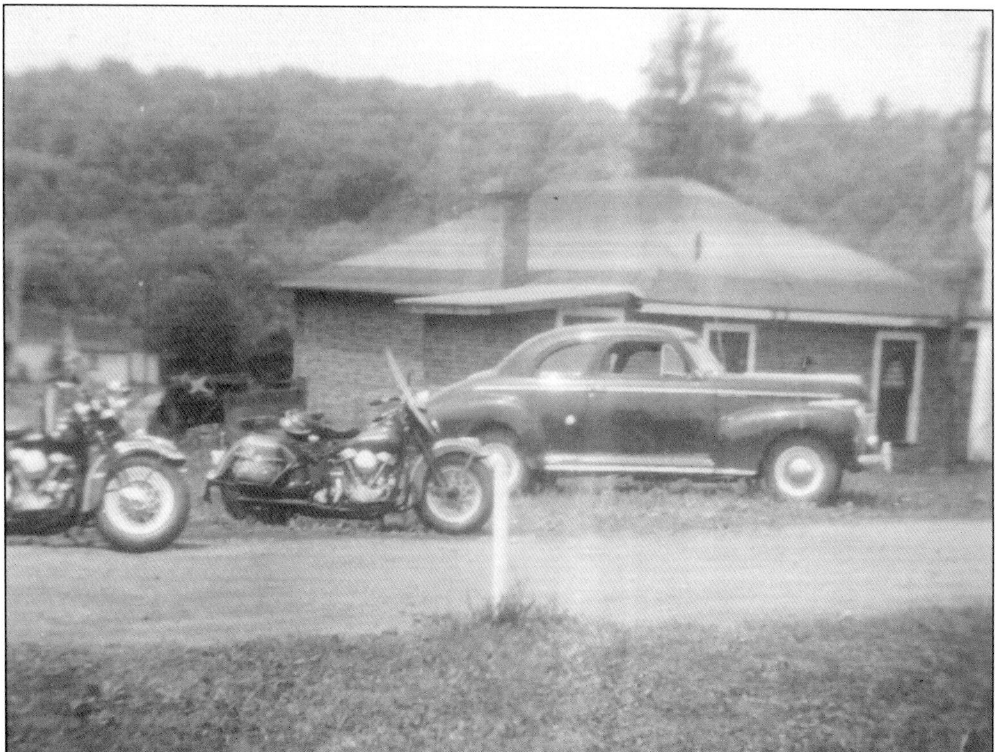

Nine

OIL CITY

THE HUB OF OILDOM

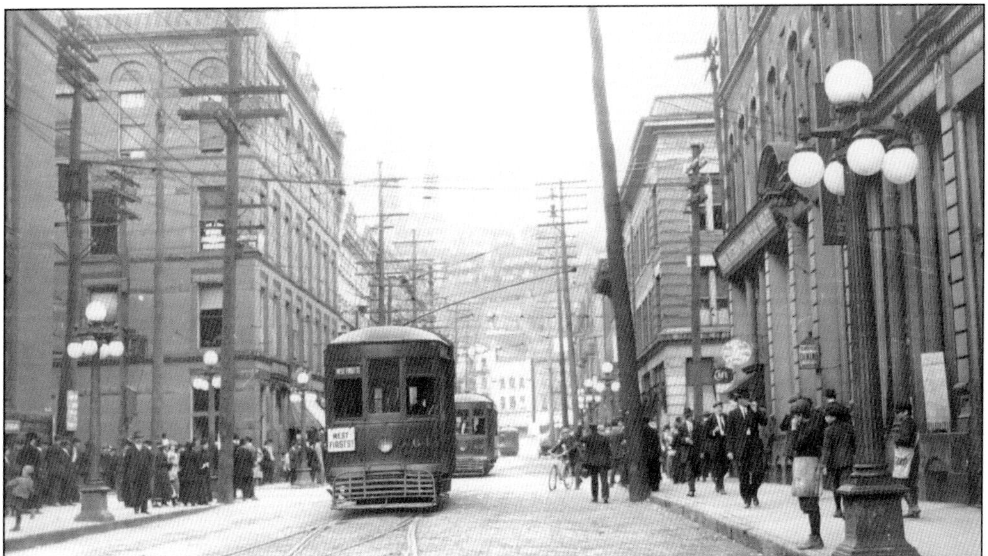

By 1900, Pithole had completely vanished, and Plumer was once again a quiet little village on the hillsides of Cherry Run. However, Oil City was undergoing a second renaissance. Although always beset by devastating floods and fires, Oil City took these disasters as opportunities to build new business and strengthen old ones. This view of Central Avenue, c. 1919, could be Manhattan. Margie Hummel's father is the Western Union boy on the bicycle on the right. (Photograph courtesy John and Margie Hummel.)

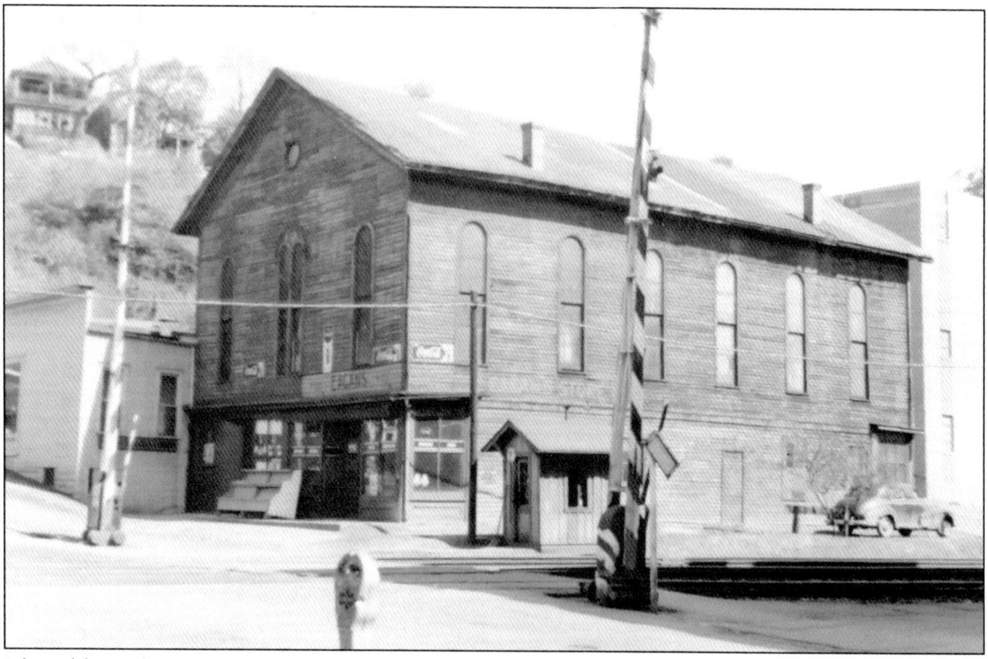

The old Presbyterian church moved to Oil City after Pithole's demise and became a fixture on Central Avenue until it was demolished in the mid-1950s. (Photograph courtesy John and Margie Hummel.)

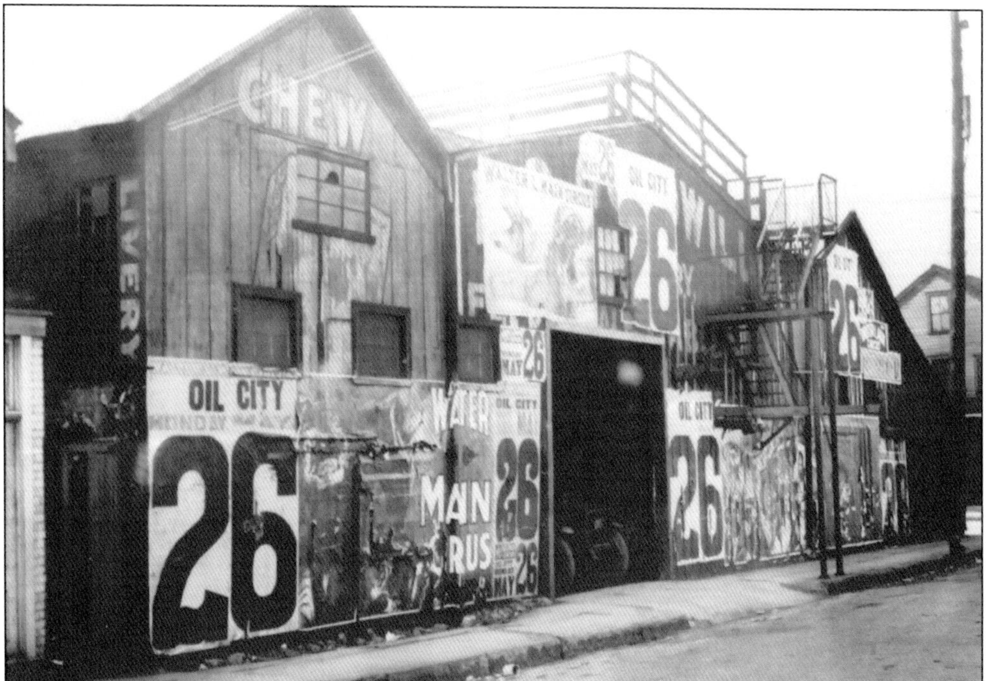

This view of Elm Street in 1926 shows wooded structures that had been a part of Oil City since the mid-1860s. These buildings were soon replaced by new buildings. (Photograph courtesy John and Margie Hummel.)

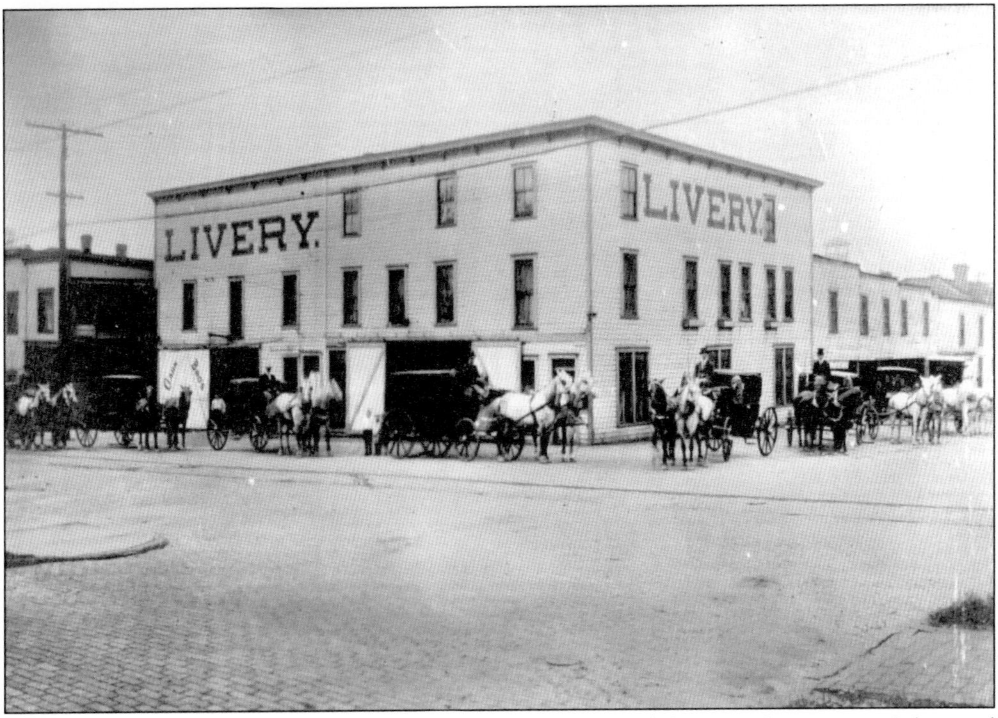

Clark's livery stable was in use into the 20th century. (Photograph courtesy John and Margie Hummel.)

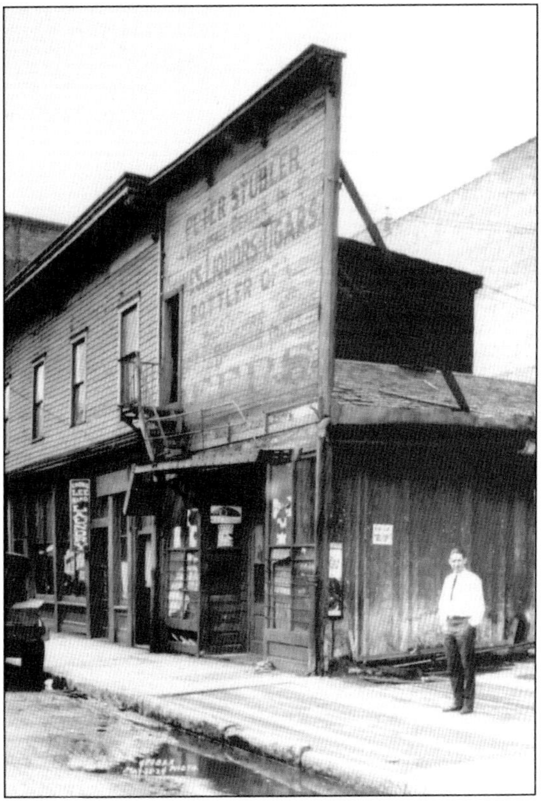

Stublers Beverages on Elm Street was later relocated to Second Avenue. (Photograph courtesy the Oil City Genealogical Society.)

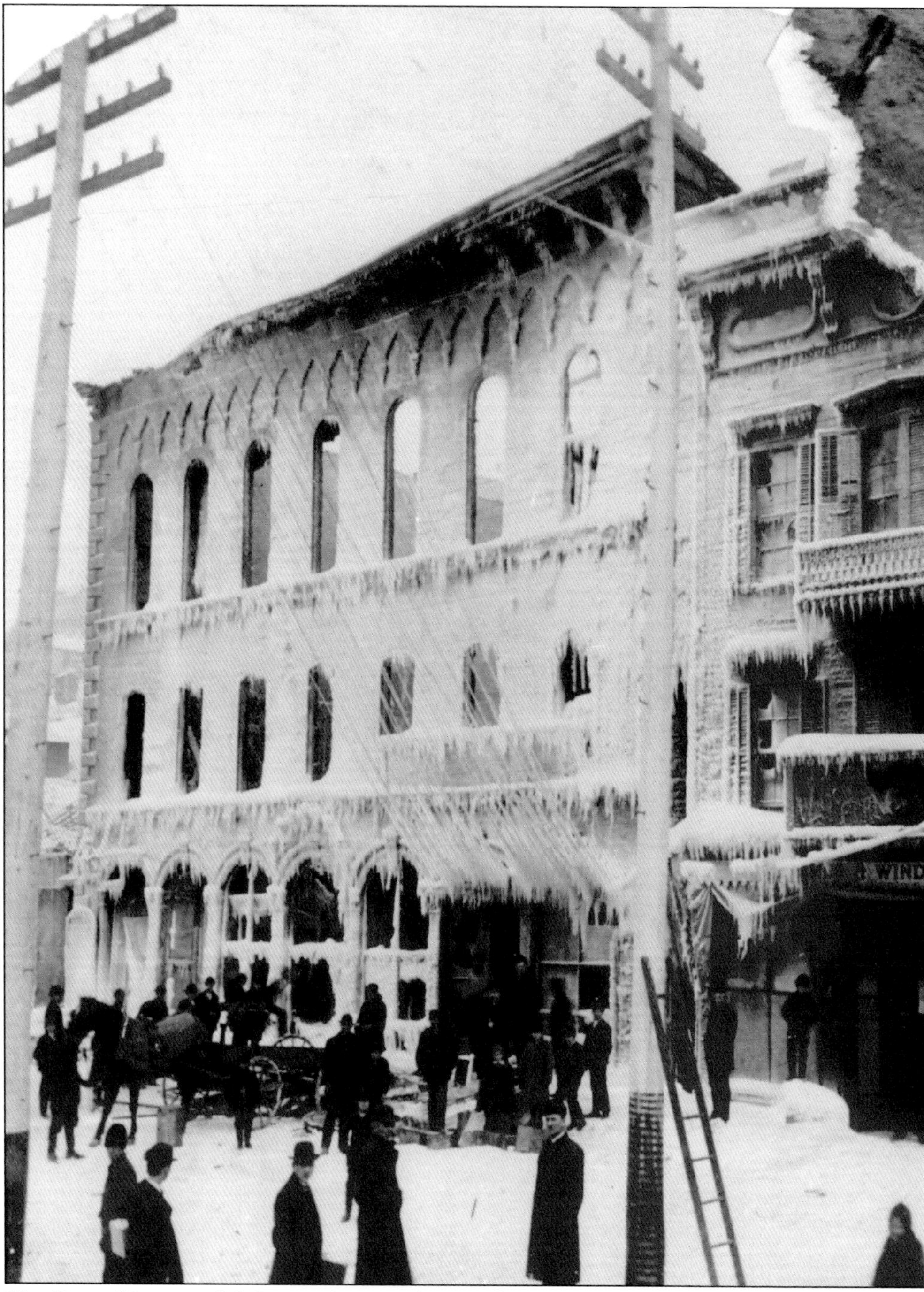

The Opera House in Oil City at the top of Central Avenue was almost destroyed by fire in the 1890s. It is shown here covered in ice from the firefighters' efforts to control the blaze. It was rebuilt and hosted many vaudeville stars, some who went on to even greater glory in motion pictures. (Photograph courtesy John and Margie Hummel.)

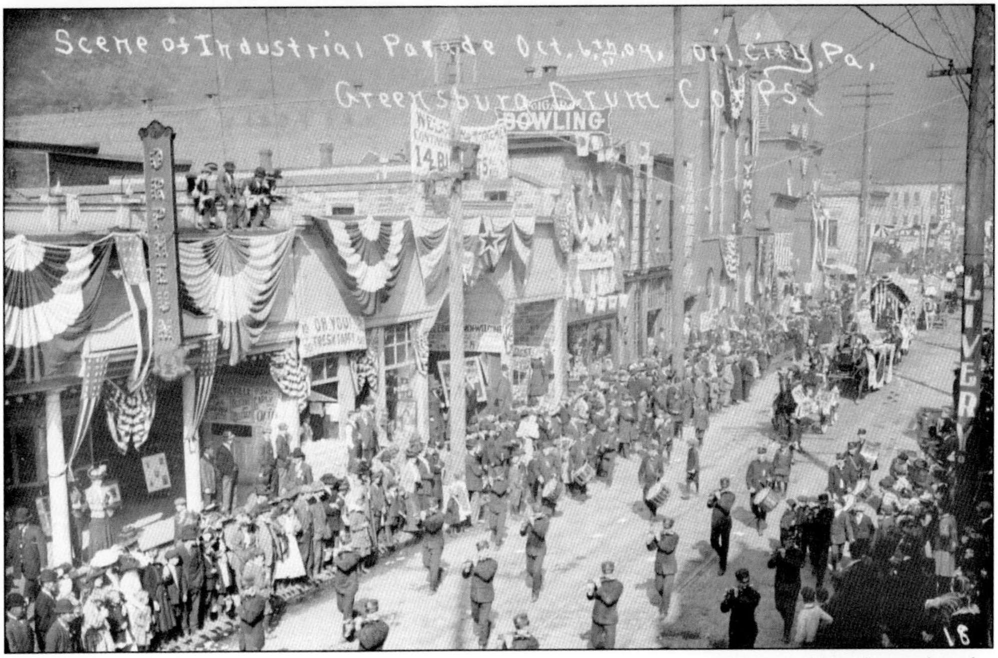

The Industrial Parade, held in Oil City in October 1909, drew participants from far and wide. The Greensburg, Pennsylvania, Drum Corps is shown marching. (Photograph courtesy the Oil City Genealogical Society.)

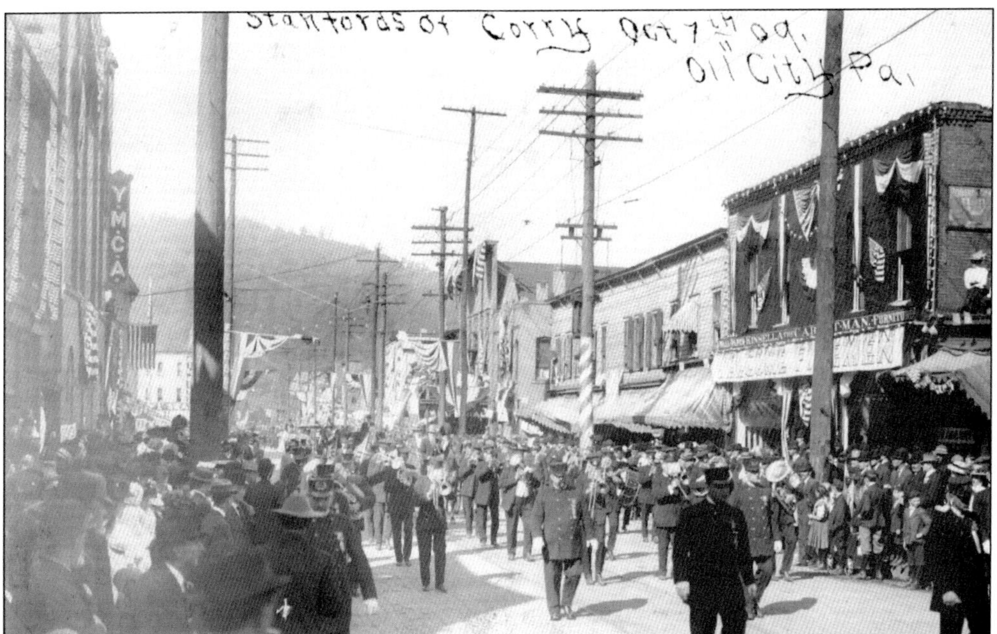

The Corry Band is pictured here in the 1909 Industrial Parade. (Photograph courtesy the Oil City Genealogical Society.)

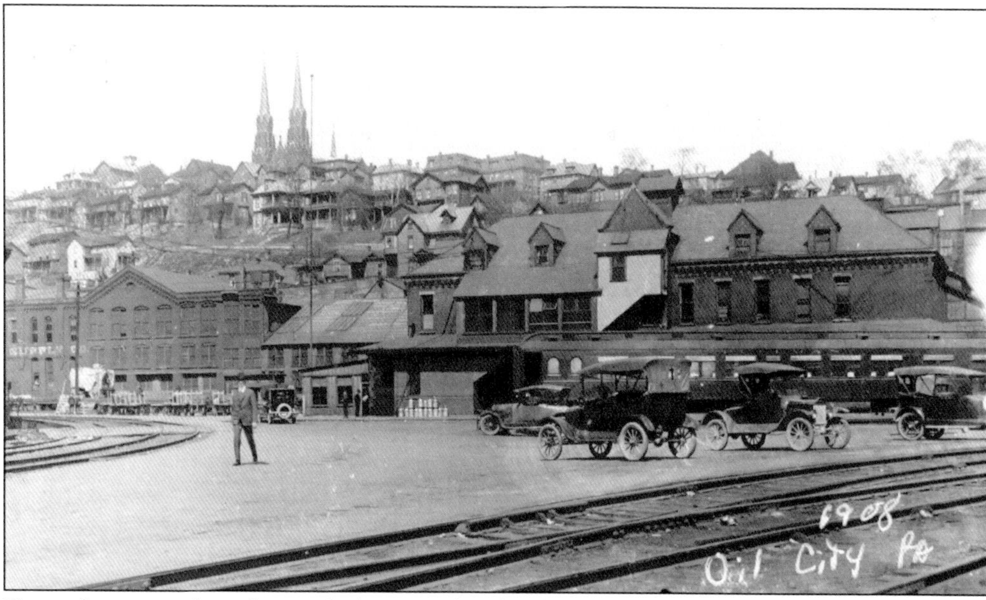

Trains have greatly influenced the growth of Oil City. The Penn rail yard appears here, c. 1908. (Photograph courtesy John and Margie Hummel.)

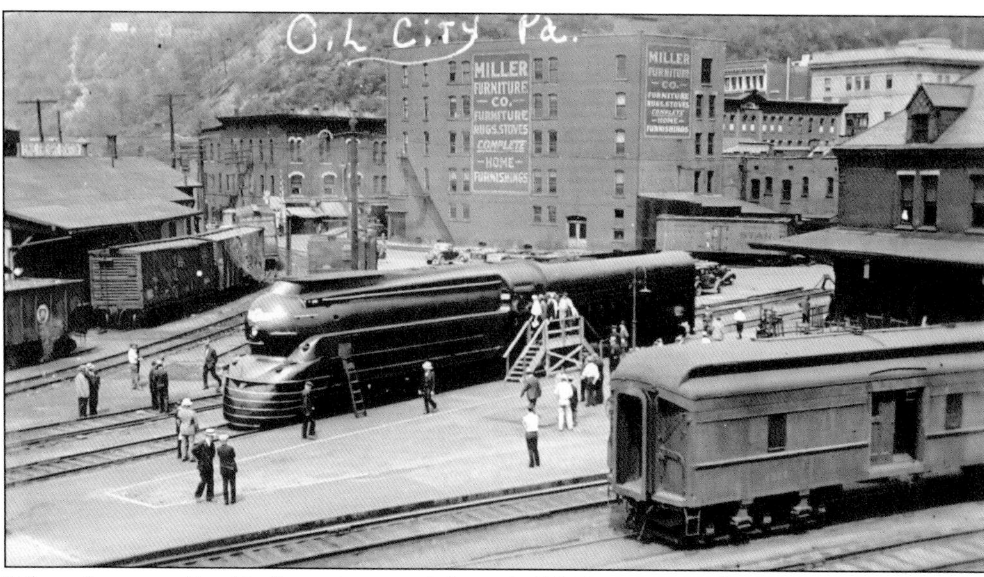

When the streamlined bullet train passed through Oil City, it created quite a sensation, shown here c. 1930s. (Photograph courtesy John and Margie Hummel.)

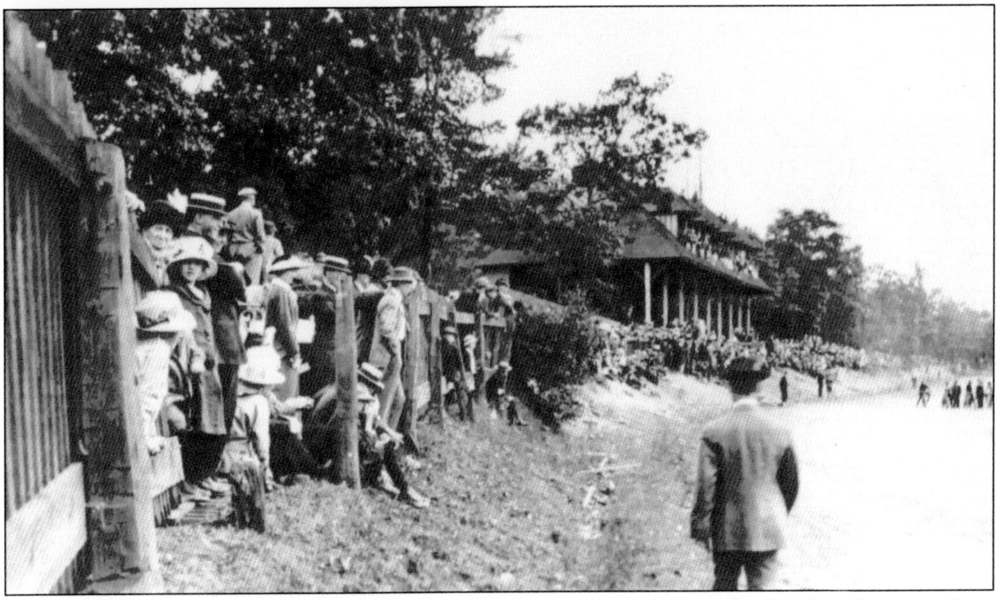

Hasson Park, on the top of Hasson Heights, has been a favorite spot for families for more than 100 years. Here, huge crowds watch the horse race on Labor Day 1914. (Photograph courtesy John and Margie Hummel.)

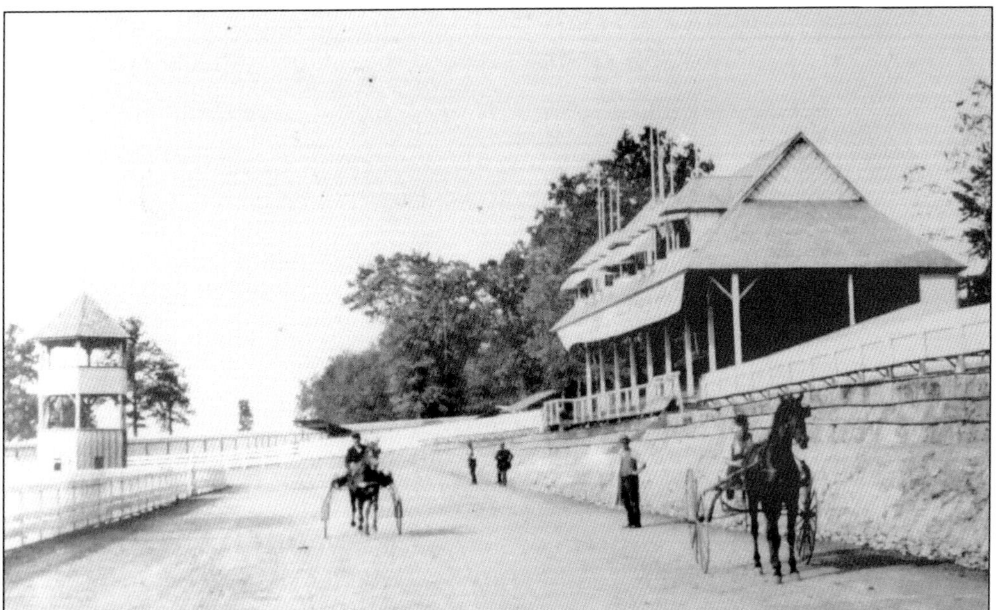

Harness racers take practice laps around the track at Hasson Park in 1898. (Photograph courtesy John and Margie Hummel.)

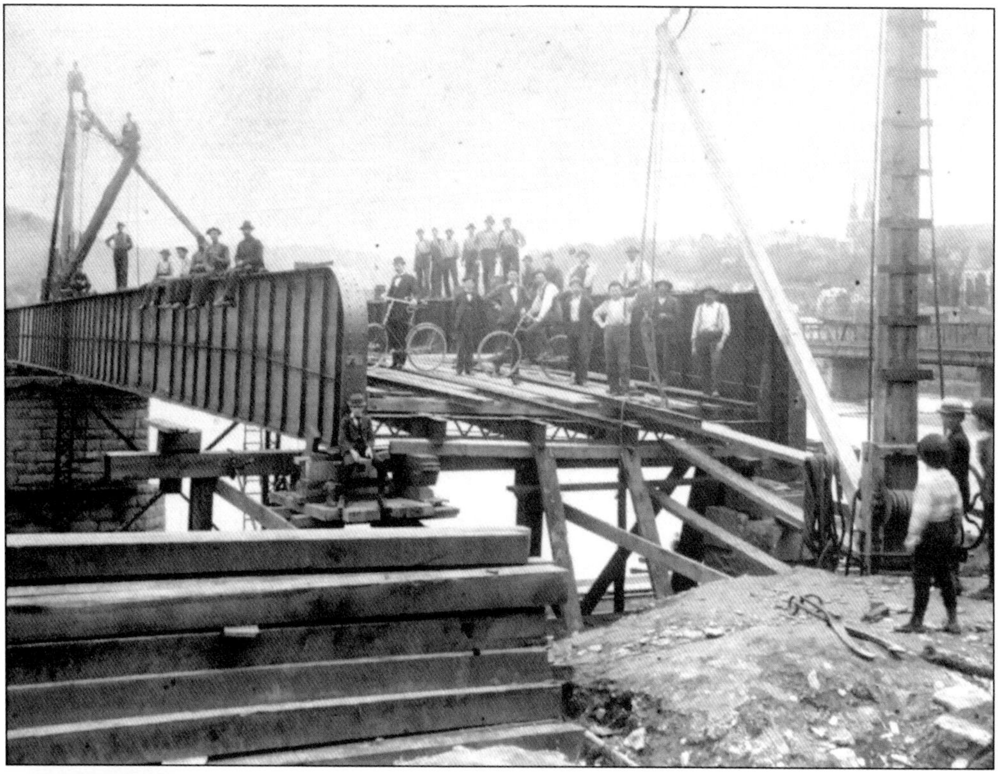

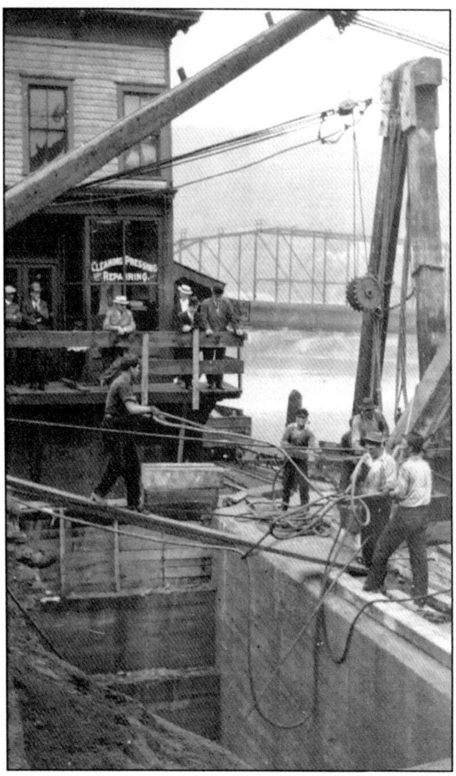

Oil City, at the mouth of Oil Creek on the Allegheny River, has always been a city with multiple bridges for foot traffic, trains, trolleys, and automobiles. Ice jams and continual flooding have caused the city to constantly rebuild old and build new bridges. The photograph above shows steel decking being installed. On the left, new cisterns are being excavated. (Photographs courtesy the Oil City Genealogical Society.)

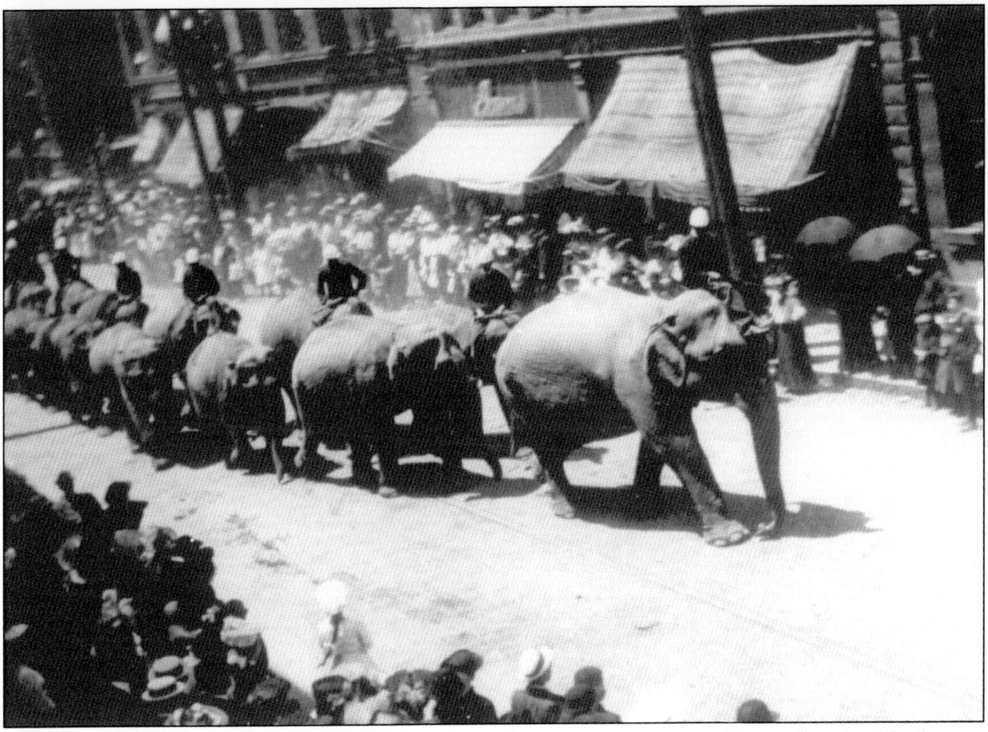

The circus has long made Oil City a major stop when it visits western Pennsylvania. Elephants, shown *c.* 1916, were the best advertising you could use. Visible in the lower photograph is a more traditional way of announcing the arrival of the circus. (Photographs courtesy the Oil City Genealogical Society.)

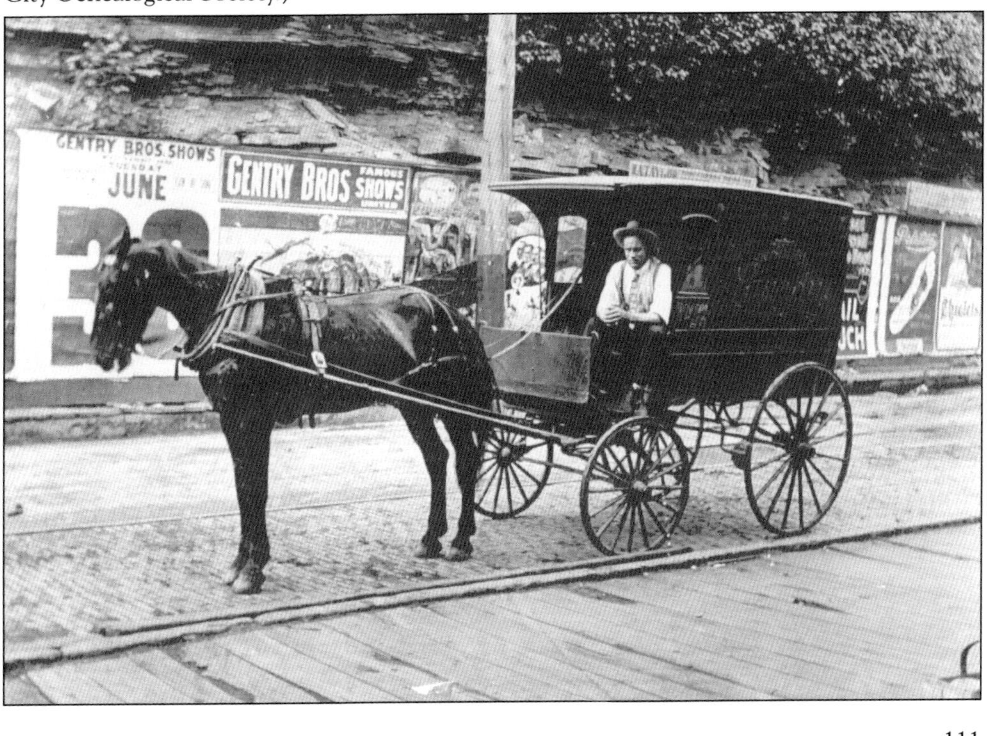

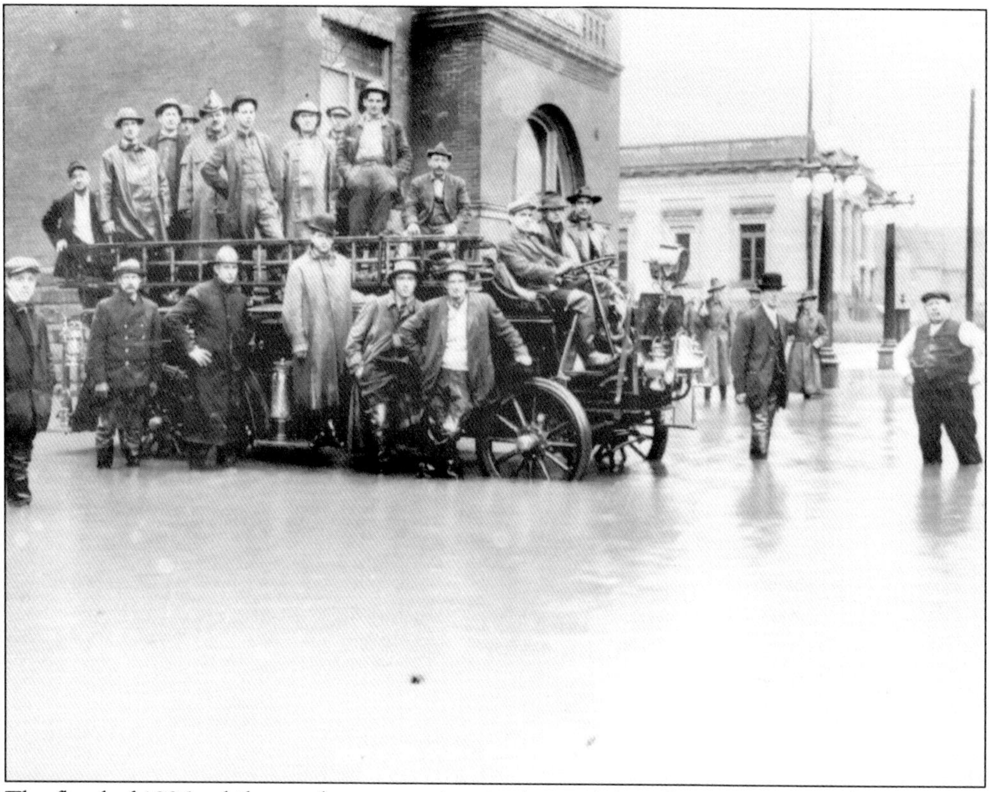

The flood of 1926, while not the most serious in the city's long history, was very destructive to many of the original frame structures that still stood. Oil City has always found ways to cope with natural disaster. (Photograph courtesy the Oil City Genealogical Society.)

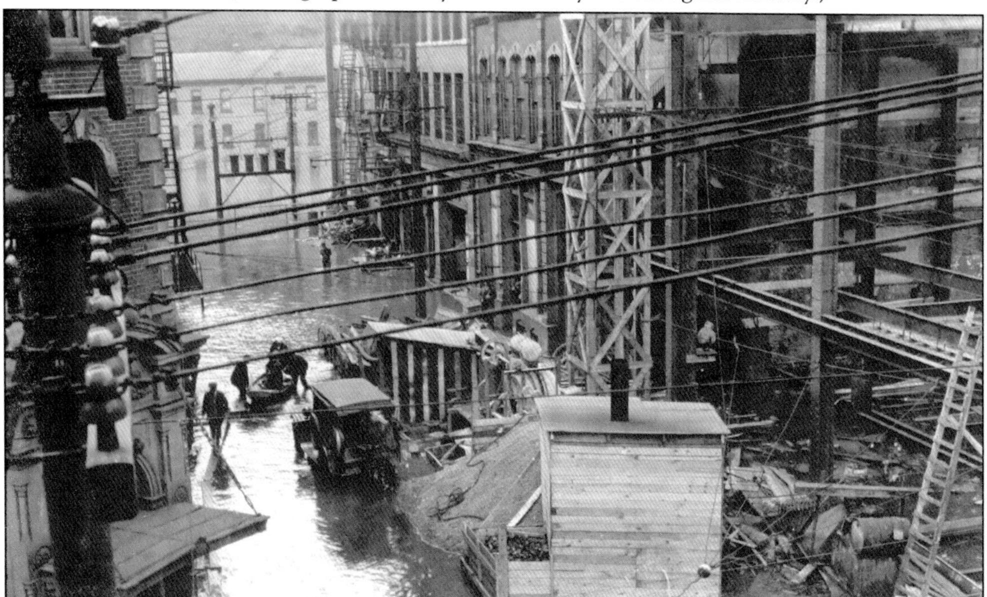

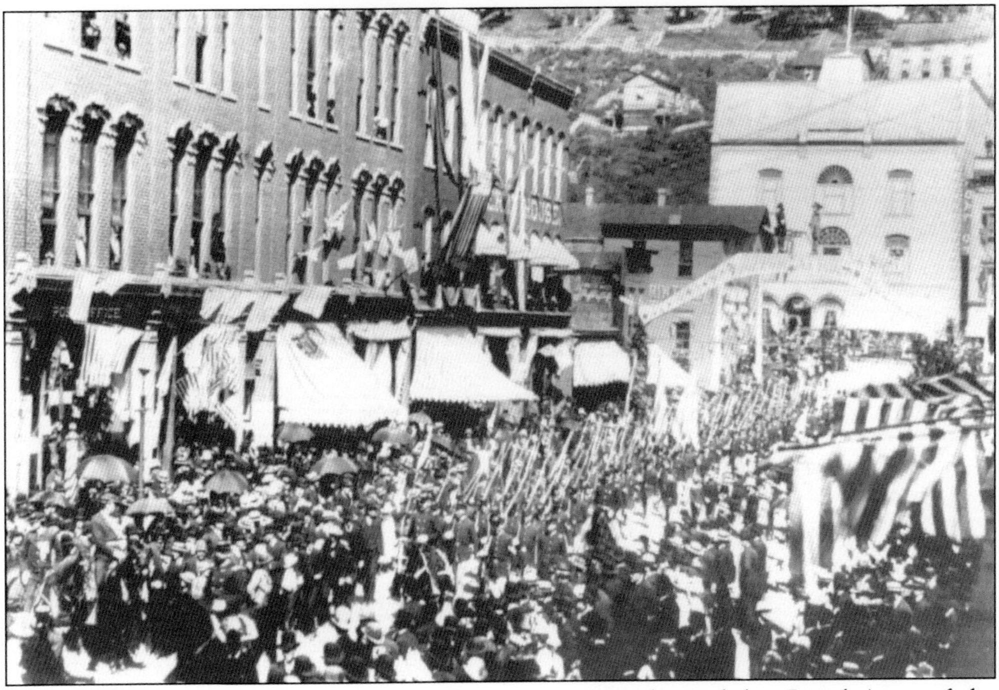

This view shows a ceremony honoring the surviving members of the Grand Army of the Republic in 1886. (Photograph courtesy the Oil City Genealogical Society.)

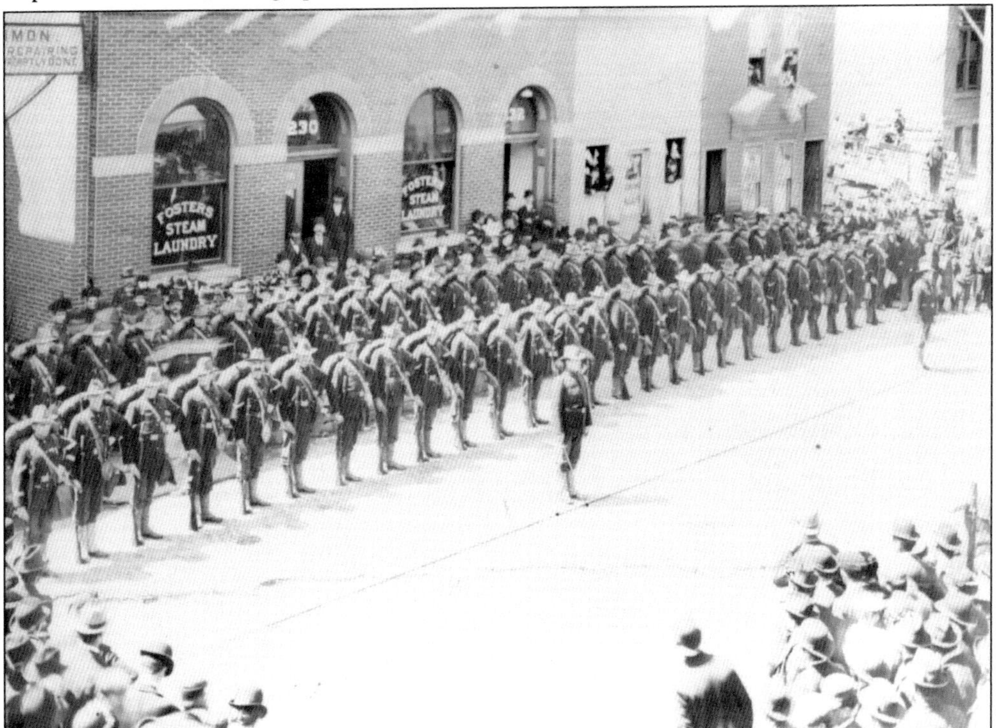

Our brave young lads from Oil City are about to leave for the long trip to Cuba, c. 1898, at the start of the Spanish American War. (Photograph courtesy the Oil City Genealogical Society.)

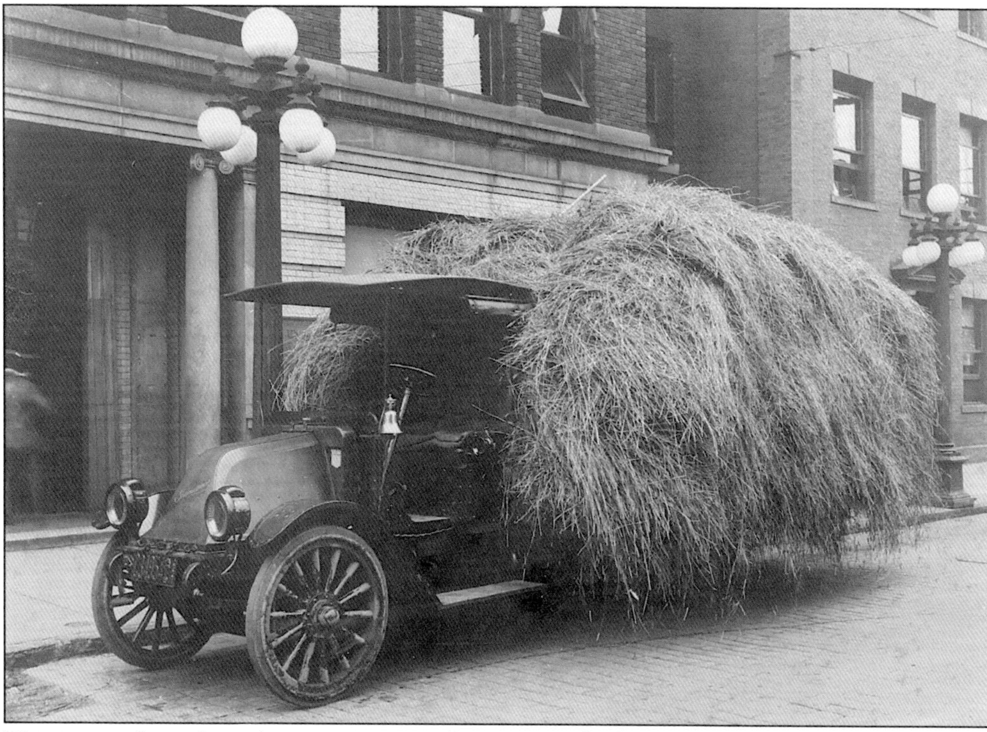

This image shows how the economy was changing at the beginning of the 20th century. The brand-new International is parked in downtown Oil City, not with a load of oil, but a load of hay. (Photograph courtesy of Joe and Jerri Saunders.)

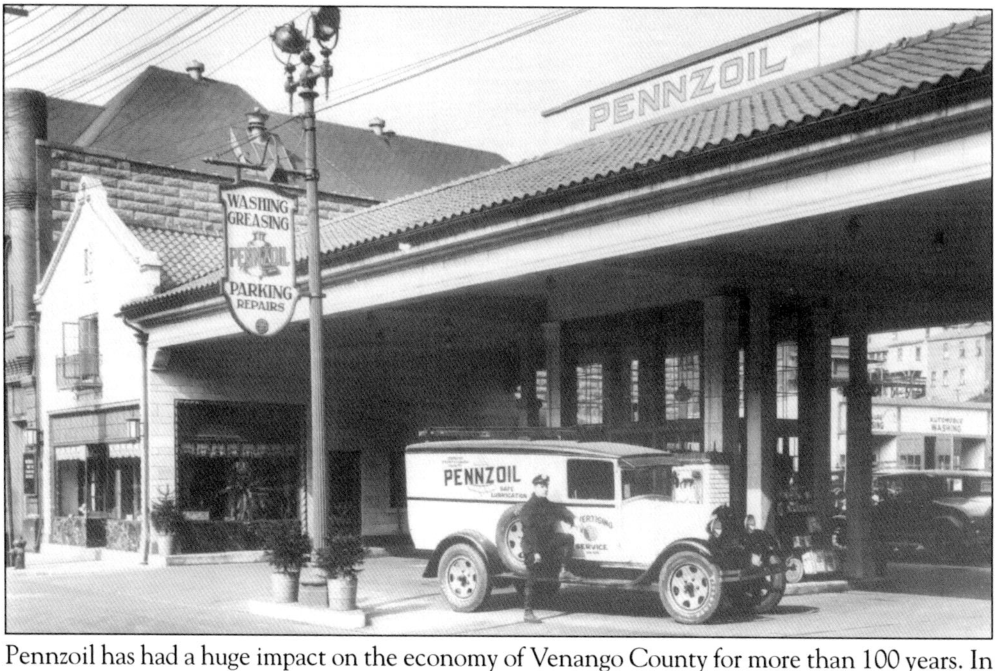

Pennzoil has had a huge impact on the economy of Venango County for more than 100 years. In June 2000, Pennzoil closed its last refinery in western Pennsylvania at Rouseville. (Photograph courtesy of the Venango Historical Society.)

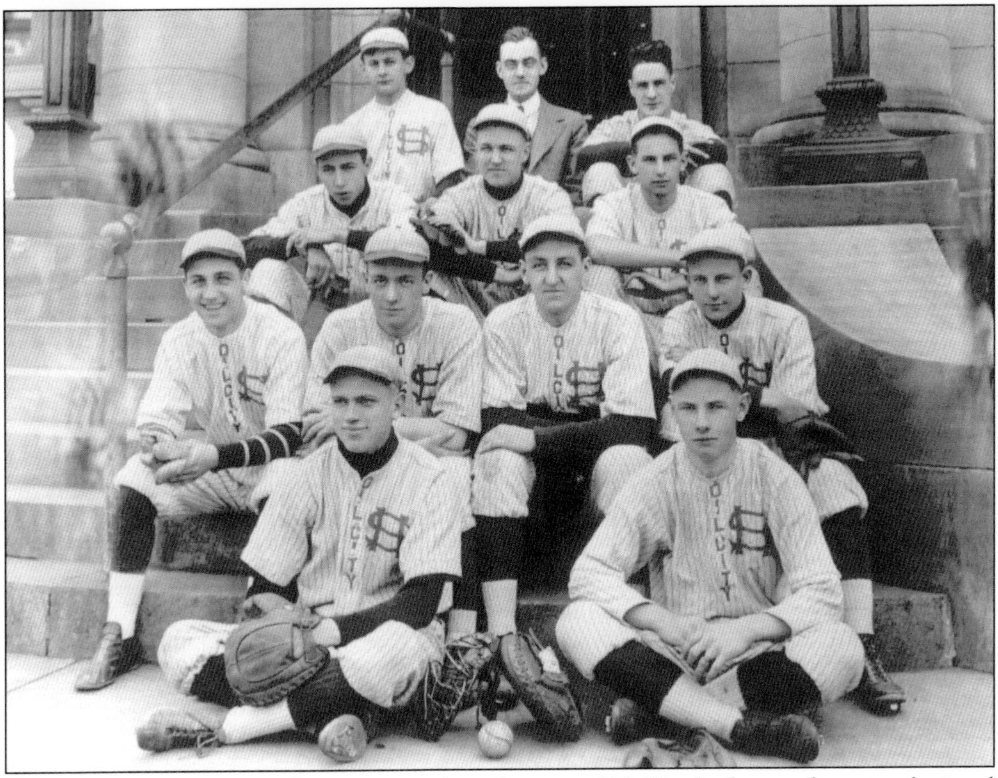

Baseball has always reigned supreme in the oil region. Oil City had several semiprofessional leagues up through the 1930s. Many fine players have played ball for Oil City High School. This image dates from c. 1920s. (Photograph courtesy the Oil City Genealogical Society.)

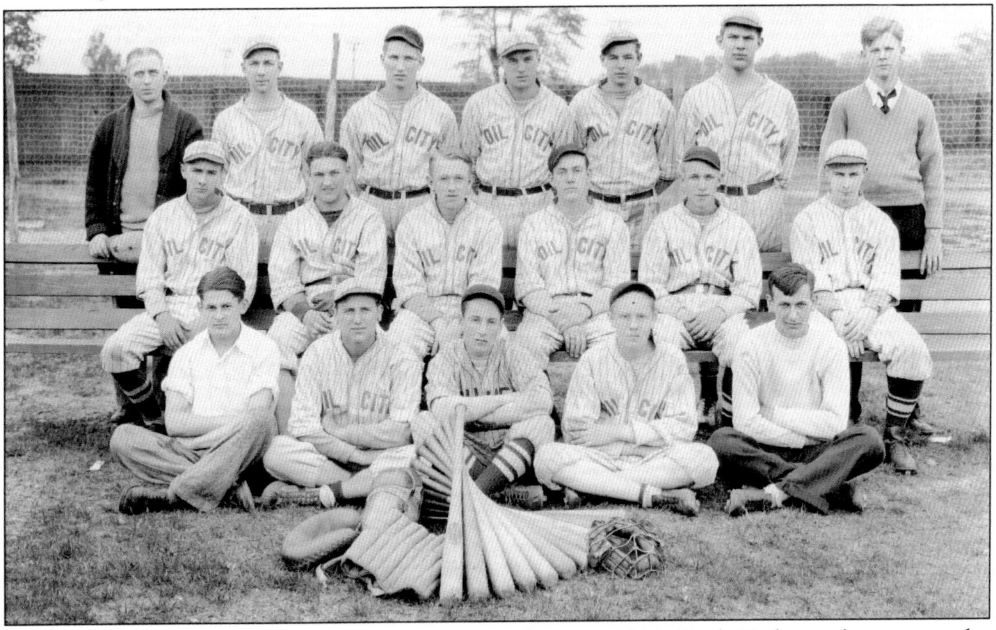

Dick Turk's Oil City High School team appears here in 1931. Dick Turk can be seen at the upper left in the back row. (Photograph courtesy Dick Turk.)

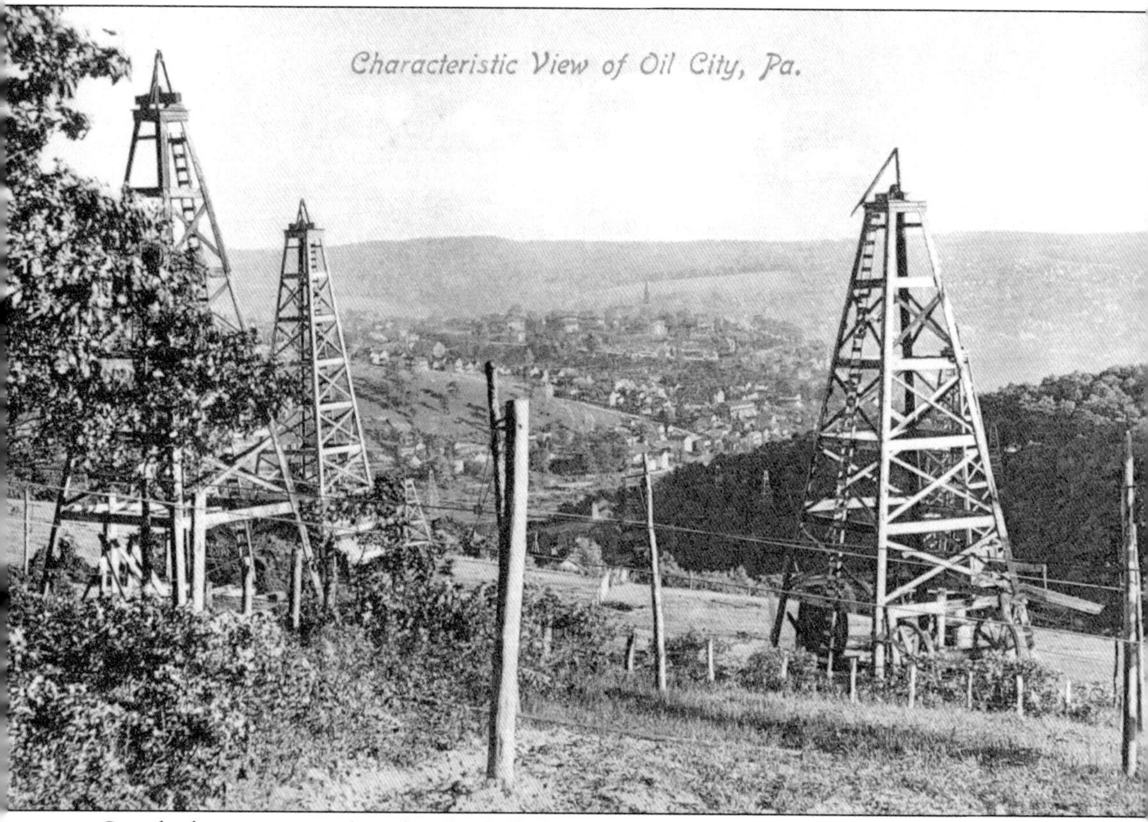

Standard rigs continued to dot the hillsides around Oil City through the early 1900s. They were replaced with drilling machines, central power stations, and strings of small pumping jacks. Crude is still pumped every day in Venango County, but now natural gas is being drilled at depths reaching a mile with very favorable results. Oil City will long be known as the hub of oildom.

Ten

PLUMER'S SCHOOLS AND THE OLD HOME DAYS

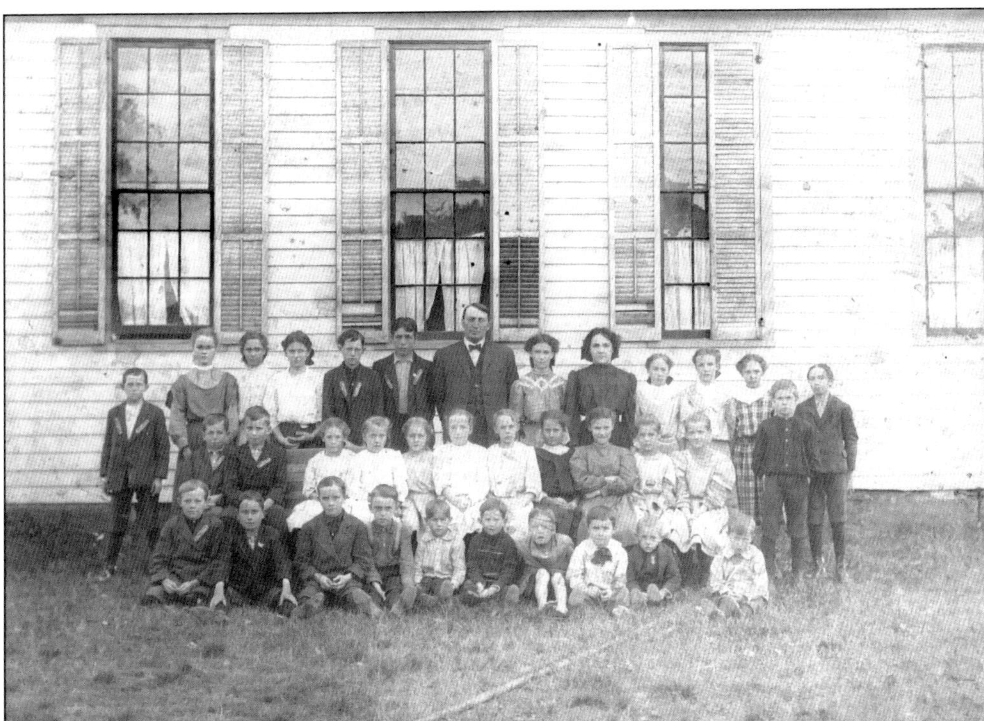

Plumer has had a school since 1839. This class outside Plumer School was photographed c. 1890s. (Photograph courtesy Lois Horner.)

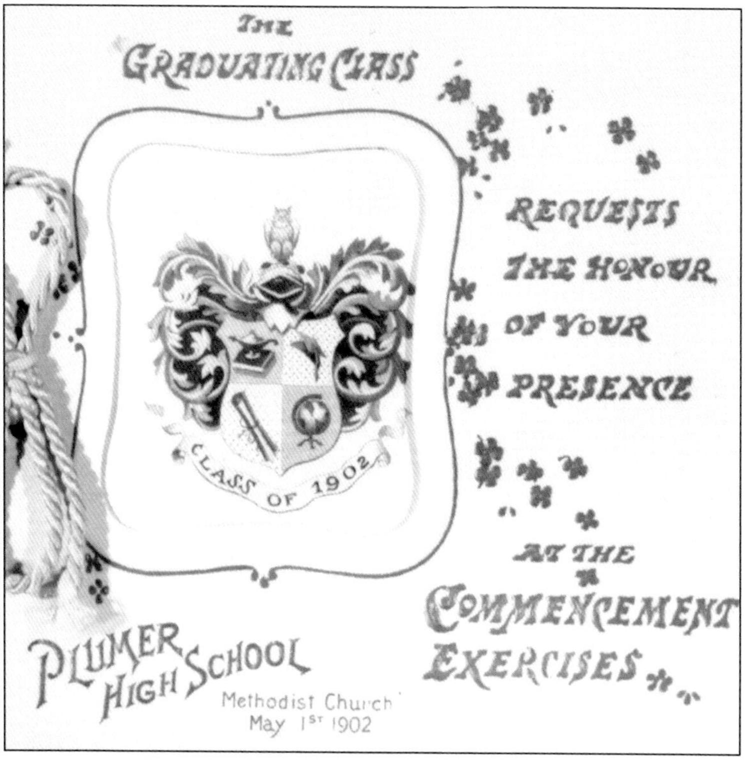

The Class of 1902 was the only high school class to graduate from Plumer School. The graduation ceremony was held at the Methodist church in May 1902. The graduating class is pictured below. (Photograph courtesy the Gene Burt Tyred Wheels Auto Museum.)

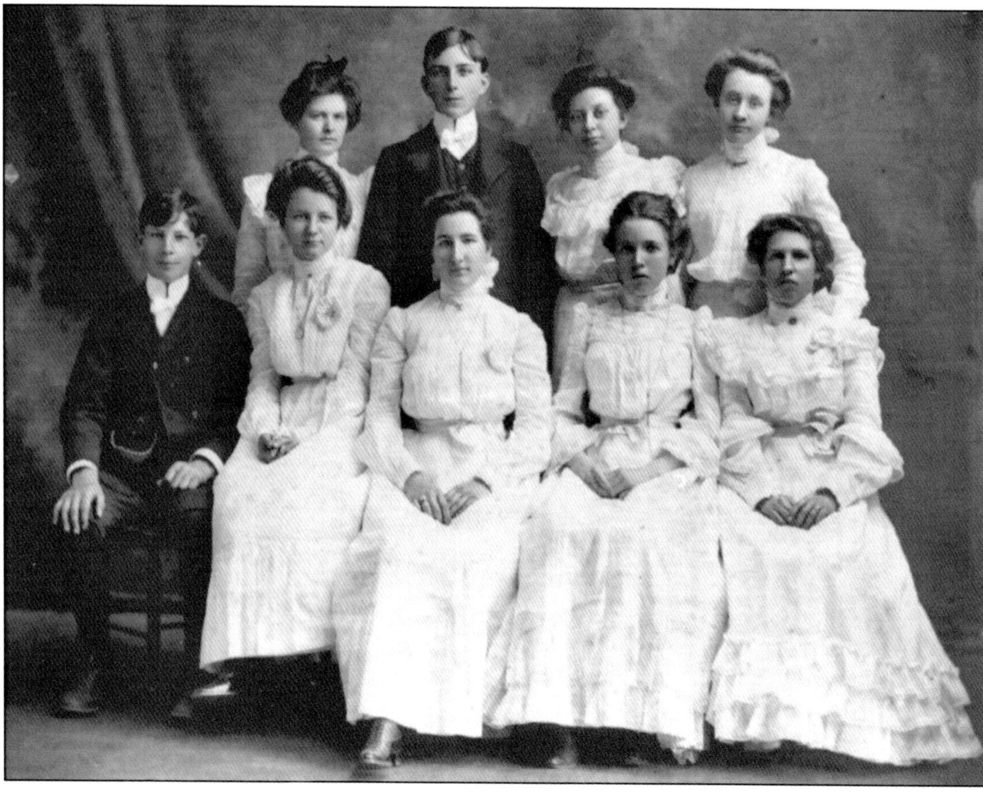

Cornplanter Township

Plumer School Room No. 2

Term of 1898-9

The 1898 to 1899 school season was one of the largest enrollments in years. (Photograph courtesy the Gene Burt Tyred Wheels Auto Museum.)

NAMES OF PUPILS.

1. JAMES BARNES,
2. LOUIS CAMPBELL,
3. JACOB PORTER,
4. EDW. HATCH,
5. GEORGE BRECHT,
6. LAWRENCE HUTCHINSON,
7. CHARLES PORTER,
8. FRANK SUTTON,
9. URBIE McCLINTOCK,
10. JOHN BEGLEY,
11. JAMES RUDISILLE,
12. CHARLES BOALES.
13. ORMA TURK.

1. HAZEL CHRISTIE,
2. BELLE McCLINTOCK,
3. CORA IRWIN,
4. CLARA TENBUS,
5. MAGGIE HAUPT,
6. GRACE PORTER,
7. HATTIE RULAND,
8. EDNA RULAND,
9. JENNIE HATCH,
10. EDNA CAMPBELL,
11. BLANCH BOYD,
12 CLARA ENSLE,
13. RETTA ENSLE,
14. EDNA BEGLEY,
15. LIZZIE IRWIN,

E. L. BUCHANAN. Principal.

SOUVENIR

.. Plumer School, Room No. 2 ..

Cornplanter Township

VENANGO COUNTY, PENNSYLVANIA

1904—1905

H. ROY WALLACE, Teacher

SCHOOL OFFICERS

Hon. Peter Berry, Pres.; J. E. Cunningham, Sec'y; A. S. Browne, Treas.; C. H. Wilson, J. S. Wallace, W. J. Kirkwood; B. V. Riddle, County Sup't

The Plumer School list from 1904–1905 contains many names that are still recognizable around Cherry Run Valley.

NAMES OF PUPILS

EIGHTH GRADE

Sara Christie	Flora Haupt	Thomas Russell
Laura Friggle	Nellie Russell	Edward Roemer

SEVENTH GRADE

Lizzie Porter	Gertrude Smith	Ralph Irwin
Anna Selden	Ivan Thomas	Jefferson Rodgers

SIXTH GRADE

Bessie Luzier	Leola Friggle	William Haupt
Ida Ruland	Fred Smith	Frank Selden

FIFTH GRADE

Mildred Christie	Nellie Porter	James Friggle
Olive Irwin	Hazel Wolf	George Caldwell
Dora Smith	Beulah Pritchard	Louis Roemer
	Rosa Behringer	

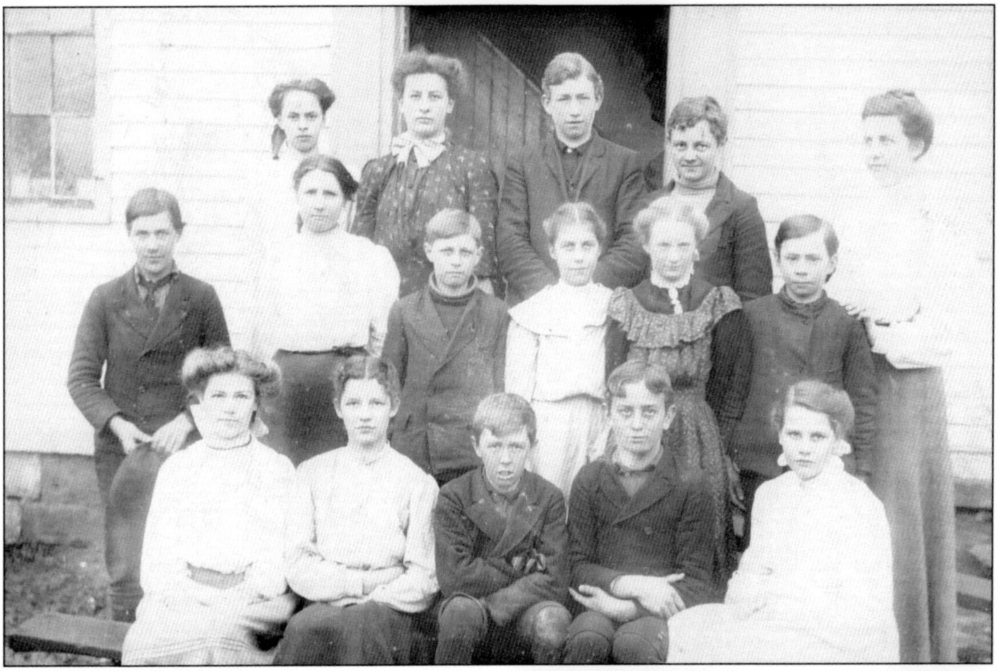

This Plumer School class was photographed outside the old framed schoolhouse, c. 1907–1908. (Photograph courtesy Lois Horner.)

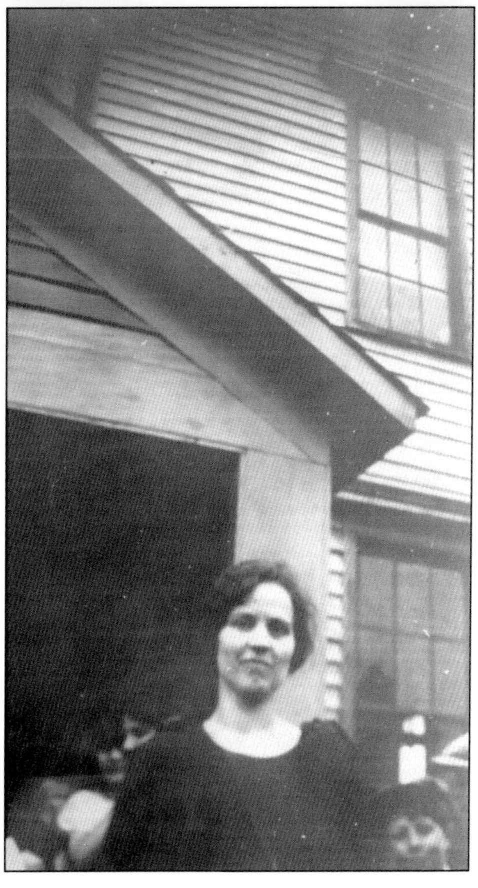

Elsie Heeter was a teacher at Plumer School before 1920. She was said to be one of the most feared teachers at the school. (Photograph courtesy Dick Turk.)

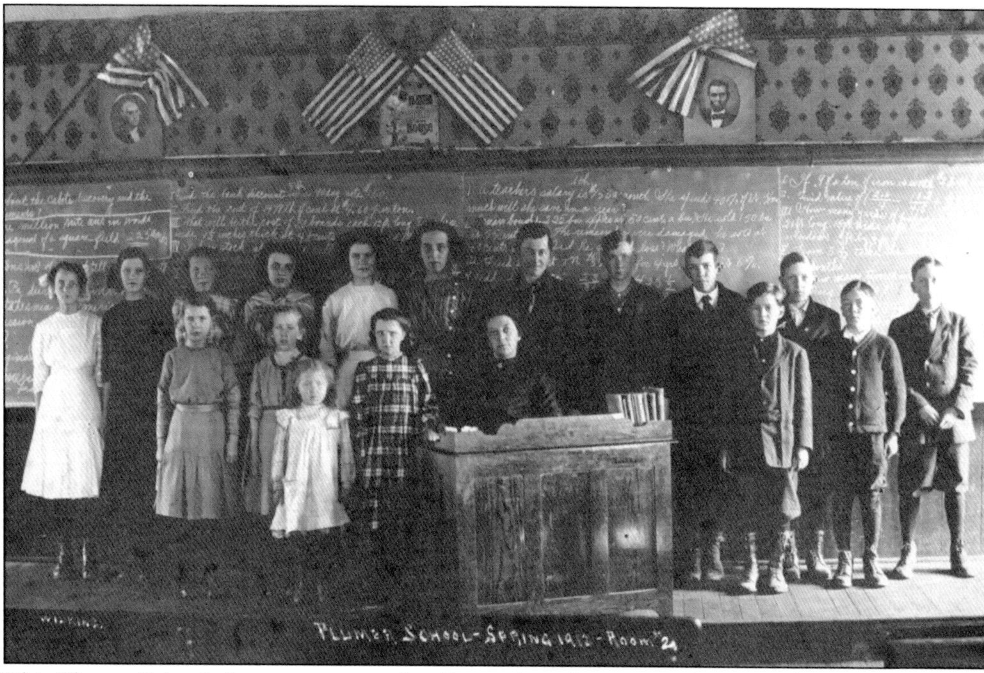

This Plumer School class was captured in Room 2 in the spring of 1912. (Photograph courtesy Dick Turk.)

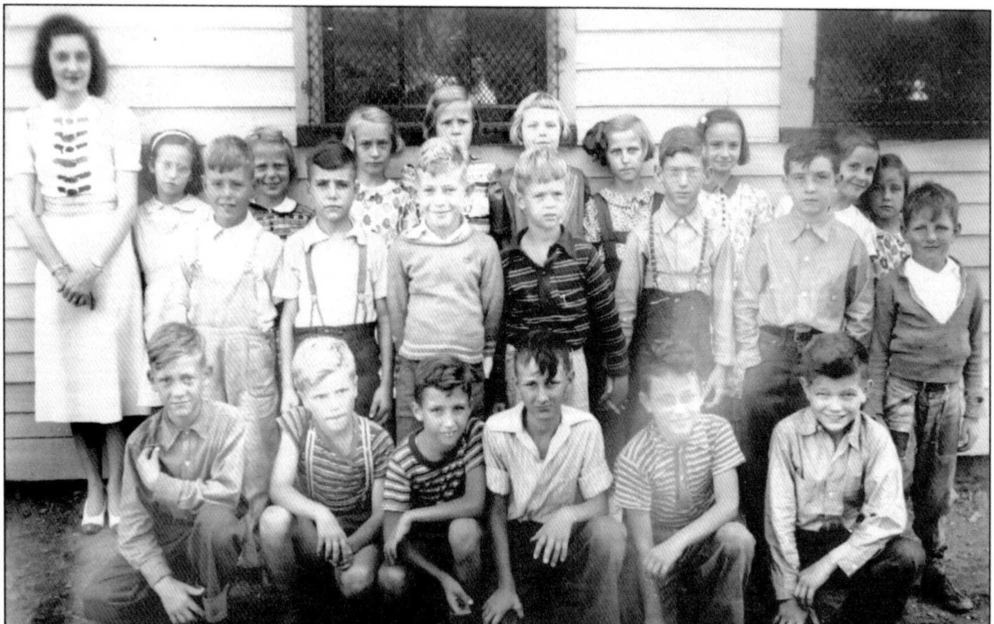

The third and fourth grades of Plumer School, c. 1939–1940, are shown from left to right: (front row) Bob Gibson, Eugene Snyder, Bob McSparren, Arden Pader, David Hites, and Bud McGee; (middle row) John Russell, Harry Turk, unidentified, Bill Applequist, Maurice Ross, Lester Dearment, and Guy Forbes; (back row) teacher Opal Horner, Alice Black, Mary Lou Hilton, Lois Beightol, June Russell, Carolyn Applequist, Betty Ross, Christina Behringer, Amy Meabon, and ? Britt.

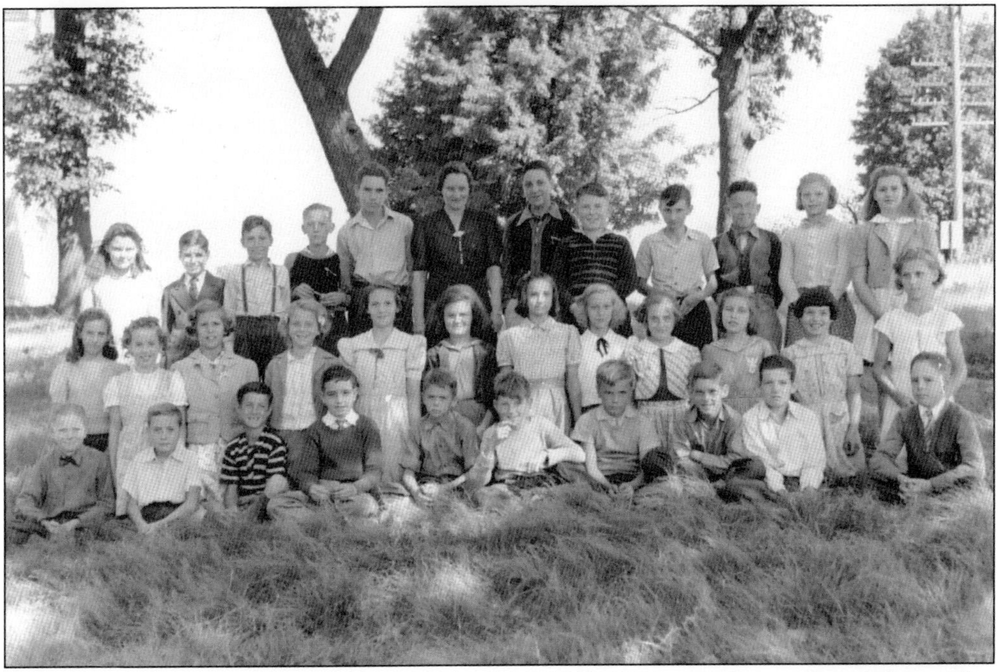

The fifth- and sixth-graders of Plumer School, *c.* 1940–1941, are shown, from left to right: (front row) Joe Goodman, Charles Moon, Emmanuelle DeMarches, Lester DeArment, Bill Applequist, Guy Forbes, Eugene Snyder, Maurice Ross, Frances Sullivan, and John Russell; (middle row) Alice Black, Dolores Burt, June Russell, Mary Lou Hilton, Amy Mealon, Zanah Proper, Christina Behringer, Lois Beightol, ? Straub, ? Britt, Mary DeMarches, and Betty Ross; (back row) Betty Goodman, Harry Turk, Bob McSarren, Bob Gibson, Archie Horner, teacher Mildred Heeter, Bob Finnegan, Bob Nelson, Arden Paden, Dave Hites, Carolyn Applequist, and Elaine Russell. (Photograph courtesy June Russell Pearson.)

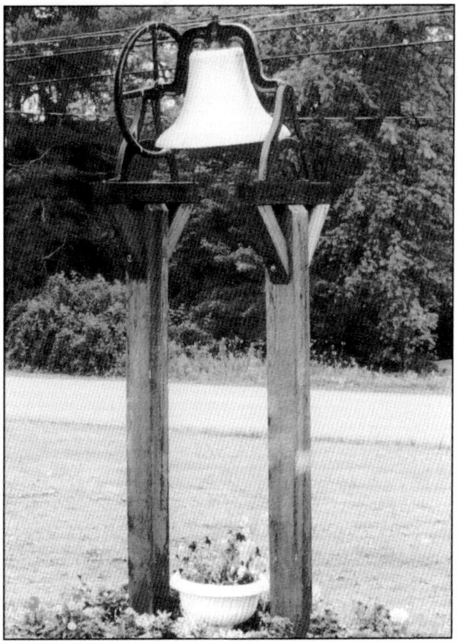

The old Plumer School was last open in 1942. The next fall, a new school opened across the street. That year, Plumer consolidated the schools at Petroleum Centre, Pithole, and Plumer into the new brick school in Plumer. The bell from the old Plumer School is located in the front of the new school. The brick school was closed in 1967 and all the students were sent to the Hasson Heights School in Oil City. (Photograph by Jim Stoudt.)

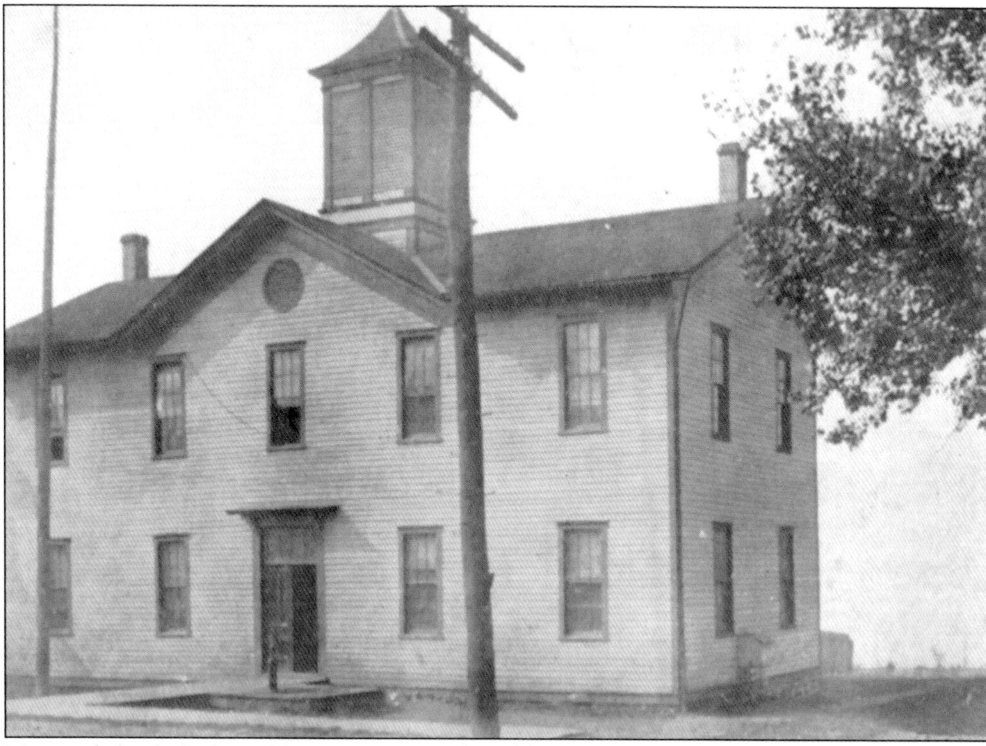

Many of the kids from Plumer went to the old Rouseville High School on Main Street. (Photograph courtesy John and Margie Hummel.)

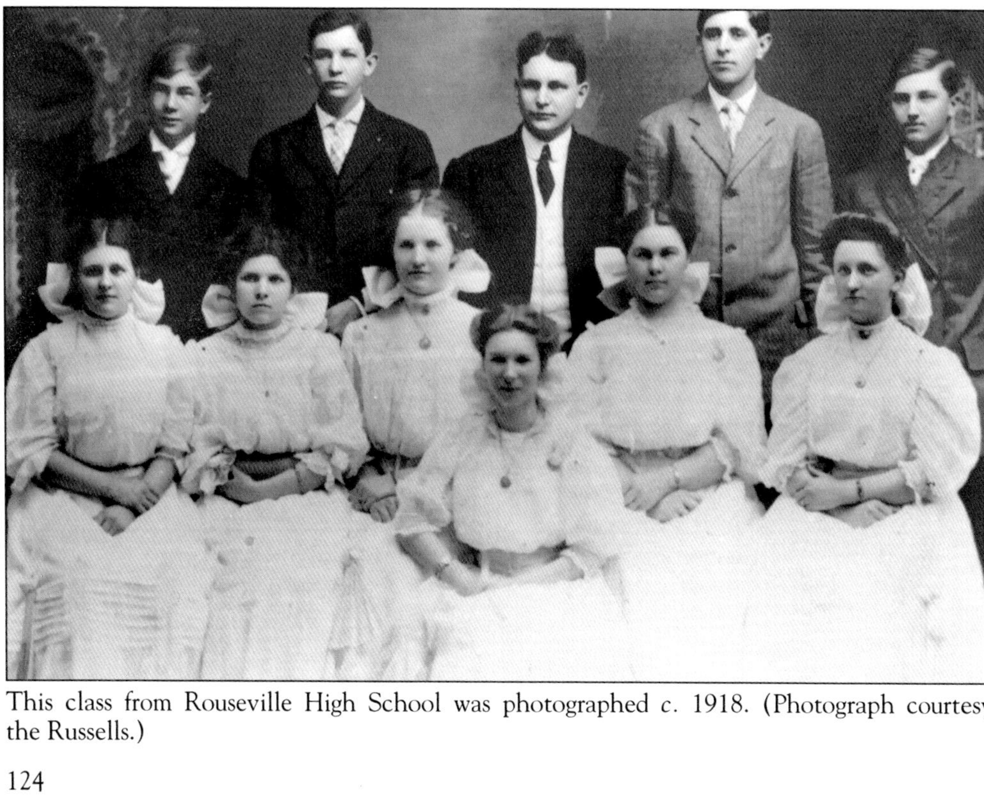

This class from Rouseville High School was photographed *c.* 1918. (Photograph courtesy the Russells.)

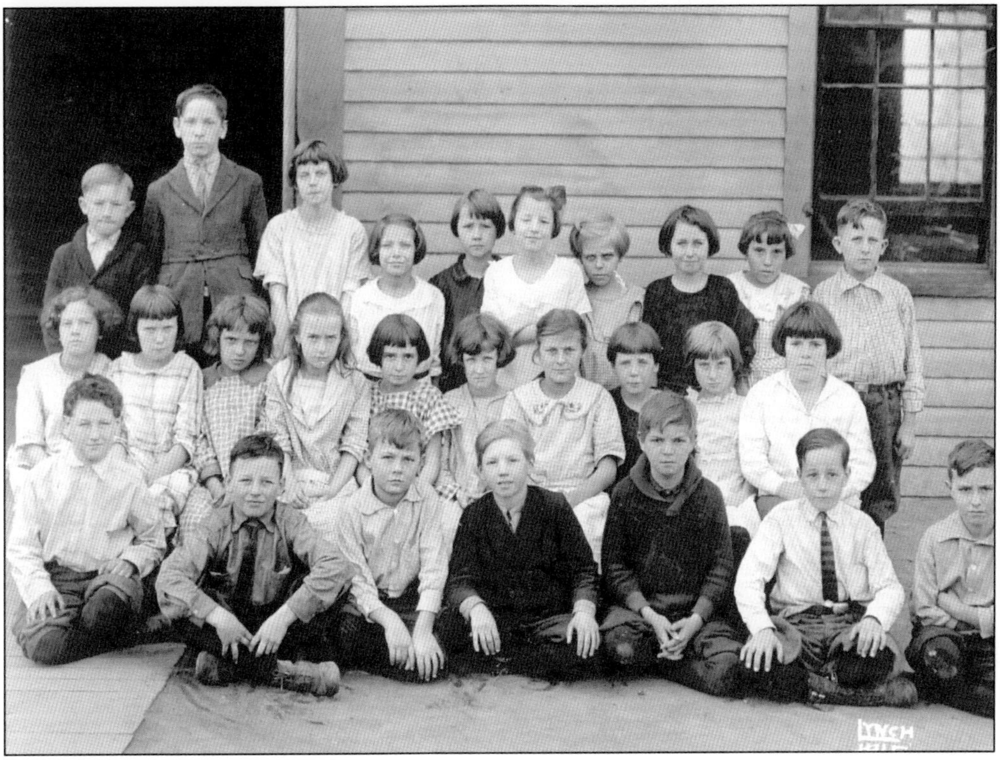

This class attended a Rouseville school sometime in the late 1920s.

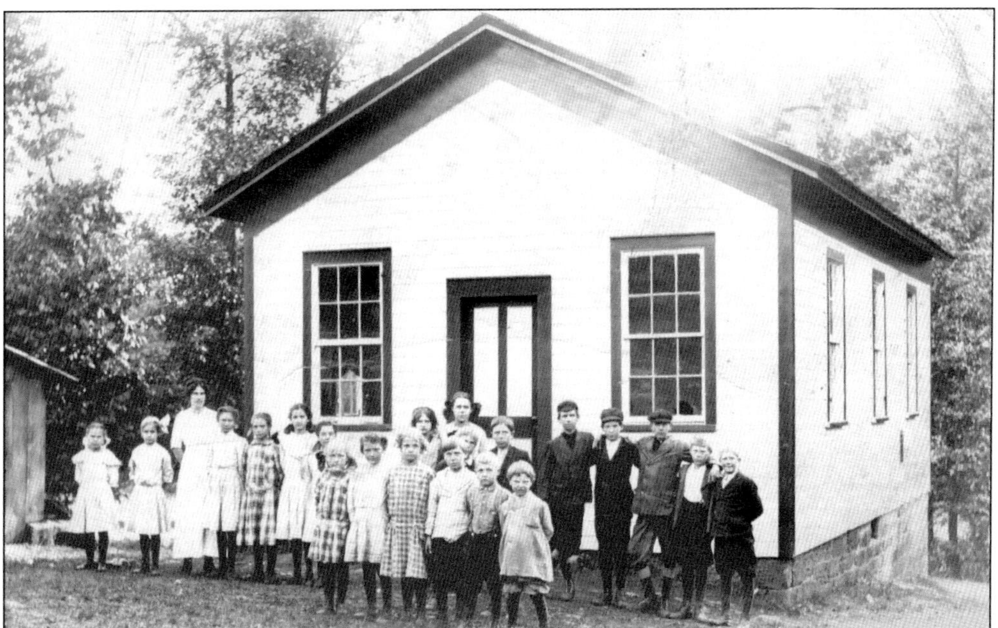

This Pithole school was photographed *c.* 1900. Thomas Holmden's brother, Walter Holmden, was the school superintendent. (Photograph courtesy Dick Turk.)

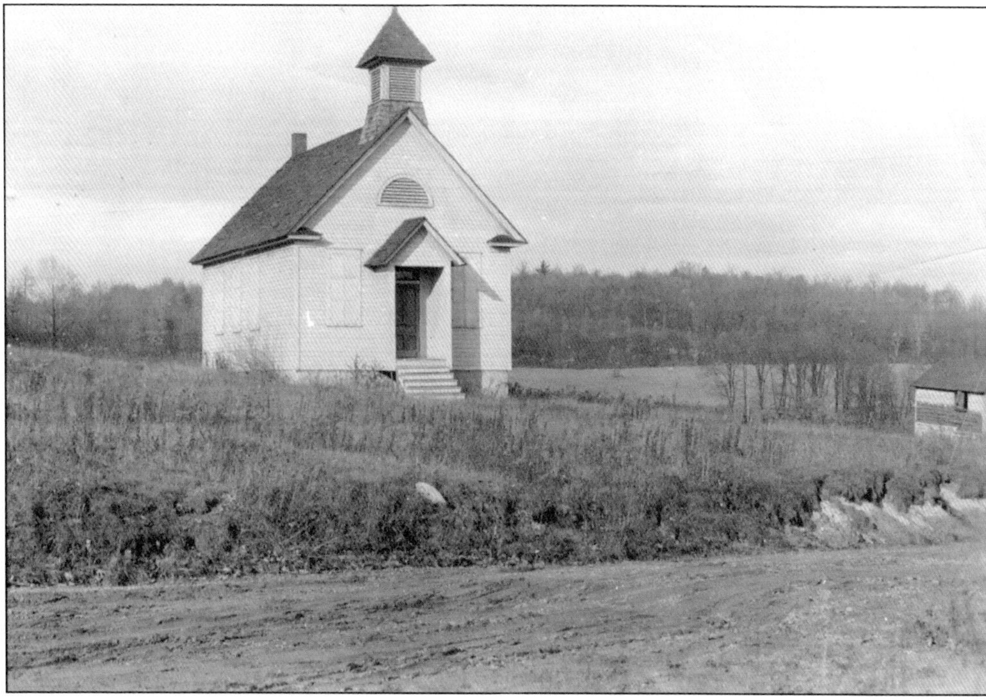

This old school was located at Russell Corners just northwest of Plumer. Russell Corners had originally been settled by the Russell brothers before the oil boom. (Photograph courtesy Dick Turk.)

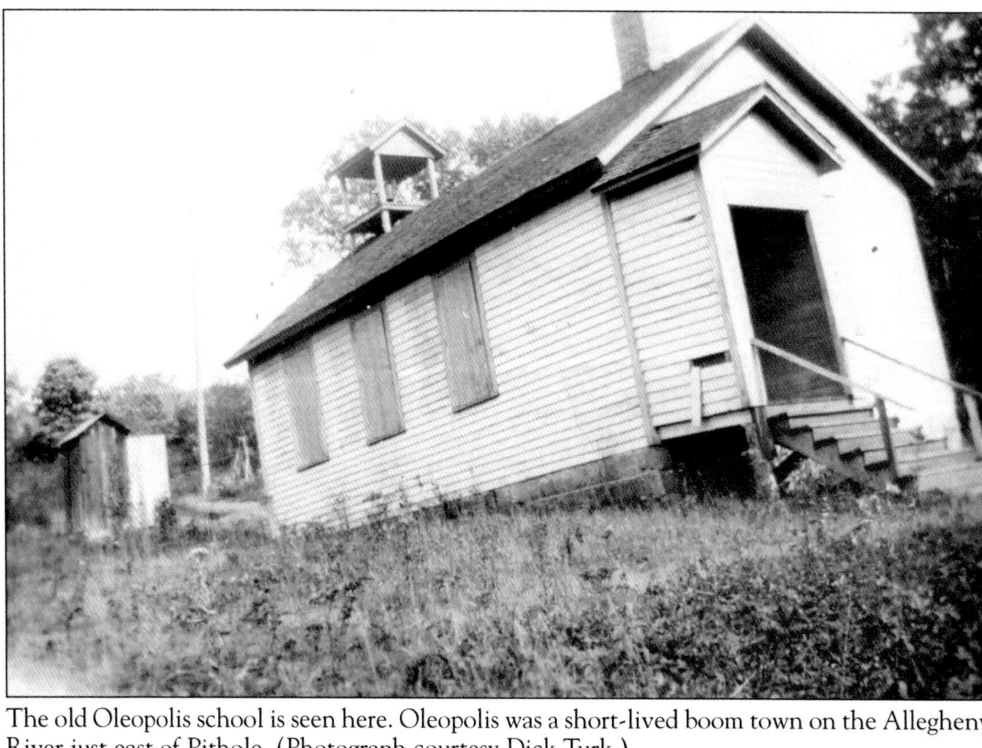

The old Oleopolis school is seen here. Oleopolis was a short-lived boom town on the Allegheny River just east of Pithole. (Photograph courtesy Dick Turk.)

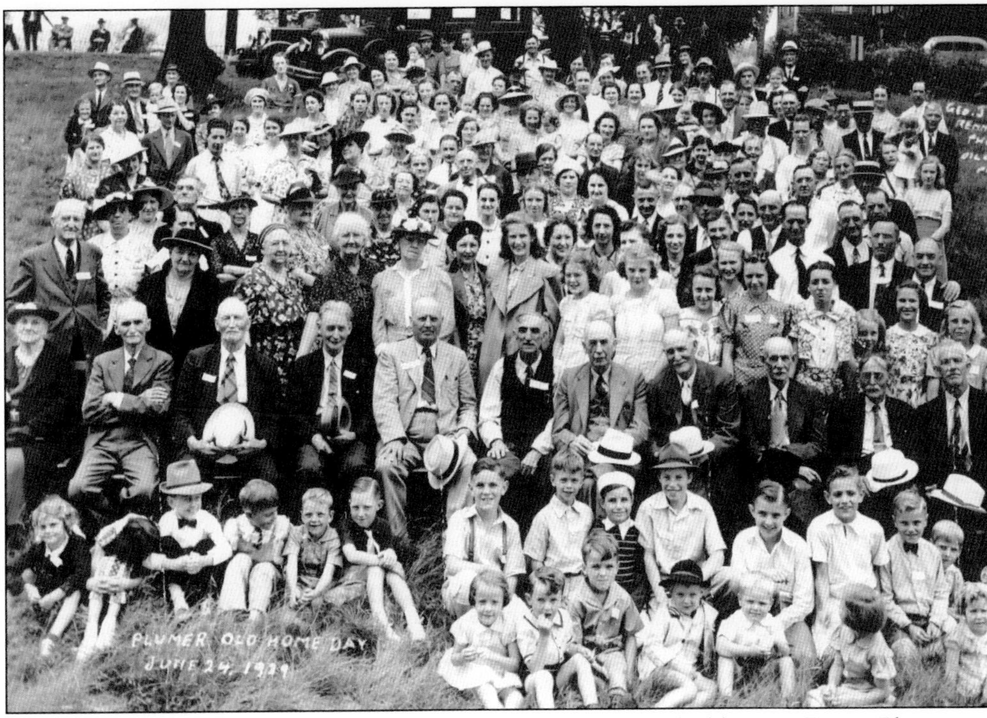

This Plumer Old Home Day took place in 1939. The tradition of Old Home Day in Plumer can be traced back to the Drake Day Festival held at Beers Camp in 1922. It has been an annual event since the late 1920s.

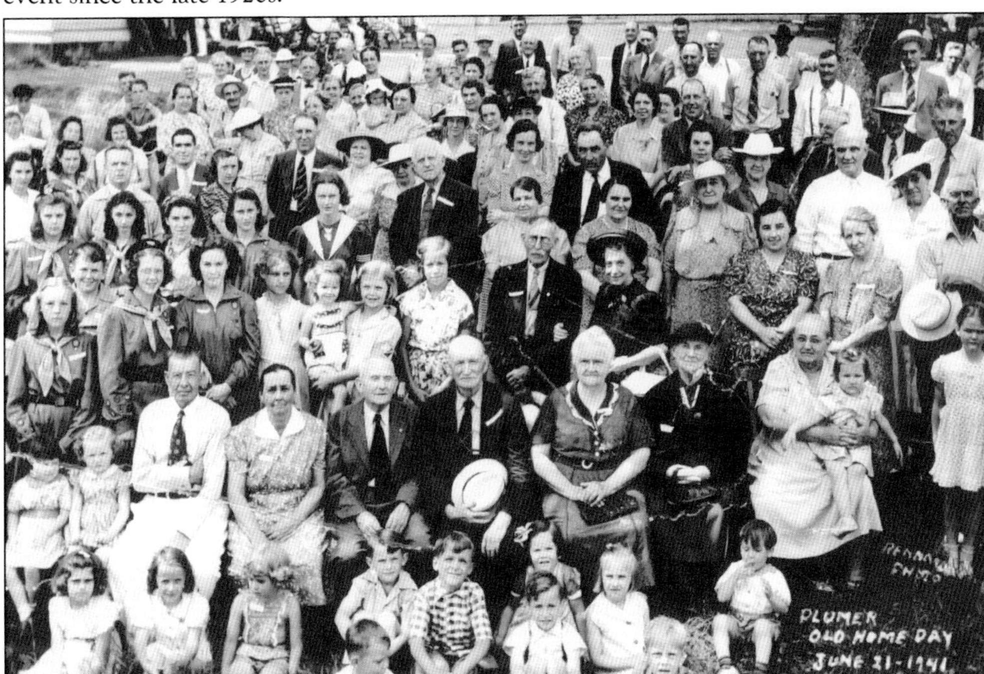

This Plumer Old Home Day took place in 1941. A band heightened the festivities as everyone gathered outside the Plumer Presbyterian church. (Photograph courtesy Bill Huber.)

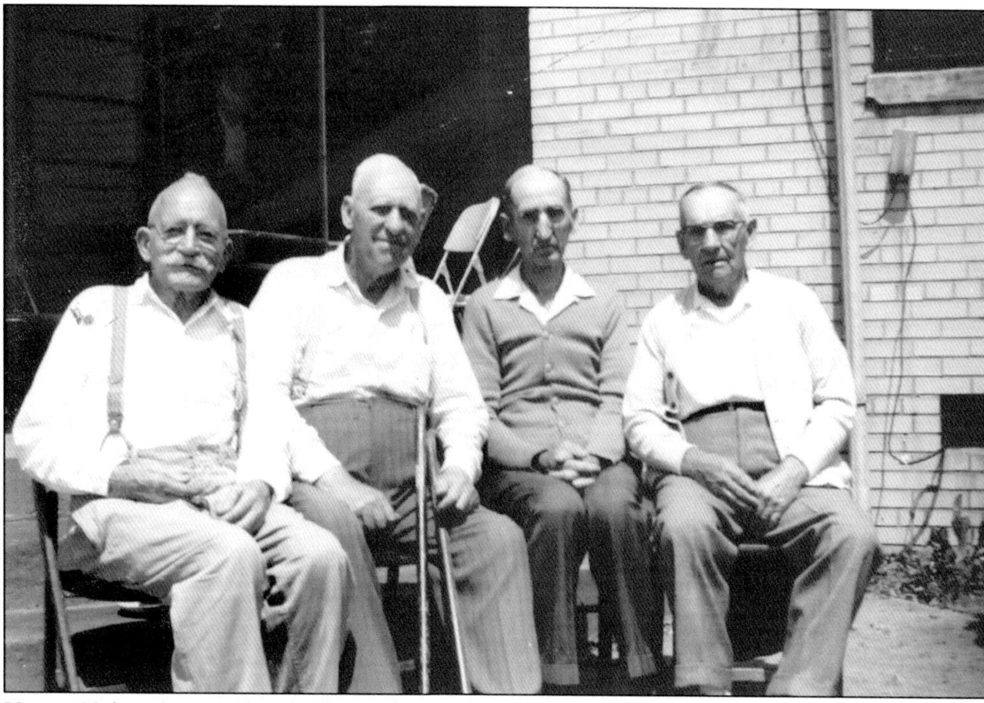

Henny Huber, Oma Turk, Charlie Ensle, and Willis Stephens appear at an Old Home Day in the 1950s. These four old-time oil men of Cherry Run gathered for one of the last times in Plumer.

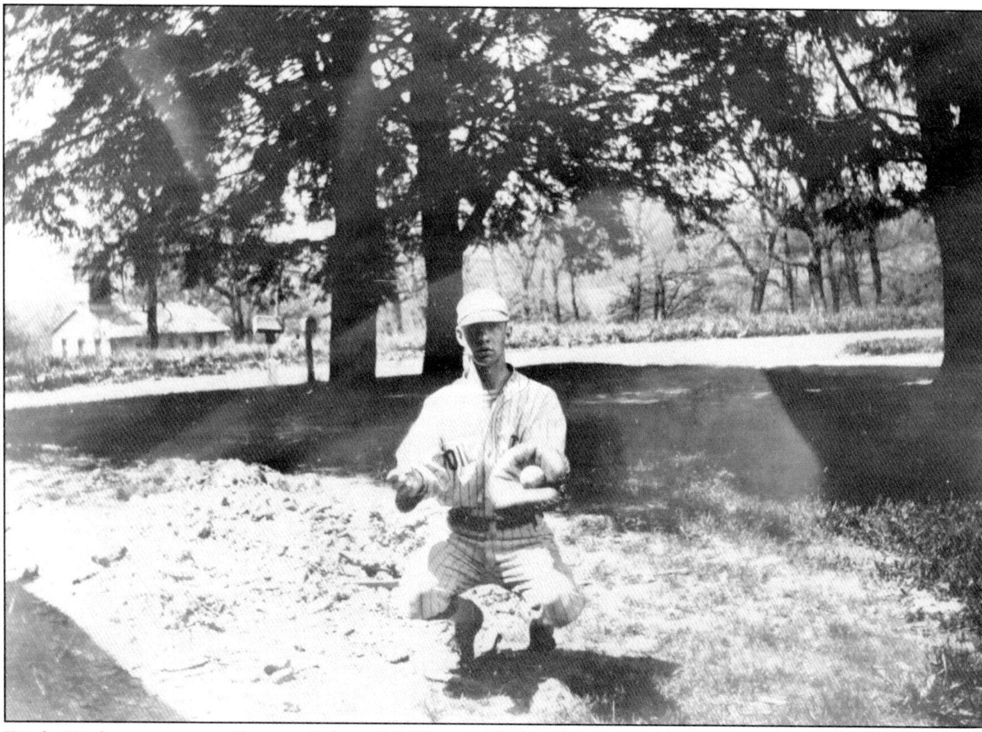

Dick Turk appears in front of the old Plumer School, *c.* 1929. Dick, who was born in 1913, continues to make Plumer his home.